The Archaeology of People

Alasdair Whittle's new work argues powerfully for the complexity and fluidity of life in the Neolithic, through a combination of archaeological and anthropological case studies and current theoretical debate.

The book ranges from the sixth to the fourth millennium BC, and from the Great Hungarian Plain, central and western Europe and the Alpine foreland to parts of southern Britain. Familiar terms such as individuals, agency and structure are discussed, but Whittle emphasises that they are too abstract to be truly useful.

Instead, he highlights the multiple dimensions which simultaneously constituted Neolithic existence in concrete and complicated situations: the web of daily routines, group and individual identities, relations with animals, and active but varied attitudes to the past.

The result is a vivid, original and perceptive understanding of the early Neolithic offering insights for readers at every level.

Alasdair Whittle is a research professor in the School of History and Archaeology at Cardiff University. His previous publications include *Europe in the Neolithic: the creation of new worlds* (1996) and (with Joshua Pollard and Caroline Grigson) *The Harmony of Symbols: the Windmill Hill causewayed enclosure, Wiltshire* (1999).

D1067275

The Archaeology of People

Dimensions of Neolithic life

Alasdair Whittle

Routledge
Taylor & Francis Group

LONDON AND NEW YORK

First published 2003
by Routledge
11 New Fetter Lane, London EC4P 4EE

Simultaneously published in the USA and Canada
by Routledge
29 West 35th Street, New York, NY 10001

Routledge is an imprint of the Taylor & Francis Group

© 2003 Alasdair Whittle

Typeset in Garamond by Exe Valley Dataset Ltd, Exeter
Printed and bound in Great Britain by MPG Books Ltd, Bodmin

British Library Cataloguing in Publication Data
A catalogue record for this book is available from the British Library

Library of Congress Cataloging in Publication Data
Whittle, A. W. R.
    The archaeology of people: dimensions of Neolithic life/Alasdair Whittle.
        p. cm.
    Includes bibliographical references and index.
    1. Neolithic period–Europe. 2. Human remains (Archaeology)–Europe.
    3. Europe–Antiquities. I. Title.
GN776.2A1W44 2003
936–dc21   2002037161

ISBN 0-415-30407-5 (hbk)
ISBN 0-415-30408-3 (pbk)

For Liz, Clare, Anna and Natalie

Contents

Figures

Acknowledgements

My greatest debt in the writing of this book has been the support given to my research by the former Vice-Chancellor of Cardiff University, Sir Brian Smith, and by his successor, Dr David Grant. For information and help, I am indebted to: Eszter Bánffy, Alex Bentley, Amy Bogaard, Richard Bradley, Ingo Campen, Vicki Cummings, Richard Evershed, Detlef Gronenborn, Lamys Hachem, Gill Hey, Tim Ingold, Stefanie Jacomet, Eva Lenneis, Theya Molleson, Mike Parker Pearson, Francis Pryor, Erich Pucher, Colin Richards, Ulrike Sommer, Peter Stadler, Harald Stäuble, Julian Thomas, Anne Tresset, Peter Walter, James Whitley, Howard Williams, Michael Wysocki and Andreas Zimmermann. I am grateful to Howard Mason and John Morgan for their preparation of figures and photos. John Evans provoked several of the thoughts here on sociality. Rick Schulting helped with teaching and the Ecsegfalva project, and I am indebted also to the rest of the Ecsegfalva project team. Vicki Cummings helped with figures, and a critical reading of draft chapters. It is hard, finally, to thank my wife and daughters enough for their loving encouragement. This book is for them.

Preface

What was it like, being there? Sometimes a remote past can seem tantalisingly close. So with a little imagination, it is not too difficult to picture oneself, say, inside one of the great timber longhouses characteristic of central Europe in the second half of the sixth millennium BC. Perhaps it is a day in summer, and the light inside the house seems dark in contrast to the bright day outside. A woman is framed in the sunshine at one of the few doors. Roof timbers creak faintly. Outside there are a few other voices, a dog barking half-heartedly, and some mud-caked pigs asleep in the shade of the eaves. Other longhouses a short distance away bask in the heat, and the surrounding woodland has the faded green of high summer. The rest of the people and animals are elsewhere, in gardens and woodland. Or, perhaps not quite so easily, we could picture ourselves watching as a body was brought to one of the great house-like long cairns or barrows in southern Britain in the middle of the fourth millennium BC. Such a scene is often reconstructed in darkness, with the light from torches accentuating the faces of the mourners and creating deep shadows which conveniently hide details of which we are less than sure. But suppose this too is a fine day in summer. People are sweating after carrying a body some distance. The corpse is pale and the sun brings out the smells of death. The light is good enough for the bodies of people previously interred to be glimpsed by those close enough, and if permitted, to peer into chambers: a mixture of whole skeletons, ligaments and disarranged bones, skulls and longbones prominent, suggesting the gradual melting of the human form back into the mass of waiting ancestral remains.

Like nearly all reconstructions of this kind, however, these are only snapshots. Of more extended attempts, which at least offer plot and development, the best example I know is in fact in comic-strip format (Figure 0.1) (Houot 1992), following the interactions of two neighbouring villages in the Alpine foreland in the third millennium BC.[1] Rather more often the past can seem remote, not only because of the conditions of preservation, but also because of the way in which we write about it. Partly this is a matter of scales, which I can illustrate with some of my own past work. Either we write at a level of wide-ranging synthesis, in my case about Europe in the Neolithic period (Whittle 1996), or we focus on particular sites in specific regions, in my case recently Neolithic monuments in a particular area of southern Britain (Whittle 1997; Whittle et al. 1999). Broad synthesis may miss the details

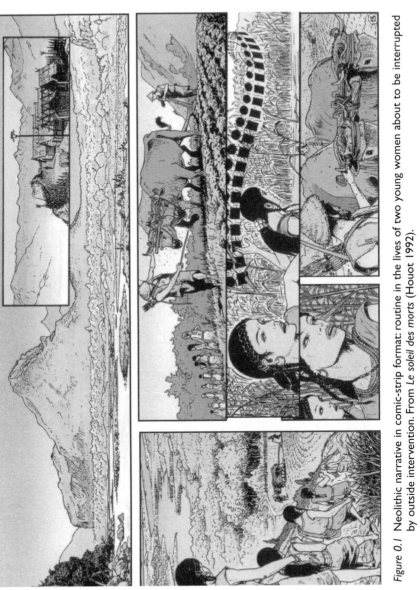

Figure 0.1 Neolithic narrative in comic-strip format: routine in the lives of two young women about to be interrupted by outside intervention. From *Le soleil des morts* (Houot 1992).

and diversity of particular situations, and site reports may be too full of detail to draw out central features of the broader context in which the individual monument or settlement was located. In both cases, however, another dimension is normally missing: a fuller sense of the range of values and goals that motivated different people in different ways, of what bound people together and what individuals were like, of the detail of daily lives and the ways in which these were guided by but at the same time themselves created central features of a worldview. This lack has fostered, I suspect, the current popularity of short narrative reconstructions, and it is certainly behind the recent and current interest in both gender and agency.

Literary flourishes will not on their own make remote pasts closer. Debate in archaeology tends to lurch from one fashion to another. We need to combine scales of writing much more often, to avoid compartmentalisation, to investigate daily contexts and the diversity of individuals, but also to unite these with a renewed interest in shared values and culture. We need to consider how the conditions in which people acted affected how things changed, and whether things always changed as rapidly in the past as our own worldview presupposes us to think. From this perspective, the examples with which I started pose as many problems as they provide insights. What was the composition of households, and what was the wider significance of the longhouse? Did people come and go in this system, and if so, how did people maintain an identity at once individual and collective? Apart from the important technical issue, long debated, of whether fleshed corpses or already disarticulated bones were normally deposited in long cairns and barrows, what was the relationship between the living and the dead? Were these regular funerals, or rather rarer ancestral commemorations? If ancestors were indeed involved, what sort of figures were these? Were these more important at one time than another? And in both cases, how were central concerns acted out in daily life? What was the woman at the door thinking? Did mourners think with their bodies as they carried a corpse?

This book is a preliminary attempt to suggest ways forward. I am interested especially in the many-sided, perhaps often ambiguous nature of what it meant to be an individual in the past, in how individuals related to wider social groupings, in how the flow of daily life carried central and shared concerns forward, and in whether the combination of the conditions of daily life and prevailing worldviews served together to make change very slow. I will draw widely on the evidence from the Neolithic period in Europe, principally from the Carpathian basin westward to Britain and Ireland, and so draw on examples mainly from the sixth to the fourth millennia BC. In detailed case studies I mostly focus on the first few centuries of regional sequences, but I briefly discuss some later situations towards the end of the book in order to investigate the question of change. In many ways, I would prefer to be able to drop the blanket term 'Neolithic' altogether, but it remains convenient (though dangerous) as shorthand. I will draw on a wide range of theory of various kinds and from various sources, though this is not primarily a theoretical tract. At times, I will use analogies of various kinds. These have obvious limitations, and it has been suggested that some kinds of analogy, basically more general ones, are safer than others. It is always possible, however, to convert a specific kind of analogy into a more general form, so this separation is barely helpful. Like others, I use analogies to widen the imagination and to open up possibilities of interpretation, though it is clear that analogies do not come from a timeless world (e.g. S. Hugh-Jones 1995, 226). But I also follow the anthropologist Marilyn Strathern (1988; 1992a; 1992b) in using analogies to challenge our own western way of thinking about the world.

I have already set many questions, both general and specific, but this book makes no attempt at all at completeness. At this stage, it is the kind of question asked and the style of answer suggested that may be important.

Chapter 1

Being there

This book is about being there: about the nature of past lives at a time remote from the present. It tries to capture something not only of the central concerns but also of the many-sidedness and frequent messiness of existence. It seeks to show how we can avoid reducing social existence, and the people who constituted that, to a single dimension. It is about different ways of looking at scales of action and thought, which resist the common tactics of choosing one scale over another or of lapsing into unhelpful abstraction. In taking this theme, I hope also to open fresh ways of looking at the recurrent tensions between the individual and the collective, diversity and uniformity, and change and stability.

Two examples

Two initial examples, from my own recent research, help to set out the nature of the questions at stake. The causewayed enclosure at Windmill Hill, Wiltshire, in southern England, was constructed around or perhaps a little before 3500 BC, some centuries after the beginning of a different way of life in its region (Whittle *et al.* 1999). At a general level, this construction can be seen as a powerful statement of identity and central values. Its very form, concentric rings of interrupted ditches, may recall, whether consciously or unconsciously, that of much earlier constructions on the European mainland, which date back over 1,500 years (Figure 1.1). As such, it could be seen as an idealisation of a notion of ancestral settlement, a mythical form from a distant past (Bradley 1998a), all the more startling because this was not the first kind of construction to be attempted; in our jargon, other 'monuments' such as long cairns and long barrows had already been built in this region. More down to earth, the form of the enclosure might also draw on the shape of either contemporary camps or natural clearings and man-made clearances in woodland, and the placing of the vast construction in probably little altered woodland must raise the question of how people regarded their surroundings. These are the first of a series of probable metaphors, the defined space of this carefully constructed arena and the many things deposited within it standing for a string of ideas and concepts. As often commented, the segmented ditches may symbolise the disparate groups involved in construction and perhaps use of the site. In the ditches, the placed deposits, principally of animal bone, may evoke the importance of animals and their ambiguous relationship with

Figure 1.1 Excavation in 1988 of the middle ditch (Trench E) on the north side of the Windmill Hill enclosure, southern England. Abundant but small bone deposits were contained in a complex stratigraphy, close to the terminal of the ditch segment in question. Photo: author.

people, and the central place of gathering and feasting in contemporary social existence. Animal bone deposits may also stand for the deposits of human bone encountered in larger quantities in other constructions, shrines, ossuaries or tombs housed in long barrows and cairns; the necessity to kill animals, as well as the social imperative of valuing them alive, may also be bound up with fear of killing people and the uncomfortable facts of inter-personal violence. Other things deposited, such as potsherds and stone artefacts, may stand for social interaction and relations with neighbours and allies, on the one hand, and the very fact of contemporary domestic existence on the other. At another level of abstraction, the dominant metaphors worked and re-worked at this site may present ideas of transition, transformation and renewal: a further set of attitudes to time and consciousness of self.

With so much to say about this one arena, and with so many other enclosures, barrows and cairns from the same period and area to consider, should we be content with this evidence and these kinds of interpretation? There are at least three problems. Research over the last two decades has shown that no one enclosure is quite like any other. Even regional groupings by form and layout may have been much exaggerated (Barclay 2000). From site to site, people might be seen as having drawn on a repertoire of common ways of doing things, but as having used these according to local circumstance and choice. We hardly yet understand this diversity, though it has often been described. Was it the product of deliberate statements about difference and otherness, or the accidental result of relative isolation and rituals infrequently performed? Did people come from far and wide to participate, or were these exclusively local affairs?

The second problem is how to relate these enclosures to their local contexts. The now over eighty or so enclosures of southern England (Oswald et al. 2001) are found in a considerable range of settings, none of which we yet comprehend very well. Around Windmill Hill, for example, other evidence, apart from that of barrows and cairns, is frustratingly limited to occasional pits, lithic scatters and fragments of old occupation surfaces preserved under earthworks. Much can be done with these, especially in areas where a density of monuments provides close sampling spots, as in Cranborne Chase (M.J. Allen 2000), but there is little getting round the fact that the dominant metaphors explored above tend to float above their local contexts. Whether or not this matters may depend on the view one has of ritual. Some ritual, like myths (J.F. Weiner 1988, 16), may simply operate in different domains from other aspects of life and thought. In that case, discussion of causewayed enclosures could legitimately be self-contained, and their dominant metaphors be taken as those of a realm of special consciousness. In other views, ritual is not to be so easily disconnected from other activity. Ritual, or better, rituals, may be a formalisation of other activities (Bell 1992), and part of their role at least may be to transform for people their understanding of what is understood in other contexts (Bloch and Parry 1982, 19). In this case, we badly need to know more about other contexts. Around Windmill Hill, this kind of evidence is meagre. What is principally suggested is a series of rather simple depositions in pits and other contexts, as part of what may have been quite transient and short-lived occupations, such as outside the enclosure on Windmill Hill itself (Whittle *et al*. 2000) or at Cherhill (Evans and Smith 1983). People may have been routinely accustomed to small-scale gatherings and attendant depositions.

This brings us to the third problem. The emphasis given in our discussion of the dominant metaphors of the Windmill causewayed enclosure sits uneasily with more detailed consideration of the deposits in question themselves. We analysed these carefully, Caroline Grigson giving especial attention to species, body parts, fragmentation and weathering, and Joshua Pollard to the wider evidence from earlier excavations at the site for combinations of finds (Grigson 1999; Pollard 1999a). We suggested some recurrent kinds of deposit, based on form, composition and possible history before final deposition (Whittle *et al*. 1999). In the end, a stark contrast remains between, on the one hand, the big ideas possibly represented by the totality of the site and the big-scale event that its original conception and construction must surely have marked, and on the other, the generally small-scale and perhaps often rather mundane nature of what was placed in the ditch segments of the site once active: the partial remains of an animal or two, sherds of broken pottery, some stone implements, sometimes charcoal, ash and blackened soil. How then were the supposed dominant metaphors of the site actually conceptualised, and what was really different in the use of the arena compared to 'out there' in the landscape? Was it in the end the power of memory, the recognition of a special setting, and perhaps the monumentality of the construction itself that mattered, rather than the ensuing commemorative acts of deposition?

Until we have better models of individual action and its relationship to collective practice, and of how people think in and across different domains of their existence, the interpretation of this kind of situation, intriguing and evocative though it is, will remain problematic. More or less the same difficulties recur in the quite different setting of my second example, and this recurrence indicates the general problem with which I am concerned.

We know very little about settlement of the river systems of the Carpathian basin before the late seventh and the very first part of the sixth millennia BC. We know something of quite concentrated forager populations in the Danube Gorges (Radovanović 1996), whose diet seems to have been based firmly on the resources of the Danube (Bonsall *et al*. 1997; 2000), and a little about forager populations in the hills to the west and north of the Carpathian basin. Some of these latter may have been quite mobile, while in the Gorges there may have been both periodic (or longer) aggregations of people, and connections to much wider regions seen in movements of raw materials (Chapman 1993). We may therefore have to think of systems operating at a regional scale. This may have included people making forays into the Carpathian basin itself, though the evidence is very sparse, apart from newly discovered but still imprecisely dated occupations on the northern edge of the Great Hungarian Plain, north of the Tisza valley near Szolnok (Kertész 1996). This is the necessary preamble to what happens next, before 6000 BC in the southern part of the basin (in the northern part of former Yugoslavia), and after 6000 BC in its central part (on the southern half of the Great Hungarian Plain).

From these dates, a series of changes ensue. People living off sheep, goats and other domesticates, as well as a wide range of wild game, fish, birds, cultivated cereals and probably other wild plants, came gradually into the Carpathian basin, probably from south to north (Figure 1.2). Their occupations can now be found plentifully along the watercourses of the basin, as far north as approximately half way up the Great Hungarian Plain (e.g. Kosse 1979; Jankovich *et al.* 1989). These consist of pits dug into the subsoil, and where they are preserved, thin occupation levels; some surface structures, perhaps shelters or small houses, are known. Finds of animal bone, pottery and other artefacts are abundant, for example at the small occupation of Endrőd 119 in the Körös valley (Makkay 1992).

Research on this phenomenon has concentrated for decades on big questions of the identity of this population (generally favouring the idea of some kind of colonisation by people coming up from further south in the Balkans), its choice of settlement location (strongly waterside as we have seen), its main means of subsistence and the general character of existence (generally seen as sedentary and agriculturally based). These remain important questions. The problem of identity can be seen in fresh light as continued research has shown how indigenous people in the Gorges were directly involved in these changes, and how, although new forms of settlement spread at first only so far across the Hungarian Plain, there were contemporary changes involving the use of very simple pottery and the building of houses on the west side of the Danube at least as far north as Vienna (Whittle *et al.* 2002). It is possible that local or regional populations were involved in or were part of these processes of change. One study of lithics has suggested that although obsidian raw material was procured from sources well to the north, in the hills of southern Slovakia and northern Hungary, well beyond the limits of the new phenomena on the southern half of the Great Hungarian Plain, the style of flint working and use owed little to indigenous traditions (Starnini 2000). In other cases, however, the details of lithic reduction and point technology may suggest some such continuity, as at Brunn outside Vienna and Ecsegfalva 23 in the central part of the Great Hungarian Plain (Peter Stadler, pers. comm.; Mateiciucová 2001). The very broad spectrum of resources used in the waterside environments of the Great Hungarian Plain, including plentiful fish, small game, freshwater shells and birds (e.g. Bökönyi 1992; Takács 1992), could speak for the continuation of forager subsistence traditions, even though it is likely that sheep, goats and cattle provided more food than all these other resources put together. Though no ancient DNA has yet been obtained from samples of this early date on the Great Hungarian Plain, study of mitochondrial DNA in modern populations has suggested a general European picture of only about one-fifth of the population being of non-European descent (Sykes 1999). It may therefore be appropriate to begin to model a complex process of limited, gradual and perhaps targeted northward colonisation by population from the south, combined with adaptation and change among local or regional indigenous populations.

These are important questions, and if one is optimistic, the 'impenetrable whodunnit' of identities (Halstead 1989, 24) could be seen as now a little closer to resolution. They remain, however, questions set at a very general level. Rather less

Figure 1.2 Excavation in 2001 of the occupation at Ecsegfalva 23, one of a series of sites near the northern limits of the Körös culture on the Great Hungarian Plain, showing remains of a burnt structure. Photo: author.

attention has been given to variation or individuals in these situations. On the Great Hungarian Plain, people clearly lived in varying settings. The overwhelming majority of these were waterside, but while some occupations were on the edges of active river systems, others were strung out along older alluvial deltas, and some, as at Ecsegfalva and Szarvas, on large still-water meanders. We do not yet understand the significance of such variation, though it might be to do with seasonal prefer-ences. The occupation of place may have been significant in the construction and maintenance of identity. This is particularly so around the Ecsegfalva meander, where occupations appear relatively small but concentrated on particular points in the landscape, which were avoided at later dates.

We also know rather little of the day-to-day conditions of existence. One or two small structures or houses are known (e.g. Raczky 1983) but the evidence is often elusive, as at Endrőd 119, where burnt daub was concentrated at the top of large infilled pits (Makkay 1992). Likewise at Ecsegfalva 23, careful recovery has so far shown considerable quantities of burnt daub, but few signs of postholes or stake-holes. It is possible that light, reed- and daub-covered structures are in question. One possibility is that the quantities of daub observed would only be produced by deliberate firing of these structures (Ammerman et al. 1988). A series of excavations has shown the existence of large and small pits, and both Endrőd 119 and Ecsegfalva 23 suggest that light structures could have been accompanied by at least one large pit complex and accompanying space around it. Most pits were deliberately rather than naturally filled. A complex cycle of comings and goings may be likely, the taking of places being marked by digging into the ground, and abandonment being marked by deliberate re-filling, as well as by the burning of small houses. It may be that the pollution of death was regarded as one good reason to shift from place to place (Chapman 1994).

The evidence of one such burial puts the question of scales of analysis into sharp relief. Excavation at Ecsegfalva 23 in 1999 found the skeleton of one adult woman (Figure 1.3) (Whittle 2000a). The skeleton was crouched and the body had presumably been tightly bound, before being placed on the ground, not in a grave, above filled up shallow features at the edge of the occupation; it is hard to envisage contemporary occupation close by while the body decomposed. In itself, there is little unusual in this, as burials of mainly women and children have been found on many Körös culture occupations, in varying body positions and degrees of complete-ness (Trogmayer 1969; Chapman 1994). Intriguingly, the woman at Ecsegfalva had bad teeth. There were large cavities in the sides of her molars, and her front teeth, like the others, were worn well down. Across the ground surface of her upper two front teeth, there was a narrow groove, worn into the surface of the teeth, pre-sumably by some repetitive action such as the working of sinew (Ildikó Pap and Rick Schulting, pers. comm.).[1]

We are confronted with a series of questions at different scales and it is hard to bring these together. At one level, we can investigate a general transformation in identity, choice of settlement areas and the use of new subsistence resources. At another we can investigate regional variation in such transformation. We can

Figure 1.3 A woman of the Körös culture (or the succeeding AVK) from Ecsegfalva 23, notable for her delicate skeleton and bad teeth. Photo: author.

examine not only preferred locations for occupation, but also the use of place as a means of creating local identity. There is the problem of what occupations looked like, how long they were maintained and the circumstances in which they were abandoned. Or we can concentrate on individuals. The evidence of the Ecsegfalva woman suggests rather different perspectives on the wider phenomena. Perhaps her diet did not particularly suit her, giving problems with her teeth, unless she was predisposed to such difficulties. In either case, the experience of her adult life was presumably strongly coloured by pain. The particular use of her front teeth as a 'third hand' might suggest not only repetitive and unglamorous but also boring activity. How conscious would such a person have been of the wider histories of which she was part? The radiocarbon dates from the site so far may allow for memory of beginnings a few generations earlier. The woman presumably understood and probably took part in a range of subsistence activities. The facts of domestication may have been partly taken for granted, though people may have also been very conscious of the difference between wild and tame. On the other hand, the provision of food and drink in social gatherings, symbolised perhaps by the pottery so abundantly found in all these occupations, may have been much more important than the source of such food in itself. The cycle of occupations, and the significance of local place, may have been at least as important in the consciousness of people as the means of subsistence which have dominated the literature for so long. Place was hand-made, the walls of structures being framed by bundles or mats of reeds, and covered with clay which still bears finger impressions.

In both examples, we need much better integration of routines and daily activity with what went on at special times and places, of individualism with the ties that bind, of the present with the past and memory, and of people with their animals. In both cases, there are competing possibilities for what was thought significant, and what was remembered. We need a far better sense not only of how people acted, but also of how they thought, as both individuals and collectivities.

Structure and agency

The starting point of this book is that while a lot of research has been concentrated on particular aspects or scales of the kinds sketched so far, rather little has been offered by way of integration. It is an appropriate time to try, as these sorts of issue have begun to be widely debated. Ian Hodder has drawn attention to the need in studies of the British Neolithic to take account of individual action (1999, 132–7; cf. Hodder 1986), and Mark Edmonds has written an unusually empathetic account of the southern British Neolithic (1999). The relationship between what have come to be called structure and agency has begun to be widely debated in archaeology (e.g. Hodder 1999; Dobres and Robb 2000a; cf. Layton 2000), typically some time after the initial debates in the field of social theory and social anthropology. The principal sources have been Bourdieu and Giddens, each in turn influenced by a number of earlier and contemporary writers, including Mauss in the case of Bourdieu, and Bourdieu, Goffman and Garfinkel among many others in the case of Giddens

(Gosden 1999, 125; Baert 1998, 94–100). Some initial description is useful at this point, but it will be brief, since it has been offered already many times elsewhere (e.g. Baert 1998; Gosden 1999; Dobres 2000, especially chapter 6; Dobres and Robb 2000b).

Bourdieu was concerned with daily action and the engagement of the body in it, with the minutiae of life as well as the realms of more conscious thought (Gosden 1999, 125). This was expressed in his important concept of *habitus*, the bare definition of which is somewhat forbidding at first sight:

> systems of durable, transposable dispositions, structured structures predisposed to function as structuring structures, that is, as principles of the generation and structuring of practices and representations which can be objectively 'regulated' and 'regular' without in any way being the product of obedience to rules, objectively adapted to their goals without presupposing a conscious aiming at ends or an express mastery of the operations necessary to attain them and, being all this, collectively orchestrated without being the product of the orchestrating action of a conductor. (Bourdieu 1977, 72)

Habitus is a generative or enabling disposition, generally absorbed or learnt unconsciously; it is a second nature and a 'feel for the game'; 'people produce thought, perception and action without thinking about how they are doing so, but in a manner which has its own logic' (Gosden 1999, 125–6). As Bourdieu also puts it (1977, 78), *habitus* is 'the durably installed generative principle of regulated improvisations'. Agents or subjects, both terms used by Bourdieu, are in part portrayed as not really knowing what they are doing:

> It is because subjects do not, strictly speaking, know what they are doing that what they do has more meaning than they know. The habitus is the universalizing mediation which causes an individual agent's practices, without either explicit reason or signifying intent, to be none the less 'sensible' and 'reasonable'. (Bourdieu 1977, 79)

Habitus, finally, is historically grounded; 'the system of dispositions . . . is the principle of the continuity and regularity which objectivism discerns in the social world without being able to give them a rational basis' (Bourdieu 1977, 82).

Bourdieu was concerned to go beyond the opposition between 'subjectivism', or the search for how people experience and conceptualise the world, and 'objectivism', the search for underlying structures, independent of people's knowledge, concepts or purposes (Baert 1998, 30). In a sense, this was also the goal of Giddens (1979; 1984), but is expressed by him in a wider theory of action, which draws not only on Bourdieu but also on a number of other sources, and is presented as applicable to a broad range of historical situations, especially recent ones in complex modern societies, as opposed to the more circumscribed settings analysed by Bourdieu. For Giddens, agency is a blend of tacit knowledge and practical consciousness (Baert

1998, 105); agency is not necessarily the same as intentionality, 'purposive' rather than 'purposeful' (Baert 1998, 101; Giddens 1984, 9). Agency is a 'continuous flow of conduct' (Baert 1998, 101), 'a stream of actual or contemplated causal interventions of corporeal beings in the ongoing process of events-in-the-world' (Giddens 1979, 55). There is also the conviction that people are knowledgeable and are always able to act otherwise (cf. Baert 1998, 101). Structure is marked out from system (the patterning of social relationships across time and space), and defined as 'a set of social rules and resources which are recursively implicated in interaction', and 'located outside space and time, existing only in a virtual way as memory traces, to be implemented in spatially and temporally located interaction' (Baert 1998, 101–2). At the heart of this model is the idea of the duality of structure and its realisation in structuration (Giddens 1984, 25). 'Structure allows for agency, which in turn makes for the unintended reproduction of the very same structures'; 'structures, as rules and resources, are both the precondition and the unintended outcome of people's agency' (Baert 1998, 104).

This range of ideas has been widely influential, but should not be treated uncritically, especially since there is a tendency for archaeology to pick up theories from other disciplines some time after their original formulation and discussion. Both Bourdieu and Giddens are better at describing some of the conditions in which social order is reproduced than at dealing with change (cf. Baert 1998, 33 and 110). Both downplay other, more conscious forms of thought, whether or not these characterise or are part of the routines of daily life. Despite drawing in part on Bourdieu, Giddens presents rather disembodied agents. Both present a rather shadowy picture of structure or structures, and the distinction in the case of Giddens between structure and system is artificial and reductionist.

The number of archaeological studies taking this body of theory as a starting point has multiplied recently. Barrett (1994) discussed the notion of knowledgeable agents in an extended case study of the Avebury region, but these agents remain somewhat faceless, lacking motive or value. Dobres (2000) has attempted to bring people back into the study of technology, within the context of a wide discussion of agency. There is less direct discussion of structure or context, and the detailed case study here (Dobres 2000, 187–209) consists essentially of a demonstration that in a specific late Palaeolithic regional context there was variability in artefact manufacture and repair, which may relate to age and gender differences on the one hand, and perhaps to a non-aggressive use of material culture as a means of social display on the other. One of the more detailed discussions so far has been of the conditions in which changes in container technology were adopted in one region of the eastern United States, from about 4500–3000 BP (Sassaman 2000). Starting from the proposition that 'actions to build consensus or norms are likewise agential in that they derive ultimately from efforts to create rules or traditions in opposition to other structures', Sassaman (2000, 149) argues that there was considerable conflict between insiders and outsiders, and that women were of central importance in a residential system with matrilocality and unilineal descent. Women may have made pottery, while men were committed to an older tradition of soapstone cooking slabs. In time, soapstone vessels appeared, possibly to assert more inclusive relations among regional populations (Sassaman 2000, 163). Agency can be seen in collective action and in collectivities. It is not clear in this account whether agency is to be seen as consistently conscious and intentional, or unconscious and habitual. There seems no reason why it should not have been both, and a very general term is being called upon to cover a very wide range of situations (rather as though we were to approach the study of literature with a central concept of literacy).

While attention to the structure–agency debate is undoubtedly proving fruitful in archaeology, these examples also illustrate some of the difficulties as far as archaeology is concerned. Perhaps at least three recurrent problems can already be identified. First, there is a tendency to brevity. Sometimes this takes the form of programmatic statements, with little or nothing by way of supporting case studies. Thus Hodder has used the convenient example of the Ice Man to illustrate his view of how individual agents could be seen to fit into and influence the historical situations to which they belonged (1999; 2000). The Ice Man is probably in fact one of the least good examples to choose, despite the immediacy of his presence as given by the remarkable circumstances of preservation, since his death was isolated and it is hard to relate him to his contemporary context. Besides, it is equally legitimate to see him as a routine figure, of a kind long familiar in high places, rather than as a new kind of persona symbolising the emergence of a more aggressive, separate and male-oriented world.[2] In either case, the argument needs to be much longer. Another, thought-provoking, programmatic statement on agency distinguishes between structural conditions and structuring principles, to emphasise the distinction between daily routines and what people thought and valued, but no examples are given (Barrett 2000, 65).

Secondly, there has been a tendency merely to substitute one scale of analysis for another: simply shifting from one end of the telescope to the other. This is not confined to archaeology. Marilyn Strathern has commented on the strong tendency in social anthropology to offer 'single relationships' at the expense of more complex, overlapping and sometimes contradictory ones (1987, 29), and J.F. Weiner has fundamentally criticised the 'belief that cultures, particularly those of small-scale societies, can be typified by a single set of structured propositions' (1988, 1). Archaeologists have been prone to substitution: in differing ways over recent years for example, meaning for function, symbolism for practicality, mobility for sedentism, and so on. In a move away from general process and the operation of systems, the individual has been emphasised and individual voices sought (Hodder 1986; Tringham 1991). The gender of whole sets of individuals has been sought, and even where the concern for gender alone has been extended to a wider interest in 'life-process' (Derevenski 2000), analysis has tended to seek the signature of the individual life course, rather than simultaneously embrace the history of the collectivity to which individuals belonged.

Thirdly, the very terms of the structure–agency debate tend to favour abstraction. Both structure and agency tend to be conceived in abstract ways, whether in the distinction already mentioned between 'structural conditions' and 'structuring principles' (Barrett 2000, 65) or in the definition of *habitus* already cited. Agency is often unhelpfully seen as something universal (Gero 2000, 37), and collective agency is often ignored (Sassaman 2000, 149). Agency is often seen in opposition to structure (Moore 2000, 260), and quite clearly agency can be and has been defined in multiple ways (Dobres and Robb 2000b). Such a multiplicity of valid definitions for a single very general term in itself indicates the difficulties. If 'culture' should not be seen as something monolithic (Kuper 1999), then a far wider range of agencies, as the conditions and capabilities for action, must also be considered.

Some of the initial outcomes of this debate, at least as far as prehistoric archaeology has been concerned, could be summarised briefly as follows. People, whether as individuals or collectives, act within settings, practices and situations. Some of their actions are conscious and deliberate, others routine and almost unthinking. Some are strongly guided if not determined by the context, whereas others may be aimed at changing, challenging or otherwise subverting the context. Sometimes people act on their own, but it is clear that agency is not to be reduced only to individuals; in other cases, groups or collectives of people may act together. The effect of action depends on context. Where the setting is stable and values strongly normative, individual or other agency may serve mainly to maintain what was already in place, where less stable and with values and goals fluid, it may lead to rapid change. There may also be unintended consequences to action. In no situation is it really legitimate to separate agency and structure, since one does not exist without the other.

It is not that this debate has been unhelpful, but rather that in archaeology it has generally not gone far enough beyond substitution and abstraction, to allow better demonstration in particular cases of these general points. Because the debate has so far largely failed to engage in detailed studies, it has also failed to give any sort of nuanced sense of what it was like to be an acting person or agent in times remote from the present. A wider discussion is needed, if a better sense of being there is to be achieved. There is great scope for a closer look at the unglamorous routine of many aspects of past lives. This will bring in a discussion of what has been called the taskscape and the dwelling perspective, a sense of people bodily engaged in a world that was never separate or pre-formed, awaiting their interpretation of it. Ingold, for example (1996, 120–1), has suggested that 'apprehending the world is not a matter of construction but of engagement, not of building but of dwelling, not of making a view *of* the world but of taking up a view *in* it'. On the other hand, this kind of treatment of the *habitus* can ignore the worldview of people. How people take a view of the world may depend crucially on how they are encultured. It is dangerous to ascribe too much to culture (Kuper 1999), but perhaps equally unwise to leave it out of account altogether (Sahlins 1999). As one particular dimension of this, values, ideas, ideals and emotions could be seen as the framework of a moral network or a moral community, and constitute a vital part of the 'structures' within which agents act, though one largely ignored so far by prehistoric archaeologists. (One exception, perhaps, is the term 'structuring principles' advocated by Barrett (2000, 65), though only in a general discussion.) Thirdly, all these possibilities need to be illuminated by a much better sense of how people thought. Debate has so far mainly concentrated on a rather simple distinction between conscious and unconscious thought, the latter often restricted to the operation of routine. 'What goes without saying', however, may encompass major issues and central concerns (Wagner 1967, 223; Bloch 1998). In any given situation, people may hold a range of overlapping and sometimes contradictory ideas, in what has been called 'hybridisation' (Latour 1993). There is a tension between the possibility that ritual, for example, is a formalisation or intensification of other activities (Bell 1992), and the likelihood that myth, as another example, exists as a separate domain, a valid but alternative 'as if' within particular settings (J.F. Weiner 1988). Many worldviews might be seen as a series of central concerns, rarely expressed as a whole and held in non-linear fashion (Bloch 1998). And finally, there is the opportunity to give a more specific sense to both 'agency' and 'structure' by considering what constitutes individualism and identity on the one hand, and networks of interaction (Latour 1993; M. Strathern 1996) on the other. There is much still to consider.

Taskscape and dwelling

As already noted, there has been rather general discussion (drawing on Bourdieu and beyond him Mauss, and other sources) of the *habitus*, the setting of existence in which habits and unthinking bodily action maintain a sense of understanding of the world (Gosden 1999, 124–27; cf. Dobres 2000, chapter 5). An overlapping recent strand has been the 'dwelling perspective', derived in large part ultimately from Merleau-Ponty (Tilley 1994, 12–14) and Heidegger (Thomas 1996), and further considered in a series of important papers by Ingold (1993; 1995; 1996; cf. Harris 1998; 2000). This, parallel to the idea of *habitus*, discusses how people act in a world which is never separate, pre-formed or a prior given. The dwelling perspective (Ingold 1993; 1995; 1996) seeks to give a better sense of how people get on in a world which is not pre-given, 'taking the human condition to be that of a being enmeshed from the start, like other creatures, in an active, practical and perceptual engagement with constituents of the dwelt-in world' (Ingold 1996, 120–21); according to it, 'knowledge of the world is gained by moving about in it, exploring it, attending to it, ever alert to the signs by which it is revealed' (Ingold 1996, 141). This kind of approach conveys well a sense of people *attending to* their world, in ways which may not have changed much over long periods of time. As Bloch has noted (1998, 5), we are sometimes guilty of seeking too much diversity, a question that will be one of the themes of this book. Paradoxically, diversity may be a constituent of long-term stability.

The initial formulation of the taskscape ended with a scene taken from a Bruegel painting, *The Harvesters*. Ingold (1993, 164–71) uses this to show how people might have attended to a series of social relations while the task of getting the harvest in was being carried out, in a landscape formed by experience and movement through it. The challenge remains of using the approach with archaeological evidence. Edmonds (1999) has discussed the woodland setting, and in a general way the use of animals, but I can think of no detailed accounts of the routine socialities that may have been played out in either plant cultivation or animal husbandry. This then is one challenge which should be attempted with archaeological evidence.

The approach is also incomplete. It seems to give insufficient attention to learning and to socialisation. These may be long processes during childhood, in their turn almost unconscious or casual (e.g. Mead 1943), but there are also stages, such as initiation, when instruction may be much more direct, and when, as among the Hua of Eastern Highland New Guinea (Meigs 1990), gender ideologies may be at their most accentuated. The taskscape approach seems to give insufficient attention to the weight of collective tradition or culture (cf. Sahlins 1999) – however that may be taken up or contested by individuals – which may affect *how* people acquire 'the skills for direct perceptual engagement' (Ingold 1996, 142) with the world. It seems an extreme claim that people never make a view of the world, and it is possible to propose that people act at different times and in different situations from varied perspectives. *The Harvesters* painting itself may promote a certain moral stance, a particular view of the world. The dwelling perspective is best at giving a general sense of the flow of life, but less satisfactory at showing how people can do basic things in very different ways, or how they cope with innovations. The issues of diversity and uniformity, and of change and stability, recur again.

Culture, values and the moral network

Culture has been having a bad time in some circles, but lives happily on in others. Prehistorians of a theoretical bent have largely ignored it since the 1960s and 1970s, culture in some collective sense being replaced by material culture, active, almost an agent in its own right, particular, used to contest and subvert as much as to bind or to express either unthinking or conscious solidarity. This mirrors the diversity of use of symbols in cultural studies. A recent critique by a British social anthropologist of the American tradition of cultural anthropology recognises the general sense of culture as simply a way of talking about collective identities (Kuper 1999, 3), though it proposes that in the end the concept is an unhelpful (and unhealthy) lumping together of too many disparate processes (Kuper 1999, 247).

Such diversity and many-strandedness are one of the main themes of this book, but it seems useful to revive interest in the ties that bind, and in a sense of collective agency. It has been strongly argued that even the 'codgers' of the American cultural anthropology tradition such as Boas or Linton did not see culture as 'universally shared, monolithic or otherwise coherent socially or consistent logically' (Sahlins 1999, 405). Wagner has described, with reference to the Daribi people of New Guinea, how, though alliances can take many forms on the ground, 'community' is a popular tactic of clan interaction and principles of exchange, expressed as belief in consanguinity (1967, 211, 216). But even if invented and tactical, a sense of collective identity can nonetheless be very real, especially in small-scale societies. We shall come back to questions of who might have been included in the varying uses of 'we': 'We, the LBK people' as well as 'We, the Tikopia'?[3]

As one way of talking about collective identities, I should like to focus more attention on values, ideals and emotions. These are important, as they are all in a sense ideas, which are unlikely in any case to have been generated by single individuals, and the scale of collectivity involved is left open. Most of the individuals sketched so far by an interpretive, post-modernist archaeology lack any or much sense of shared values. While the *domus* can indeed stand as a quite rare example of an explicitly formulated value system that includes everyone involved, the same cannot be said of the *agrios*, which only seems to have affected adult men (Hodder 1990). The Ice Man's self-sufficiency is enough to make him stand as a representative of a whole ideology (Hodder 1999). I have argued instead that there was a long-lived general set of values in the European Neolithic, incorporating ideals of participation, sharing, non-accumulation and commonality but also the pursuit of prowess (Whittle 1996). This is not to claim that values in the European Neolithic were uniform in all times and places, or that actual behaviour always accorded with such ideals. Nor is it to restate a Durkheimian position in which society makes its individuals. But there is socialisation, and each individual does not take up a view in the world *de novo* and unaffected by others; what others have done in the past and are doing in the present must affect *how* people acquire 'the skills for direct perceptual engagement' (Ingold 1996, 142) with the world, unless we are to argue that engagement with the physical and social world is something of universal character.

Analogies suggest a wide range of possibilities. In an Aristotelian sense of being concerned for the response of others, it is possible to see exchange for example as a moral activity (Hagen 1999). In arguing that exchange among the Maneo of eastern Indonesia (note the first of many examples where it seems to make perfectly good sense to refer to collective identity, even though this can also be broken down or analysed at other scales) has in this sense a vital moral dimension, not reducible to its social effects, Hagen has suggested that the Maneo are not guided by specific moral principles such as would mandate sharing (1999, 362). In many cases in the historical or recent Mediterranean world, individual personal responsibility is held in the 'triangle of honor, shame and luck' (Douglas and Isherwood 1996, 23). Referring to Kabyle society in Algeria, Bourdieu (1977, 48) has observed:

> The ethic of honour is the self-interest ethic of social formations, groups or classes in whose patrimony symbolic capital figures prominently. Only total unawareness of the terrible and permanent loss which a slur on the honour of the women of the lineage can represent could lead one to see obedience to an ethical or juridical rule as the principle of the actions intended to prevent, conceal or make good the outrage.

The western terms 'ought, 'want' and 'must' may not be easily applied to the Daribi of New Guinea, whose moral law is based on 'relative, political intergroup situations' (Wagner 1967, 29). In other cases, however, imagined moral life and moral language seem to be more centrally linked to an ethical sense, tied to ideas of the person and identity, and generating powerful emotions within a shared value system. Among the Amuesha people of central Peru, greediness and meanness are regarded as immoral, irrational and antisocial, and 'power is legitimate only when its holders are seen as loving, compassionate and generous life-givers' (Santos-Granero 1991, 229). Among the Rauto people in Melanesia, ceremonial exchange carried out in the right way creates a 'cultural landscape of memory and emotion', and the emotions generated can be considered as a kind of moral perception; emotions 'define and render compelling a particular moral stance towards life', the result of choice between this and more individualistic alternatives (Maschio 1998, 86, 97). Among the Western Apache, as described by Basso (1984), certain historical narratives served to link past events to named places, in stories which 'stalked' their listeners with their moral force; and native American appropriation of the landscape has been envisaged as being effected by 'an act of imagination which is moral and kind' (Momaday 1976, 80). These are all examples of values and emotions with a central place in social relations and living in the world. Among the Etoro of Papua New Guinea, however, male-dominated social inequality is constructed as a moral hierarchy or hierarchy of virtue, grounded in cosmology and worldview (Kelly 1993). A moral sense need not in itself be neutral, and there is certainly no need to idealise or whitewash it. Concerning the Daribi again, Wagner (1967, xxviii) has written of 'their dour, almost boastful pride in a culture which is a curse, whose demons are named for diseases, whose powers are the ill-wills of the wronged, whose triumph is the negation of a negation'; the individual Daribi reacts with anger to the ways in which the outside world possesses the soul and may bring sickness, weakness and madness (Wagner 1967, 42).

The concept of a 'moral community' has been used in a discussion of the Nuer, to connote those participating in a common value system (Johnson 1994, 327–9), as well as with reference to the Amuesha (Santos-Granero 1991, 119); the related concept of mutuality has also been discussed by Moore (1988) and Gosden (1994), and the practice of 'moral coalitions', though with a greater sense of conflict between sets of gender-based values, has been discussed by Robb (1994). Adapting these ideas, the idea of a moral network can be proposed; the extent to which others are involved and affected may define the moral network, which like other networks is liable to remain local at all points (Latour 1993, 117–20) but may also be open and unbounded. Values may be seen to act as sanctions on behaviour; there were limits to what individuals or limited interest groups could attempt or hope to get away with, and there may have been limits, within this perspective, to what they could conceive as possible. In this way, we can perhaps begin to put some flesh on what Barrett has called 'structuring principles' (2000, 65).

How they thought

It is not enough just to suggest kinds of thought and value, as it were alongside patterns of bodily action. It is also necessary to pay more attention to how those were expressed. This may vary. There may be at least four significant aspects: non-explicit performance of ideas, non-linear expression based around central nodes or concepts, alternative 'tropes', and historical hybridisation. The dwelling perspective discussed above evokes a rather active, conscious kind of attention to the world. This may not be how people think all the time. The anthropologist Maurice Bloch (1992) has explored a sense of 'what goes without saying' in Zafimaniry society in Madagascar, by looking at attitudes and beliefs, rooted in practice and material experience, which are central to people but which seem so obvious that explanation of them to outsiders seems pointless. These concern ideas about such subjects as people themselves, trees, sex, gender and houses. The relevance of elaborate house decoration is not easily put into words – what goes without saying – as it is simply part of the right way to treat the living and growing house (Bloch 1995a). Once again, some kind of collective dimension is involved. Not all relevant ideas can be seen as confined to the practice and material experience of a single generation. The concept of the maturing house (in which the hardening of its wood is a metaphor for the growth and success of the household) relies on a considerable passage of time and presumably some active transmission from generation to generation. However it is passed on, this is also a powerful model for thinking about enduring beliefs over very long periods of time (even though the historical Malagasy situation has been far from static or timeless: Bloch 1998).

Another dimension of this study was a use of 'connectionism' (see also Bloch 1993), or the non-linear ways in which people often actually seem to think. Speed of thought and the ability to react instantly in different social situations suggest that thought can be held in central nodes or concepts, such as again in the Zafimaniry case to do with what people are like and how they mature, the differences and similarities between men and women, and what good marriages, trees and wood, and houses are like (Bloch 1992). In the Zafimaniry case, these could be seen to make up some sort of coherent worldview, though that might never or rarely be expressed as a single unified whole. Or at least, there is little obvious contradiction or opposition between these suggested nodes of thought.

In other cases, the propositions of a 'culture' may exist on different planes, as it were on separate drives as well as in different folders. This has been explored with reference to myth, song and dream by J.F. Weiner among the Foi people of Papua New Guinea (1988; 1991). We shall come back to myth in chapter 5, but a preliminary discussion is helpful here. Weiner argues for a number of views of the world, a 'series of successively embedded metaphors' in which central concerns with male–female relations can be played out (1988, 285). Myth does not serve, however, to mirror exactly the facts of daily social existence, but is another and equally valid rendering of those (J.F. Weiner 1988, 5, 16). In a slightly different way, song and dreams open up different ways of looking at and re-ordering the world. For the Foi, it is important to communicate with the ghosts of the dead in dreams, an activity in which males are often engaged (J.F. Weiner 1991, 1–8). These ghosts, however, are ambiguous and elusive, inhabiting an upside-down world, part ill-disposed towards the living, part benevolent. Men seek a link with the power of ghosts through dreams. Women also have a central role in looking after the newly dead. It is they who create songs, which link names and places in the flow and movement of Foi life (of which more later), but it is men who perform such memorial litanies, preferably in the intense and public sociality of their longhouse villages, rather than in more isolated and ghost-haunted bush houses. Knowing the world is thus a complex process, involving several concepts or nodes, the dead as well as the living, play between genders, and gendered creativity and performance.

Compartmentalisation of thought may also in part be the outcome of histories. In a discussion of post-1989 Europe, it has been proposed that we do often think in compartmentalised ways, a pattern or mixture which has been called hybridisation (Latour 1993). At the present time, we may be said to retain elements of pre-modern, modern and post-modern thought (Latour 1993, fig. 5.1). This model certainly fits the discipline of archaeology in its present state. Thus the discipline still happily encompasses many concepts based on evolution (from the nineteenth century), regularly uses the concept of process from the modernist phase of the 1960s and 1970s, and has engaged since the early 1980s in post-modernist self-reflexivity; only the manifesto writers see themselves as outside such a mixture of approaches. This is a very general but potentially important and useful way to think about modes of thought in the past across horizons of change and over long periods of time. Bloch has noted one small example of this, in the way in which some Malagasy farmers speak to their animals not in their native tongue, but in French, the language of colonial power (1998, 193–5).

Individuals and networks

We keep coming back to questions of scale. The discussion of the taskscape in the dwelling perspective, or of the *habitus* and its *nexus*, the body, offers the possibility of looking closely at individual action. Many of the basic routines of past existence may have been persistent, and widely shared. They may also have varied subtly from situation to situation, encompassing both diversity and the potential for change. The tendency so far has been to treat agency as individuality, in the terms of Rapport (1996), or the ability to act, rather than as individualism, or the potential to act in distinctive ways. As we shall see in chapter 3, individuals have so far been regularly treated as universal agents, largely unchanging, atomised, mostly faceless, and lack-ing emotions and values. There has been little attempt to consider the very varied ways in which identity and concepts of the individual may have been constituted, and their significance for questions of diversity and change.

On the other hand, 'structure', in the varied guises of 'society', 'community' and 'archaeological culture', has generally been seen as a closed system, and the challenge has been conceived as one of working out the play between internal dynamics and external pressures. In this regard, the alternative notion of network may be more helpful, as it leaves the question of closure unanswered. The notion of closed system has been a powerful one, including in social anthropology. With reference to descent, it has been shown how the model of closed, unilineal descent was for a very long time forced on to the ethnographic evidence, suiting our own view of the world better than the evidence on the ground (Kuper 1988). The idea of network raises other possibilities, with open – perhaps bilateral – systems of descent, ties that go on for ever, and alliance and co-residence at least as important as kinship and descent. Leach argued such a position for the Kachin of highland Burma (E. Leach 1954), suggesting, as Tambiah (1998, 312–13) has summarised it, 'an open system of many lineages linked in circles of wife givers and wife takers, communicating with one another diacritically through variations of dialect, dress, and other local differences, and capable of dynamically generating . . . as well as contesting tendencies towards extra-local hierarchical political formations'. But it has taken a long time for archaeology to consider its implications (see also E. Leach 1973). It has been argued that even the longest networks (from global corporations to railway systems) can be seen as local at particular times and places (Latour 1993, 117), and that we are accustomed to cutting the network, in order to make sense of things within the framework of our own lives (M. Strathern 1996). These abstract propositions should be regarded with suspicion. We cannot generalise the character of every network in advance. Whether situations were seen as purely local, or whether the local was strongly bound into factors much further afield, requires careful examination in specific instances. Much may depend on the stage in the 'life course' (cf. Derevenski 2000) of individuals concerned and the kinds of sociality possible or required.

The Ice Man provides an initial, limited example. It has been argued that his way of life increasingly stood for something outside the bounds of lowland agricultural life in the later fourth millennium BC, his independence and self-sufficiency representing the separate male world of the *agrios* (Hodder 1999; 2000). Seen as part of a network or perhaps better a series of networks, the situation may seem rather different. Many people before him had gone into and across high places. Trans-Alpine contacts go back to the early Holocene period (though they probably did gradually intensify through time). There is some general support for the notion that males among foragers can range quite widely, at a lifetime scale, in search of mating partners (MacDonald and Hewlett 1999), though there is no need to restrict such movement to males (as we shall see in chapter 2). The Ice Man was clearly in contact with lowland communities. He must therefore have been enmeshed in various networks, and habituated to different kinds of sociality in varying settings, places and seasons. Perhaps such skills came best to an older person, with more experience. Whatever precisely he was doing on the trip that led to his death, his existence cannot be reduced to a single dimension.

The argument that follows

These preliminary concerns define the argument that follows. In chapter 2, I look at routines, from the scale of the body to those of residence and landscape. Routines are never neutral; they are embodied ways of dealing with the world. They thus show how much was held in common in daily life, but also the possibility for diversity, not least because acting in the world, being there, requires the presence of others and demands sociality. Paradoxically, from this structural condition may have come not only widespread diversity but also long-term stability. In chapter 3, I look at analogies to consider the many-sidedness of individualism and identity, and go on to look at the ties that bind and the possibility of different kinds of network. This also involves consideration of values and the moral community, and I shall argue that this was another factor in long-term stability. In chapters 4 and 5, I shall bring in other important parts of this world, animals and the past, to illustrate not only further central concerns, but also again ambiguity and fluidity in several important dimensions. In chapter 6, I try to pull these ideas together in short case studies from central Europe to southern Britain, to offer concrete examples instead of endless analogy and generalisation. These are mainly from early situations, and will bring us back, among others, to one of the examples with which this chapter started. In the last brief chapter, I take a longer time perspective, and suggest that the many-sidedness of past existence is part of why things may have changed more slowly than we have been accustomed to think.

Chapter 2

The daily round

Routines are the stuff of life: innumerable, repeated actions, which time after time keep the world in existence. It is impossible to envisage a Neolithic world in any detail without thinking about the conditions in which people, day after day, and from season to season, cooked, ate, gathered, talked, resided, looked after their animals, or moved through and attended to the landscapes which they inhabited. Routines comprise things that have to be done for life to go on, their very repetition creating what has been called a sense of 'ontological security'. Because they are quite varied, though each one in itself is repeating, routines embrace different kinds and scales of social interaction or sociality, in varying settings. Many routine actions may be carried out unthinkingly or unconsciously, though not necessarily all of them, and their cumulative effect may often be what has been called the 'unintentional reproduction of structures'. Routines are embodied, but rarely neutral in meaning or on reflection. They may be both generated by and in their turn help to generate culturally specific principles and worldviews. Because of this varied nature, routines are at the heart of considerable diversity and yet also of much that was held in common among people widely separated in space and time. They have been discussed widely in other disciplines, but rarely thought about in detail in interpretive accounts of prehistory. Rather, in the ways we divide up and write about our subject, the emphasis has tended to be on largely disembodied and asocial, separated procedures: residence as questions of numbers or duration; crop processing and animal husbandry as techniques and procedures; landscape as static settlement patterns; and so on. Routines are a potentially rich field of enquiry, and this chapter is an exploratory attempt to examine their importance for winning a better understanding of being there.

It is important to resist reducing routines to single dimensions. Giddens, for example, has used the insights and experiments of 'symbolic interactionists' and 'ethnomethodologists' like Goffman and Garfinkel, as well as the approach of Bourdieu, to suggest that people are normally predisposed to see their routine existence maintained, which promotes the unintentional reproduction of structures (Giddens 1979, 218–19; Baert 1998, 80, 106). Goffman studied small slices of contemporary society in America, to examine encounters and the skilful accomplishment of order and predictability by the individuals concerned. His central concern was with the performances, guided by tacit and practical rules and by a sense of situational propriety, of people in interaction with an audience of others (Goffman 1963; 1969). Garfinkel too was interested in the routine of life, and in how people make sense of things. He suggested that people do this constantly, by 'reflectivity of accounts', without explicit recourse to conscious knowledge of the rules (1967, 7–9). His experiments with how people react to breaches in trust were designed to show what happened when routines were disrupted, including the considerable reluctance of people to alter their use of implicit rules and ways of going about things. 'Ontological security' (Giddens 1979, 219; cf. Dickens 1990), no matter how vague a concept that may be, is something that people are normally reluctant to let go, and this may be an important factor in promoting or enabling continuity of practice.

Routines are powerful, complex and varied. Many operate by recourse to shared rules and procedures, because otherwise there would be no intersubjectivity or awareness of the feelings and attitudes of others. This raises again the question of the consciousness with which routine actions are carried out. The literature seems to reflect two positions. On the one hand, there is an influential lobby for the view that routine action can be and is normally carried out unthinkingly and unconsciously, with the further effect of unintentional reproduction of 'structures'. This has already been noted above from the work of Goffman and Garfinkel, and of Giddens (1979, 216–30), and, unsurprisingly, is also to be found in discussions by Bourdieu (e.g. 1977, 218, note 44; and see below), though precisely how intersubjectivity is created through the *habitus* does not seem to be explicitly addressed. On the other hand, Ingold (1993; 1995; 1996; and see chapter 1) has advanced a dwelling perspective, drawing in large part on Merleau-Ponty and Heidegger, which brings in a sense of people engaged in dealing with the world, attending to what needs to be done in their taskscape. The dwelling perspective seeks to give a better sense of how people get on in a world which is not pre-given, 'taking the human condition to be that of a being enmeshed from the start, like other creatures, in an active, practical and perceptual engagement with constituents of the dwelt-in world' (Ingold 1996, 120–1); 'apprehending the world is not a matter of construction but of engagement, not of building but of dwelling, not of making a view of the world but of taking up a view in it' (Ingold 1996, 121); and finally, 'knowledge of the world is gained by moving about in it, exploring it, attending to it, ever alert to the signs by which it is revealed' (Ingold 1996, 141). The sense of active attention to the world is demonstrated in the example of Bruegel's *Harvesters*, noted in the previous chapter (Ingold 1993, 164–71). Stressing the way in which the world is constantly being carried forward, the account also places people in the centre of the taskscape, active, responsive to each other, aware of their past and future, and in tune with the landscape resonating around them (Ingold 1993, 170–1).

As with the discussion of agency in the previous chapter, I believe that it is important to avoid having to choose one of these positions at the expense of the other. Routine action is part of agency, and both are complex and varied, and not to be reduced to simple propositions. Some action may normally be carried out unconsciously or unthinkingly, with people barely aware of its wider potential meaning.

Other action may be done with a kind of submerged consciousness of its significance, as in the case of the decorative carving of houses in Madagascar (Bloch 1995a), such that questions about it from outsiders seem ludicrous and pointless to the people involved. In other cases, motivation and intentionality may be much more squarely in the foreground.

Learning may be a useful example. There is evidence to suggest that learning begins in the womb, with the primary absorption of both language and a sense of bodily orientation (Gopnik *et al.* 1999). Bodily orientation may come to be central in later life, as James Weiner (1991, 73; and see below) has suggested for the Foi of Papua New Guinea. Much learning probably takes place informally during childhood (e.g. Mead 1943; Lepowsky 1990). With reference to the house, Bourdieu (1977, 90) has pronounced that 'the 'book' from which the children learn their vision of the world is read with the body, in and through the movements and displacements which make the space within which they are enacted as much as they are made by it'. Much of what is vital may simply be picked up by participation and imitation. J.F. Weiner (1991, 37) has noted how the Foi individual male, to whom movement through the landscape is vital, must pick up knowledge of territory in a piecemeal fashion, but with his father or guardian showing him 'one by one the places available to him'. It is clear then that informality of learning need not always be the same as unconscious learning. And there is initiation, a recurrent though not universal formal passage to adulthood (e.g. M. Allen 1998; Meigs 1984; 1990; Power and Watts 1997). At initiation there are recurrently separation and a heightening of consciousness, and a passing on not only of knowledge and a sense of identity, related both to group and to gender (including in the process apparent gender reversals: Power and Watts 1997), but also of concepts of activity and behaviour appropriate to the initiated. These have varied from rules about food for young male initiates among the Hua of Papua New Guinea (Meigs 1984), to short-lived ritualised male homosexuality in various parts of Melanesia as a whole, important for the transference of semen as symbolic of male potency and representative of the giving of milk by mothers (Allen 1998). Among the Foi, men initiated boys into a major cult designed to promote good relations with ghosts and thereby to overcome illness and lead to success in sorcery (J.F. Weiner 1988, 56). Initiates ranged from boys of nine to young married men (J.F. Weiner 1988, 58). Some food-associated taboos for men lasted until 'advanced middle age', related to central notions of proper relations between women and men (J.F. Weiner 1988, 61). Here then are examples of explicit instruction in non-trivial behaviours, some to be longer lasting than others, which are imposed on the young from the stages of childhood up to early adulthood.

Two longer examples, not from archaeology, can give a more extended idea of the various possibilities hinted at so far. James Weiner has written strikingly about the way in which among the Foi, women interrupt the talk of men, calling, commenting and interrupting from their smaller houses which flank the longhouse, where the men reside and also sleep, when they are all together in their central settlement (J.F. Weiner 1991, 5; 1988). The people are not always together. In the drier half of the year, people are congregated in the central settlement, focused on both gardening and communal life based around the longhouse, with its attendant emphasis on 'gregariousness, competitiveness and confrontation' (J.F. Weiner 1991, 8). Public life in the longhouse collective is contrasted with the intimate sociality of the bush-house, never more than an hour away (J.F. Weiner 1988, 38), in which the smaller unit of man and wife and immediate family work closely in complementary ways to achieve their own production goals. The wetter season of the year was associated with dispersal, especially to remote and isolated hunting lodges, and men's experi-ences in this domain constituted much of the stuff of talk back in the longhouse (J.F. Weiner 1991, 35). Here, very vividly, are a series of routines and socialities. The Foi orientate themselves partly with reference to the flow of the rivers along whose banks they garden, and they make sense of life in their songs and their myths by reference to ideas of flow and movement.

In a different setting, Mark Harris (1998; 2000) has described the changing routines and socialities of life on the Amazonian floodplain. Here the fluctuating height of the river sets basic conditions. It is the dry season which leads to dispersal and movement, and the wet season to unavoidable static congregation in dispersed houses. Seasonality is not just a matter of adapting to a framework of external environ-mental constraints, but is experienced by changes in sociality and mood. The flood times, in which people are largely confined to their houses, are felt to be boring, lacking wider sociality, and yet regenerative, because focused on the individual house and relations among the immediate family (Harris 1998, 78). The dry season is associated with a revival of spirits, more food, periodic festive aggregations, inter-action with strangers, exchange and generosity, though it is linked also with an increase in tension and gossip (Harris 1998, 77). Routines, in this account, resonate with 'the rhythms of the dwelt-in environment', and are part of the 'work in motion' of bringing the world repeatedly into existence (Harris 1998, 79).

In exploring routines and sociality in the Neolithic setting, with the evidence of archaeology rather than of ethnography and social theory, this chapter will concen-trate on the body, residence, subsistence tasks, and movement through the landscape. This is a barely explored field of enquiry, which can potentially contribute to better understanding not only of any one situation but also of central questions of con-tinuity, diversity and change. I will return to those issues throughout this book.

An archaeology of the body?

The body seems a good place to start. There are the Ice Man (see Spindler *et al.* 1995) and innumerable skeletons. These have been more or less carefully examined, but with surprisingly little integration of results into a view of daily life. Skeletons are routinely aged and sexed, with the resulting data normally employed in reconstruc-tions of social formations and now gender relations, while pathologies and traumas are often regarded as unusual oddities. Only recently has a more forensic approach begun to be applied to the human body itself, with new insights into how the human body carries on it evidence of activity and lifestyle (Larsen 1997; cf Wysocki and Whittle 2000). Meanwhile, social theorists have been arguing for years the central importance of the body; indeed Weiner (1991, 63) points out that this tradition goes back to Malinowski. Merleau-Ponty (1962) was one of the first in more recent times explicitly to challenge the Cartesian separation of mind and body, and to suggest the body and its movements as the source of orientation and perception of the world. Bourdieu too, as already noted, gave great importance to the body. Sometimes this is a rather generalised, almost abstract body, as when he declares (1977, 218, note 44):

> Every group entrusts to bodily automatisms those principles most basic to it and most indispensable to its conservation. In societies which lack any other recording and objectifying instrument, inherited knowledge can survive only in its embodied state. . . . The body is thus continuously mingled with all the knowledge it reproduces, which can never have the objectivity and distance stemming from objectification in writing.

In other instances, however, especially in his study of the Kabyle house, the body is both in focus and gendered: 'whereas for the man, the house is not so much a place he enters as a place he comes out of, movement inward properly befits the woman' (Bourdieu 1977, 91). Henrietta Moore has discussed the extent to which Bourdieu's 'dumb imperatives' of the body are consistent with any sense of agency, and suggests in his defence that praxis or action is itself a moment of interpretation, and that embodiment is a never finished process (Moore 1994). Bourdieu's reference to the 'arbitrary content of a culture' (1977, 91) chimes well with many other accounts. The body is not a given, according to Foucault (1978; cf. Gatens 1992). It has been noted in one study that the way pots were held and carried was at least as important for signalling facets of identity as the shape or decoration of the vessels in question (Sterner 1989, 454).

The body has therefore been widely discussed in disciplines other than archaeology. Bryan Turner (1996, 24–7; see also Featherstone *et al.* 1991; Falk 1994) has summarised three approaches. The first is the concept of the body as a set of social practices. Bourdieu belongs to this, with a background in the notion of potentiality first explored by Mauss, namely that the body is a 'physiological potentiality which is realized socially and collectively through a variety of shared body practices within which the individual is trained, disciplined and socialized' (B.S. Turner 1996, 25). Turner also assigns Garfinkel to this group. The second approach has seen the body as a system of signs, and carrier of social meaning and symbolism. This can best be seen in the work of Mary Douglas (1966; 1996). 'The social body constrains the way the physical body is read' (Douglas 1996, 69). The central hypothesis is that the body reflects the form of the society to which it belongs; the more closed the social situation, the more formal the expression and behaviour of the body. Particular situations can be read by reference to the relationship between group or bounded social unit, and grid or rules and classifications (Douglas 1996, 59–68; Fardon 1999, 110–16). Though the body here is put centre stage, it is curiously passive and reflective, and there appears little room for either individual diversity or deliberate divergence from prevailing norms or for change. The third strand (which may well overlap with the previous one) is that which has seen the body as a system of signs standing for and expressing relations of power (B.S. Turner 1996, 27). This is a trend presaged in the writing of Foucault, and exemplified in more recent work by many others including Butler (1993).

How then to approach with archaeological evidence what Crossley (1995) has called a 'carnal sociology' and B.S. Turner (1996, 27) a 'fleshly discourse'? My approach and argument here are simple: that there is much to consider that has been neglected, that the potentiality of the body may have been realised in many different ways, that the body was rarely neutral, and that it may be possible to glimpse, or at least to begin to think about, generative schemes behind bodily action.

As a start, we can go back to growing up, learning and initiation, already discussed above. There is no doubt that from a demographic point of view children are under-represented in the mortuary record. On the other hand, they consistently appear in graves, cemeteries and an array of barrows and cairns. When were children thought to be fully socialised? I have argued that by the later fifth millennium BC on the Great Hungarian Plain, as seen in the graves at Tiszapolgár-Basatanya, at least some children, perhaps as young as five or six, were being treated in death ritual as future adults (Whittle 1996, 72–3). Girls for example wore finger rings and sashes of beads in the style of much older women, and took with them to the grave sufficient pots to display the ability to provide food, drink and hospitality. It cannot be certain, however, that this reflects the actual status of children at this time, as opposed to the standing of the group or groups who used the Tiszapolgár-Basatanya burial ground over a number of generations. In many other cases, there is evidence to suggest that children were of ambiguous status. For example, there are instances of children being buried under house floors in the tells or settlement mounds of the earlier fifth millennium BC on the Great Hungarian Plain: in the case of Berettyóújfalu-Herpály, especially at the corner of buildings, and in the company of the skulls of wild cattle (Kalicz and Raczky 1987). Adult graves, when they occur, come in small groups in spaces between or beyond contemporary houses. In the Linear Pottery culture of central and western Europe (referred to hereafter by its German abbreviation LBK) of the later sixth millennium BC, there are numerous instances of children's graves in the spaces beside and between contemporary longhouses (Veit 1996; Siemoneit 1997). This is much rarer for adults (Veit 1996; Orschiedt 1998). Children are represented also in cemeteries, normally with very few or no grave goods (Jeunesse 1997). Adults are found in much greater numbers than children in the cemeteries. The graves of children among the longhouses are nearly always very simple affairs. It is misleadingly easy to see in this simplicity a lack of emotion (cf. Rosaldo 1993; Reddy 1997; Connor 1995). It is far more satisfactory to suppose that children were highly valued, but that because they were still learning, still full of potential, they were an appropriate symbol for regeneration and continuity into the future, a link between the stages of the cycle of longhouse growth and decay. In another context, of Britain in the fourth millennium BC, it has been suggested that stone extraction sources could have been in part a place of initiation (cf. Edmonds 1999, 45), and the involvement of children or young people is certainly supported by the very narrow galleries of many flint mines (Russell 2000).

A series of examples involving adults can perhaps take us closer to routines, as well as to sociality. Bourdieu was keen to emphasise the 'gestures and movements of the body' (1977, 94), and Mauss himself used the example of walking to illustrate his notion of potentiality (B.S. Turner 1996, 25). At the pre-Neolithic and early Neolithic Syrian site at Abu Hureyra, a mass of evidence for the bearing of loads, pounding and grinding was found by detailed examination of damage to the skeleton and of muscle attachments; grinding was here probably a mainly female activity (Molleson 1994). It is clear from recent re-examination of Early Neolithic human skeletons in southern Britain, of the fourth millennium BC, that there was potentially much variation in the manner in which people walked and moved about their business, and in 'activity regimes' in general (Wysocki and Whittle 2000; cf. Larsen 1997). This is possible to detect because of variations in the effect which muscles, tendons and ligaments create at their point of connection to the skeleton. These are known technically as musculoskeletal stress markers. Though the data are relatively limited and their interpretation complex, nonetheless differences can be suggested both between sites and between males and females. At the West Kennet long barrow, for example, males may have used their right arms in rotary action, perhaps for throwing, far more vigorously and often than females, whose forearms were used together for a range of possible tasks; likewise the men seem to have used their legs for exercise such as running and jumping, or possibly longer-range travel, to a much greater extent than the women. By contrast, there are some signs that whereas the men from two south Welsh sites, Parc le Breos Cwm and Tinkinswood, were as active as their counterparts at West Kennet, the women there were not as active over the same range of activities as their counterparts.

We can only guess at how these variations might have shown themselves in the way in which people moved. There is some evidence to suggest that hunter-gatherer males may range further over a lifetime than females (MacDonald and Hewlett 1999), but both in Late Mesolithic Brittany (Schulting and Richards 2001) and in the LBK of the Rhineland (Price et al. 2001) there is new isotopic evidence to suggest the in-marriage of females.[1] I have already referred to J.F. Weiner's discussion (1988; 1991) of the importance of a sense of flow and movement among the Foi of Papua New Guinea, and a sense of movement and direction may also be visible in the strongly repetitive orientations of both LBK longhouses and long cairns and barrows in western Europe, especially Britain. Both have been ascribed to other factors, the placing of longhouses as a response to prevailing winter wind direction or the direction of the coast (Coudart 1998), and the placing of cairns and barrows as an orientation on the moon (Burl 1987). Other interpretations of the orientation of longhouses ascribe this to a gradually fossilising tradition (Mattheusser 1991) or to a sense of ancestral origins (Bradley 2001). In both cases, it is hard not to imagine landscapes in which people moved around, to varying extents, and the link I am seeking to establish is between kinds and degrees of movement carried out in daily routines and a wider sense of the importance of movement and direction in the wider cultural context.

The resting and talking body must also have been important. The evidence is unfortunately much thinner here. Negatively, there is virtually no evidence of furniture across our area, and even in the unusually preserved stone houses of northern Scotland, what do survive are mainly 'dressers' and 'beds', classically at Skara Brae, Orkney (Parker Pearson and Richards 1994). There are only a few possible individual seats in the form of very low single stones by the central hearth. This lack also extends to the wooden houses of the Alpine foreland. Presumably, therefore, for much of the time people squatted on the ground or on floors. There may be some osteological evidence for this, in the form of facets from wear on hip, knee, ankle and foot joints, though none of these is unambiguous (Larsen 1997, 185; Theya Molleson, pers. comm.). A notched kneecap at Abu Hureyra has been attributed to squatting at rest (Molleson 1994), and at the Early Neolithic site of Çatalhöyük in Anatolia the bone evidence suggests that men habitually squatted, heels together on the ground, while women adopted a variety of positions, presumably reflecting a variety of activities undertaken (Theya Molleson, pers. comm.). In Britain observations of facets on the distal anterior tibia (i.e. ankle) have often been associated with habitual squatting, but it is not possible from the samples currently available to suggest clear gender- or age-related differences (Michael Wysocki, pers. comm.). A few of the burials from the Danube Gorges were buried in a sitting position, legs splayed *à la turque*, and it has been suggested that this might have been a position appropriate to old men watching the river and its ancestral creatures (Borić 1999, 60–1). Among the Foi again, Weiner has noted important differences in the public body postures of men and women (1991, 156). Men tend to stand up, with chest and upper torso open, using their arms to emphasise and give rhythm to singing and oratory. Women normally sit, with the central body closed up; their singing is performed sitting. In this context at least, 'women's positions emphasize stasis, compactness, motionlessness; men's postures emphasize a dynamic, charged motion, an openness and potential for vigorous, rhythmic movement' (J.F. Weiner 1991, 156). Could this ever be reflected in body positions seen in graves?

In the Foi context, public communication often takes the form of ritualised singing, oratory and other kinds of performance. There is also plenty of talk, including between neighbouring houses, as already noted. The force of the institution of the men's house on Vanatinai Island off New Guinea has also been described by Lepowsky (1990, 178–9), but this is also a setting in which the opinions of women and young people are regularly voiced in public debate. Talking together presumably filled much of people's time; given that there was a spectrum of time and energy budgets across the varied subsistence regimes of Neolithic Europe, a diversity better documented in Australia and New Guinea among both hunter-gatherers and shifting cultivators (Lourandos 1980, 248), there was plenty of time to fill. The nature of talk may have varied. Basso (1984, 33–4) has referred to three kinds of speech among the Western Apache: ordinary talk, prayer, and narratives or stories, the latter of which can again be subdivided into myths, historical tales, sagas and gossip, as well as Coyote stories and seduction tales. In turn these categories can be distinguished by their temporal and spatial anchoring, and by their field of concern:

myths to enlighten, historical tales to criticise and to warn, and so on. 'In acts of speech, mundane and otherwise, Apaches negotiate images and understandings of the land which are accepted as credible accounts of what it actually is, why it is significant, and how it impinges on the daily lives of men and women. . . . With words, a massive physical presence is fashioned into a meaningful human universe' (Basso 1984, 22). This might seem as far as we can get with talking, and it is not even clear whether at this date different groups could have understood each other (cf. Renfrew 2000). But we will come back to various possible kinds of talk and speech subsequently.

Another central routine is eating. It is obvious that the consumption of food is not neutral (Douglas 1996; Gosden and Hather 1999). Food is clearly not just a matter of satisfying the needs of the body. The way in which resources are looked after and brought to the point of consumption is a social matter. Food itself may be consumed in very different ways, either very privately among the immediate group, as among the Dobu in the western Pacific (Bloch and Parry 1982, 28), or very publicly in different sorts of feasts (Hayden 1995). In the communal longhouses of north-west Amazonia, food preparation is privately done within constituent families, but eating is public and collective. Sharing is vital for the maintenance of group unity and meals are taken in communal central space within the longhouse (S. Hugh-Jones 1995, 231). Food can be a valuable used in exchange. It may also be bound up closely with notions of the essence of what it was to be a person. Among the Hua of Papua New Guinea, the central vital essence is *nu*, normally thought of as liquids, from water and blood to fat, and conceived as the source of life, vitality and fertility (Meigs 1984, 115–24). For the Hua, food and *nu* are conceptually interchangeable, with close associations and resemblances between *nu* substances, such as blood, faeces or secretions, and certain foods. Foods are seen as being permeated with the *nu* substances of their producers, and food is a mechanism of *nu* transfer between people, important for effecting changes in physical status, from growth and health to ageing and sexuality (Meigs 1984, 122–3).

Again, this might seem as far as we can take the issue of eating. This would be a sad reflection on the worth of all the reports on hearths, animal bones, plant remains, clay containers, and other relevant remains. One hypothesis worth exploring, however, is that for this period and area there was a basic contrast between private commensality and public feasting. The basic mode of consumption may well have been in small groups, such as households. For all the gross patterning in dominant subsistence staples at the scale of regions or traditional archaeological cultures (thus sheep and goats numerically dominant in the Körös culture of the Great Hungarian Plain, cattle in the LBK, and so on), there may have been much variation at local level. This may be beginning to show in isotopic and dental studies of the Early Neolithic in Britain. Thus recent stable isotopic studies of human bone from a variety of assemblages in southern Britain suggest a range of diets, from emphasis on meat in some cases to a more mixed diet in others; there is so far little sign of predominantly plant-based subsistence (Richards and Hedges 1999; Richards 2000). In one limited study of human teeth from mortuary assemblages from long cairns (and therefore possibly a not very representative sample) around the Black Mountains in south-east Wales, it was found that there was considerable variation in a small area (Wysocki and Whittle 2000). Rates of caries, enamel hypoplasia, tooth loss, crowding and eruption all seem to have varied. Though the sample is small, these variations can tentatively be connected with variations in subsistence, diet and food processing (Larsen 1997; Hillson 1996; Wysocki and Whittle 2000, 592–3). The people deposited in the various long cairns seem to have made different use of carbohydrates and meat, and to have been subject to varying nutritional deficiencies and physiological stresses. By contrast, in southern Britain as a whole at this date in the fourth millennium BC, there is a greater unity in the general dominance of cattle in animal bone assemblages, seen most clearly in those from ditched enclosures (Oswald *et al.* 2001). When such assemblages are examined in more detail, however, as noted at the start of chapter 1, there is considerable variation from individual deposit to individual deposit, as at Windmill Hill (Grigson 1999; Pollard 1999a). At that site, few individual deposits consist entirely of cattle bones, and more normally other species are also represented, to varying extents.

This requires further attention to the nature of cattle. As we shall see in chapter 4, cattle can be valued for many different reasons, far beyond their nutritional value. They are comparatively slow growing, but reach considerable size. There is growing evidence from recent lipid analysis of pottery for the consumption of milk, and the cattle may have been exploited as often for their milk (and perhaps blood) as for their meat. When they were slaughtered, adult animals could have yielded comfortably in excess of 200 kg of meat, fat and offal (Anne Tresset, pers. comm.; these issues are discussed in more detail in chapter 4). We know virtually nothing about the size of herds, but the holding of individual households might have been quite modest (Bogucki 1993), and slaughter might not have been lightly undertaken. What to do with all that meat? The amount available is too great, unless there were effective techniques of smoking, salting or other curing to allow storage. Cattle might therefore have been kept, among other reasons, as a means of participation in public consumption, as a bond either between separate households within villages, from the slightly dispersed longhouse concentrations to the more tightly nucleated smaller buildings of the Alpine foreland, or between the probably more scattered communities of southern Britain in the fourth millennium BC. It may be no accident from this perspective, that some of the cattle and deer meat in the non-enclosure consumption event at the Coneybury Anomaly, Wiltshire, was probably taken away for use elsewhere (Maltby 1990). This was an old practice, judging by its occurrence also in Late Mesolithic contexts (Figure 2.1) (Prummel *et al.* 2002).

Then as now, much of life was presumably spent asleep. We know very little of the conditions in which people slept in the Neolithic. Ethnography again suggests its possible importance. Men and women frequently sleep in different houses, at least at some times of the year, as among the Foi (J.F. Weiner 1988; 1991) and intermittently among the Hua after initiation (Meigs 1990, 106). In lowland north-west Amazonia, where people sleep within longhouses can define their identity: residents at the back, and visitors, including long-term ones, at the front (S. Hugh-

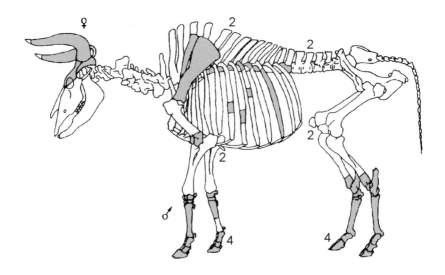

Figure 2.1 Composite diagram of the butchery patterns of aurochs found at the Late Mesolithic site of Jardinga, Netherlands; unless otherwise annotated, remains from one animal are indicated. After Prummel *et al.* 2002.

Jones 1995, 229–30). At dance-feasts, visitors spend the first night camped outside the longhouse, to emphasise their status as outsiders (S. Hugh-Jones 1995, 233). The Neolithic record is tantalisingly shorn of specific evidence for beds or sleeping places, apart from the stone side-boxes of Skara Brae and other Orkney house sites already noted above. It has been suggested that sleep in general was an important metaphor in Early Neolithic Orkney, the dead placed in cairns being regarded as merely sleeping (A. Jones 1999). If this is so, the communality of sleep might be suggested by the collective deposits of the dead. However, this is obviously not universal, since elsewhere single graves are common. In the graves of the LBK, there is a wide variety of body positions (e.g. Jeunesse 1997), from fully extended to more tightly crouched. Generally speaking, differentiated rules for the placing of the body, when they do appear, are a later phenomenon, for example in the Early Copper Age on the Great Hungarian Plain as seen in the left- and right-side positions for men and women (Derevenski 2000), and it might be possible to view this in the light of Mary Douglas's observations about the relationship between form of society and control of the body (1996, 76). Could LBK body positions in death (Figure 2.2) also in some way reflect the manner in which people slept in longhouses and elsewhere, perhaps expressing with their bodies an openness and lack of personal conformity, rather than closure and tight control? For the Kabyle of north Africa, the year can be divided into wet and dry seasons, and Bourdieu (1977, 159–60) has written vividly about how the wet season draws the village together, bringing even

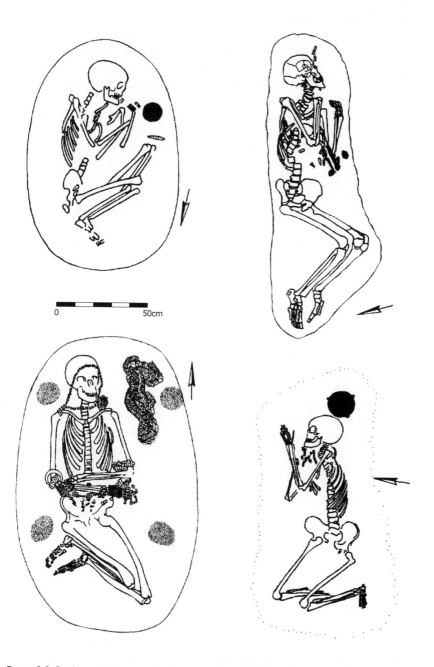

0   50cm

Figure 2.2 Body positions in LBK graves, a possible indication of sleeping poses. Clockwise from top left: Nitra 34; Stuttgart-Mühlhausen 67; Sondershausen 19; Sondershausen 15. After Orschiedt 1998.

the men, 'whose imperative duty is to be outside', back to the communal house, in a phase of self-reflection and withdrawal; there, the presence of men inhibits the normal movements of the women. The greatest possible contrast is created by the return of noise, bustle and vitality in the dry season, and the return of normal patterns of bodily movement through the space of the village. In the winter conditions of continental Europe from the sixth to the third millennia BC, it is hard not to suppose that warmth and close proximity were highly desirable, and sleeping together in longhouses and the smaller houses of the Alpine foreland might have been part of a similar routine contrast between winter and summer.

Discussing much earlier hominid development, Clive Gamble has referred to the possible importance of a 'release from proximity' (1999, 67). In the light of the discussion above of possible sleeping arrangements, proximity is likely to have remained significant long after. Among the Foi, sex takes places in the bush, furtively (J.F. Weiner 1991, 151), which is probably mirrored in many other instances (e.g. Lepowsky 1990, 191–2); the subject of sex, and sexual differences between men and women, may be the focus, however, of repeated conversation and joking (Gow 1991, 123). Bodily difference is one source of sexual attraction between Lese farmer men and Efe forager women in central Africa (Grinker 1994, 80–1). Views of conception also vary, from the uncomplicated matter-of-factness of the Jivaroan Achuar (Taylor 1996, 205) to the notion of the Foi that women must accumulate male fat or semen along with their own fluids in sufficient quantities from repeated intercourse (J.F. Weiner 1988, 50). Female sexuality may be feared, and even seen as a cause of death (Bloch and Parry 1982, 18). Among the Foi, 'morally approved sex turns a contaminating substance, menstrual blood, into new life, while sorcery conserves and enhances its debilitating properties' (J.F. Weiner 1988, 53). It seems almost impossible to find relevant evidence in the archaeological record for such moral and conceptual codes, let alone sexual behaviours. It has been suggested that some of the people, of varying ages and of both sexes, deposited after violent treatment into Danish bogs in the Early Neolithic could have transgressed moral codes (Bennike 1999, 29), but there is no specific reason to suppose sexual transgression. Much of the mortuary record revolves around a sense of gendered difference, which is enhanced through time, but this does not in itself reveal more than a recurrent sense of order, played out in the complementarities and oppositions of both single graves and collective deposits. The best example I can suggest for consideration is that of the Fussell's Lodge long barrow in southern England (Ashbee 1966). This is a collective deposit, with male and female, older and younger all represented (Figure 2.3). What makes this deposit unusual is its linear spatial separation. As in other instances (see Thomas 1988), there is some kind of opposition, or at least difference, being expressed between adult and younger people, and females are grouped with men in the terminal deposit of adults. The two proximal deposits, however, are of two sets of two females, bone groups C and D, arranged to appear to be two individuals; the females in C were of the same age, while one in D was older and the other younger (Brothwell and Blake in Ashbee 1966, 53; Michael Wysocki, pers. comm.). These proximal human deposits are in turn fronted by an ox skull.

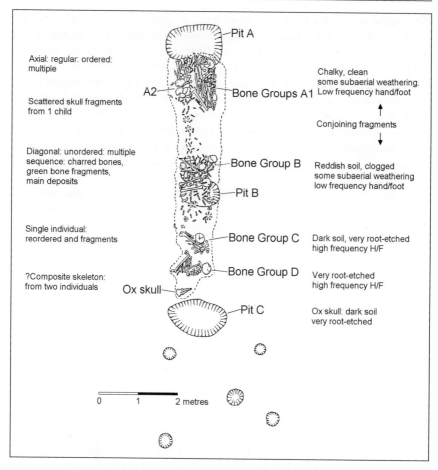

Axial: regular: ordered:
multiple

Scattered skull fragments
from 1 child

Diagonal: unordered: multiple
sequence: charred bones,
green bone fragments,
main deposits

Single individual:
reordered and fragments

?Composite skeleton:
from two individuals

Pit A

A2

Bone Groups A1

Bone Group B

Pit B

Bone Group C

Bone Group D

Ox skull

Pit C

Chalky, clean
some subaerial weathering.
Low frequency hand/foot

Conjoining fragments

Reddish soil, clogged
some subaerial weathering
low frequency hand/foot

Dark soil, very root-etched
high frequency H/F

Very root-etched
high frequency H/F

Ox skull: dark soil
very root-etched

0   1   2 metres

Figure 2.3 Layout and composition of the mortuary deposit under the Fussell's Lodge long barrow, southern England. After Ashbee, and information from Michael Wysocki.

One way to read this would be as a representation of order, balance, transformation and growth. The outer 'single' deposits are connected with the possession of cattle, and the bringing together of the remains of two pairs of women. This union, in conjunction with the presence of cattle, led on to the appearance of plentiful children and juveniles, in bone group B (and also scattered between groups B and A, and in group A), which in turn is transformed into balanced and ordered adult society, as represented in bone groups A1 and A2.

Two other features of daily routine requiring movement are the provision of water and what Mary Douglas calls 'the casting-off of waste products' (1996, 76). Water was perhaps nearly always available in sufficient quantities for the needs of people from streams, rivers, lakes and the rain, though thirsty animals like cattle may often have needed to be taken daily to a more abundant source of supply. In a few cases recently, wells have been found in LBK settlements, seemingly in locations further away from regular water, such as Erkelenz-Kückhoven in the Rheinland, where the wells were repaired on more than one occasion (J. Weiner 1998). In one of the recently discovered LBK wells at Zwenkau, near Leipzig, there is a finely decorated stick (Stäuble and Campen 1998; Campen and Stäuble 1999, fig. 10). This might of course be a deliberate deposit (or from the phase of decay or even destruction: J. Weiner 1998), but it is also legitimate to think of this as the result of a rather more casual encounter, perhaps the result of showing off or teasing among young men or women or both (Figure 2.4). Bark vessels in the Erkelenz and Zwenkau wells could have met the same fate.

Douglas (1996, 76) has commented that 'defecation, urination, vomiting and their products, uniformly carry a pejorative sign for formal discourse', but routine bodily functions have been neglected in both the anthropological and the archaeological literature. Reference is scattered and rather anecdotal. Concern for hygiene is probably one reason for periodic shifts of settlement (e.g. Politis 1996). Necessary trips to

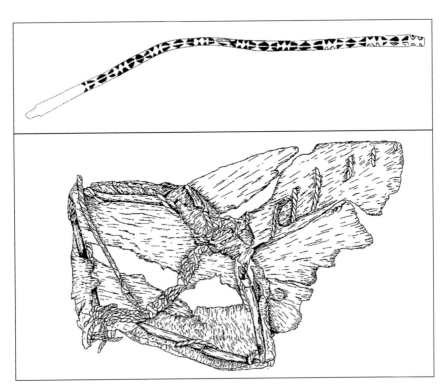

Figure 2.4 Decorated stick and birch-bark vessel from a LBK well at Zwenkau, central Germany. © Landesamt für Archäologie and Landesmuseum für Vorgeschichte, Dresden.

the surrounding bush or woodland have been noted as an opportunity for intrigue and adultery and a cause of suspicion and jealousy (Bloch and Parry 1982, 28), just as trips to water and the well might have been too. Where and how people defecate are an actively noted difference, one of a whole series of important bodily contrasts which include also colour, hair and smell, between the farmer Lese and the forager Efe; the Lese use outhouses, while the Efe use anywhere in the forest (Grinker 1994, 79–81). Conditions in the Alpine foreland have occasionally allowed the preservation of coprolites within settlements.[2] The majority of coprolites seem to be those of dogs, though pigs may also have acted as cleaners-up (Sené 1996, 748), which could suggest that people did indeed normally make trips to the woods, but in niveau VIII of the east French Jura site of Chalain (dated to 3190–3170 BC) 50 out of 182 recovered coprolites were identified as human (Sené 1996, 749). These show a surprisingly wide range of food sources, from meat to fruits, nuts, seeds and more rarely cereals. In niveau VI, dated to 3100 BC, only 7 out of 117 coprolites were identified as human, all found in one small area. Further study of parasite eggs in the Chalain human coprolites raises again the question of hygiene and disease. Eggs of various species were found both in the coprolites and organic-rich deposits of Chalain 4, dated to between 3100 and 3000 BC, including those of *Diphyllobothrium*, which can be transmitted through eating fish (Bouchet *et al.* 1995; 1997).

Water supply, defecation and infestation all raise the issue of sickness and disease. How healthy were the people with whom we are concerned? On the one hand, the Alpine foreland villages regularly lasted a decade or more before being remodelled or temporarily abandoned. On the other hand, there is scattered evidence for infestation and other problems. A single fingernail detached from the body of the Ice Man suggests three episodes of intense stress in the last months of life, perhaps related to a disease (Capasso 1995; cf. Botenschlager and Öggl 2000), and he is said to have had unusually low levels of body fat (Spindler 1996). Parasites have been found in coprolites from the Early Neolithic coastal estuarine site S3 at Swifterbant in the Dutch polders, though it is not certain whether these are human or animal coprolites (De Roever-Bonnet *et al.* 1979). Reviewing the remains of people deposited in watery places in the Early Neolithic of Denmark, Bennike (1999) has noted evidence for a range of disabling diseases and congenital abnormalities. These include fused vertebrae, secondary osteoarthritis perhaps caused by tuberculosis of the joints, and malformation of the arm, in one case probably congenital. While there are examples of violent deaths among this assemblage, including the young woman from Sigersdal with a string or cord tight around her neck, there is no sign that the diseased or deformed were subject to violent treatment.

This leads on to consideration of the way in which illness or sickness may have been regarded. The Danish evidence suggests that people with physical disabilities were tolerated or cared for, but what about those who were sick? An equation between sickness and death has been found in several societies. In Amazonia, the two are not sharply distinguished (Taylor 1996, 203). The Jivaroan Achuar of Ecuador see illness and death as the result of deliberate bewitchment, and as part of the same process of suffering, though they also regard mortality from a mythic perspective as the outcome of a minor act of transgression. Among the Bajo Urubamba of Peruvian Amazonia, sickness and death are processes involving the fragmentation of the person (Gow 1991, 188). At a conceptual level, the life of people depends on the death of the forest, while forest life is the death of people, illness coming from the 'revenge of forest animals and plants, or the active sorcery of forest demons' (Gow 1991, 191). Illness is seen as having various causes, from the revenge of natural beings, the proximity of demons, shamanic projection of objects of sorcery into the body, to serious epidemics 'sent by God'. The sick retreat from contact with others, feeling loss of physical strength and being regarded as rotten or over-ripe by the shamen who diagnose illness (Gow 1991, 180–1). Among the Daribi of Papua New Guinea, sickness is associated with possession of the soul, resulting from encounters with spirits, ghosts or sorcery, met in the bush and elsewhere (Wagner 1967, 44–5). Once again, it is hard to unite these observations with the archaeological record; they may, after all, be simply a list of exotic differences found elsewhere and at other times. But they raise important issues. The conditions of existence suggest that sickness could have been common in the Neolithic, and mortality among the young was high. How were the sick routinely regarded? Had the Ice Man in a sense been cast out because of illness?

The last aspect of an archaeology of the body to be considered at this stage is the prevalence of wounds. Inter-personal violence has come to greater attention recently, partly through a number of striking new cases, such as Talheim, Herxheim and Asparn in the LBK (e.g. Wahl and König 1987; Häusser 1998; Teschler-Nicola 1996), or Esztergályhorváti in the Lengyel culture of western Hungary (Makkay 2000), and subsequent reconsideration of older finds (Gronenborn 1999; Carman and Harding 1999). It has been tempting to suppose that inter-personal violence both increased and intensified through time, leading eventually to the more aggressive, male-oriented world of the *agrios* (Hodder 1990; 2000). I suggest that inter-personal violence was endemic and widespread, and probably of very varied causes. It may occasionally have flared, in some regions, into periods of more sustained violence, as may be suggested by the emphasis on enclosure and fortification and the series of attacks involving burnings and sporadic killings, seen at Hambledon Hill, Dorset (Mercer 1999). This may be suggested too by the group killing in at least the case of Talheim in the LBK; in the other instances, it is not yet clear whether remains were dumped after slaughter, or ritually deposited (cf. Orschiedt 1998). Elsewhere, the evidence is widespread but scattered, seemingly more to do with wounds to individuals, from the Late Mesolithic of the Danube Gorges and the Ertebølle culture, to the Early Neolithic in Ireland and the Netherlands (Cooney 2000, 87; Louwe Kooijmans 1993), and Denmark as already noted (Bennike 1999). There are large assemblages of human bone in southern Britain among which there are few wounds (though of course not all wounds would have left marks on bones), suggesting the occasional shooting with arrows (Wysocki and Whittle 2000) and from time to time clubbing to the head; parry fractures on the arms seem to be uncommon (Michael Wysocki and Rick Schulting, pers. comm.). There is, however, a case for seeing an increase in unhealed wounds in Early Neolithic contexts in Denmark (Schulting 1998).

Rather than suppose a state of perpetual warfare, I envisage a situation far more piecemeal. Clearly people did resort at times to shocking violence on groups of victims, but the evidence mainly suggests a recurrent but low level of inter-personal violence. The contexts of violence seem extremely varied in the ethnographic record, from duels carried out *within* the group, as reported among the Yanomamo (Chagnon 1968), to small-scale, inter-group raids among the Daribi as a response to the effects of sorcery (Wagner 1967, 51). In one study, of the former forager Paliyans of southern India, violence was not found to increase with the beginnings of sedentary existence, in large part because attitudes of respect for the individual and ways of safeguarding against violence were maintained through the period of change in style of residence (P.M. Gardner 2000). While warfare can be an effect of increasing social distance, among the Manambu of Papua New Guinea it was thought of 'as necessarily predicated on the prior existence of social ties between the opponents, and as remaining always embedded and encompassed within these ties' (Harrison 1995, 81).[3] Most Neolithic wounds are from arrows or axes (two kinds were inferred at Talheim from the nature of the blows). Bow and axe may have been largely male weapons, and both the acquisition of an axe, and the use of weapons if need be, perhaps when honour had been insulted,[4] may have been a recurrent validation of male identity. The male body and the female body may have been put to the test in different routines.

Movements and tasks in the routine of residence

So far in this chapter I have considered the importance of routines in general, and suggested, with the help of analogies, various aspects of embodied daily life which are normally neglected. The discussion so far has been rather out of context, lacking a sense of why such and such a way of doing things mattered in a given, specific situation: a lack of both agency and generative schemes and principles. On the other hand, routines of the kinds noted so far were part of what carried life forward from day to day. They could bring us closer to an endlessly repeated experience of the basic conditions of life, diverse and certainly not unchanging, but at the same time with enormous continuity built into them. As Bloch has noted (1998, 5), we are sometimes guilty of seeking too much diversity. In the remainder of the chapter I want to reinforce the sense of daily patterns that endured, questioning also by implication the range of difference from place to place and from time to time. Other authors have profitably explored what the processes, goals and contexts of technology can tell us (e.g. Dobres 2000; de Beaune 2000); my intention is briefly to consider movements and tasks, within patterns of residence, and then exchange and monuments, within lived-in landscapes.

Movements and tasks

Much has been made of the difference between mobility and sedentism. On the one hand, settling down and being more or less instantaneously sedentary have been axiomatically seen as part of the business of practising or adopting agriculture, over large swathes of Europe; farmers have not only stock to husband but crops to tend, and their houses show their attachment, physical as well as emotional, to place. On the other hand, there are areas, particularly Britain, where the evidence for both crop cultivation and residence is rather more fractured than in many parts of continental Europe (see Darvill and Thomas 1996; Fairbairn 2000). Partly from a British perspective, I have suggested that many situations in the continental European Neolithic were characterised by degrees of mobility, tethered but still often fluid and unstable (Whittle 1996). I subsequently suggested a perhaps more satisfactory spectrum of variation, from tethered mobility to short-term sedentism (Whittle 1997), which might do better justice to the regional and temporal variations evident in the archaeological record, including within Britain itself, and also Ireland (cf. Cooney 2000). I want briefly to reinforce this sense of a spectrum of variation. My central point here, however, is that it is not enough simply to declare a system sedentary or not sedentary, because the patterns of routine tasks and movements may serve to blur absolute differences, not least from the point of view of the socialities involved.

Ethnographically and historically, the majority of farmers seem to be sedentary. Many hunter-gatherers or foragers are mobile to varying degrees. There is variation among both sets (accepting for the sake of argument here that this is indeed a meaningful distinction). Some foragers, as on the north-west coast of America and elsewhere, had a sedentary existence, in situations of plentiful *and* scarce resources (e.g. Suttles 1990; Anderson and Smith 1996). While the lifestyle of some foragers can be characterised by high residential mobility, involving up to eighty moves per year (e.g. Politis 1996),[5] others shifted principally between winter and summer ranges, and built structures in both, such as the coastal east Siberian Nivchi (Feist and Feist 1999). There are also well-documented cases of 'mobile farmers'. The Foi, already noted several times, are one case in point, spending part of the year hunting in the remoter bush. The Raramuri, mixed farmers in the highlands of north-west Mexico, practise a bi-seasonal mobility, shifting from warm weather residences on or near the valley floor to winter residences on mountain slopes, more than a day's walk away; houses are left with many contents intact, in the expectation of return (Graham 1994; cf. Tomka 1993). In another case, of the Tsembaga people of highland New Guinea, where people are located depends on a complex range of factors, from land transfers through clan and marriage arrangements, to the pulse of ritual cycles, which tend to attract people, over a scale of a generation, to the location where the heart of things was to be found (Rappaport 1968, 21–3).

Can these cases be regarded as any more than just anecdotal suggestions? There is probably variation within every system. Thus in the LBK, for example, the existence of both herders and hunters has been suggested in the Aisne valley site of Cuiry-lès-Chaudardes (Hachem 1995; 2000; see also discussion of this evidence in chapter 3). Houses with high proportions of hunted animals are small, while those with big numbers of domesticates are more substantial longhouses; both may be likely to occur together in longer-lived sites. Short-lived sites, at least in the Aisne valley, may mainly have had substantial longhouses and have lacked smaller buildings (Hachem 1995, 202). There are too many longhouses in many LBK situations, for the numbers of people implied by these great buildings are often not matched by quantities of material discarded (see Zimmermann 1995) or the scale of local environmental impact. The longhouse in other situations can be shown to be itself a special construction, going up under particular conditions including the cementing of alliances, and not just the inevitable adjunct of regular residence (A. Strathern and Stewart 1999); among the early Iroquois, it has been claimed as a 'tool for sedentariness' (Chapdelaine 1993, 184–5). The LBK longhouse was one of the principal means by which occupation of place was claimed, renewed and maintained. How it may have been used from season to season and from year to year remains a much more open question.

Elsewhere, the existence of the house in itself does not necessarily imply long-term sedentism (though it is also not incompatible with that). On the edges of the small (and relatively high) lakes of Chalain and Clairvaux in the Jura of eastern France, people in the later fourth millennium BC constructed a series of well-built structures, many probably with planked floors raised above wet surfaces. At Clairvaux station II, Pierre Pétrequin and his colleagues (Pétrequin 1989, 196) have plausibly suggested a woodland or forest milieu, inhabited by hunters or collectors, or shifting agriculturalists, who did not expect to use any one base and its buildings for much more than ten years at a time. This was of course not necessarily the same scenario as further east in other parts of the Alpine foreland, though in fact considerable use of wild resources and similarly short site durations can be seen in many of the earlier settlements there (e.g. Jacomet and Kreuz 1999, 299–310). Likewise in Britain, there is little doubt that quite substantial buildings were a recurrent feature of the fourth millennium BC. The recent discovery at White Horse Stone in Kent joins other examples such as Yarnton (Figure 2.5), Lismore Fields and Balbridie (Current Archaeology 2000; Darvill 1996). But the frequency and character of such structures remain unclear. There are in fact good grounds, based on radiocarbon evidence and ceramic associations, for seeing these large British structures as essentially early in the insular sequence (A. Barclay 2000), suggesting again that large buildings may have been part of the establishment of new practices. Their roles may have varied. While substantial deposits of cereals have been found at Balbridie and Lismore Fields (Fairweather and Ralston 1993; G. Jones 2000), there was very little debris of any kind at Yarnton (Hey 1997; Gill Hey, pers. comm.). Large areas have been excavated at Yarnton in the Upper Thames, and only one structure of this kind was found, along with a range of other features including small pits and scattered postholes, and finds in the tops of treethrow pits; funerary and ceremonial areas have been suggested alongside domestic spaces (Hey 1997).

This evidence from Yarnton and elsewhere is compatible with a degree of mobility in the pattern of settlement. Relocation at a lifetime scale can also be documented now by isotope analysis, for example the possible movement by an adult woman from an area of origin in the Mendips to her place of burial 80 km south-east in Cranborne Chase; the children or juveniles accompanying her in the Monkton-up-

Figure 2.5 Longhouse from Yarnton, southern England. Photo: Gill Hey.

Wimbourne deposit may also already have moved between areas of different geology (Montgomery *et al.* 2000; and see above, on in-marriage).[6] What is at least as interesting from the perspective of routines is how much might have been shared in common between situations normally categorised as different on the basis of sedentism or otherwise. Yarnton, LBK longhouses and Jura forest houses all share structured repetition. There are bases in which activity is maintained and repeated, be they large house or midden. There are activities ranged out into the landscape, as people attended to the businesses of clearance, herding animals, tending crops, procuring lithic resources, and so on. There may have been relatively little permanent dwelling in any one spot or structure at Yarnton, but it seems clear that the place was routinely used and belonged to an ordered suite of activities, perhaps both up and down the valley, and ranging to neighbouring uplands. In the same way, it seems unlikely that each inhabitant of every LBK longhouse spent every day within sight of it. The game hunted from Aisne valley LBK sites and in the Jura may have taken people far from their houses, as well as many of the animals herded. We may have exaggerated the differences between tethered mobility and short-term sedentism.

Routine movements imply changing socialities. The contrasts have already been noted between the intense sociality of the collective longhouse village and the bush existence of the Foi, and between the inturned family life of the single house and the interactions of dry season gatherings on the Amazon floodplain (J.F. Weiner 1991; Harris 1998; 2000). Routine movements imply structured separations, fragmentation and fission, followed by fusion and aggregation. The scales of interactions would have varied, from groups of perhaps at times hundreds of people, down to isolated individuals. People in situations of both tethered mobility and short-term sedentism must have been adept at negotiating face-to-face relationships, not least because the routines of daily life were so varied and complex. The many tasks involved in growing, tending and using cereals are a good case in point (animals are considered in more detail in chapter 4).

Cereals must have involved different bodies of people at different stages. A lot of research effort has gone into effective recovery techniques, species identification and history, and the detailed stages of crop processing (e.g. Hillman 1981, figures 5–7). Rather less thought has been given to the socialities involved, through the processes of clearance, tillage, planting, tending, harvesting, processing, storage and consumption (Whittle 2000b). These must have varied throughout, a microcosm – in what may not have been a principal subsistence domain in many areas – of the shifting aggregations discussed above. Clearance was presumably labour-intensive. We know very little about gender-based divisions of labour in the Neolithic. One possibility, quite widely encountered in the ethnographic record, is that men were responsible for the initiation and creation of clearances, and women for their maintenance, as among the Foi (J.F. Weiner 1991, 5) or the Mende of Zaire (M. Leach 1992). The workforces assembled for clearance in primary and secondary woodland might also have varied (cf. Pétrequin 1996). Tillage (or ground preparation), and planting might have taken fewer people, perhaps women. In southern Greece, such demands were also an opportunity for the positive assertion of female identity (Seremetakis

1991). Weeding and tending could have been the tasks of those who ranged less far, perhaps children and older people as well as women. Harvesting may have brought larger numbers of people together again, though there is enormous scope for variation depending on whether plots were held by closed groups such as households or more communally, were maintained year on year or just used briefly, or were part of regular subsistence or created for special purposes. Processing, storage and cooking could again have been the preserve of small numbers of people. Hypothetically, they might again have been the domain of women. The presentation, sharing and consumption of food might again have brought larger numbers of people together, the end of the cycle matching its beginning, though close commensality has been noted above, and there is sufficient evidence to suggest considerable variation in diet and cereal use anyway. I have suggested elsewhere that the fen-edge enclosure at Etton (Pryor 1998) is a good case in point (Whittle 2000b). Pollen and insects indicate a partially cleared landscape, the enclosure being set on the edge of the braided and flood-prone valley bottom of the Welland. Cereal pollen is represented in the pollen diagrams, but insects do not suggest much by way of cultivated or disturbed ground immediately close at hand. Cereal remains were present, though not plentiful, in the ditches of the enclosure. In this one instance, itself perhaps a far from routine arena for special gatherings, cereals were just one, perhaps relatively minor part of a much more complex world.

Landscape as routine: procurement, exchange and monuments

These routines of shifting sociality would have been experienced by and through the body in varying ways, from the tasks requiring stamina, such as clearing wood, to those needing persistence rather than strength, such as sorting, sieving and grinding, and from the excitement of large gatherings to the tedium of repetitive and solitary activity. They would also have been experienced temporally in varying ways, as tasks followed one another through the seasons (Jacomet et al. 1989, fig. 74). This sense of variation through routine can be enhanced by considering wider landscapes.

Describing the Nukak in Amazonia (hunters, fishers and part-time horticulturalists), Gustavo Politis (1996) has defined five territorial dimensions in which the Nukak perceive their landscape. The general kind of divisions sounds familiar and can be found widely in the literature, but the example is especially interesting because these are the terms within which the Nukak themselves operate. These range from the band territory and regional group territory to rarely contacted distant regions, known but virtually unvisited distant places, and finally, mythical or ideological territory. Nukak bands are residentially mobile over a few hundred square kilometres, with camps within this habitual territory linked by paths, and flexible limits partly defined by rivers. Regional territory may extend over 1000–2000 km^2, within which individual band members may move quite freely, principally for social reasons, connected with ritual, gatherings, finding marriage partners and so on. Travel to distant regions is much rarer, and is sometimes done by smaller groups, including for valued raw material procurement (cane for blowpipes);

these trips take people across the territories of other bands and regional groups. Beyond this, there are places known about but hardly ever visited, and then the territory of myth, part of Nukak cosmology (Politis 1996, 496).

There is no need to force this particular analogy on to Neolithic European evidence. Apart from all the other differences, the scale of Nukak mobility is probably considerably greater than envisaged even in the concept of tethered mobility. What may remain useful, however, is a sense of routine movements around and through the landscape, at varying scales and temporal rhythms, and for varying motives and tasks, including social ones. The enormous recent literature on landscape can be seen as offering a series of perspectives: landscape as identity, biography, history, memory, myth, metaphor, power, time, narrative, and so on (Cummings 2001). I would like here to follow the line of landscape as medium and context for action (Cummings 2001, 73), emphasising especially the routine nature of this relationship. Two kinds of examples may serve to illustrate this in the Neolithic context: the procurement and exchange of lithic resources, and, briefly, monuments. These also help to suggest varying scales of routine movement through the landscape.

In the case of Hienheim, a late LBK settlement in the Upper Danube valley, no lithic raw material was available in the immediate territory, but high-quality cherts were to be found within 8–11 km (de Grooth 1997). 'Pre-cores' and initially prepared cores were brought back to the settlement for further working, probably within a household context. The quantities of material used by each household in any one year were probably not large, but sources seem to have been exploited without restriction, and a flow of procurement maintained. In the case of the LBK settlements of the Aldenhovener Platte, in north-west Germany, Rijckholt-type flints from a series of deposits some 30 km or more to the west in Dutch Limburg were preferred to more immediately available lithics (Figure 2.6) (Zimmermann 1995). The quantities obtained were, however, small (going on what has been recovered and assuming there has not been unaccounted loss in deposition and subsequently). The tallies calculated for Laurenzburg 7 on the Aldenhovener Platte were some 124 flint pieces per household per year, weighing some 1.3 kg, of which 16 were formally retouched tools (Zimmermann 1995; de Grooth 1999, 733). The range from which this flint was procured contrasts with the small variations in pot decorative styles on the Aldenhovener Platte (Kolhoff 1999), which may suggest individual and more or less independent households rooted in one place. Procurement of lithics may have been embedded in wider routine movement, and it may have had varying motivation behind it, in part strongly social as described among the Nukak above.

Wider distributions can be shown, perhaps in some cases also by direct procurement but in other cases more probably circulating by exchange. In the case of Hienheim, chert did not travel widely at a regional scale (de Grooth 1997). By contrast, Rijckholt-type flint from Limburg was found as far away as Hesse and Baden-Württemberg (Zimmermann 1995). At Bylany in Bohemia, lithics came considerable distances from a variety of sources and directions, principally Baltic erratic flint from perhaps 150 km to the north, and Jurassic Krakow flint from some

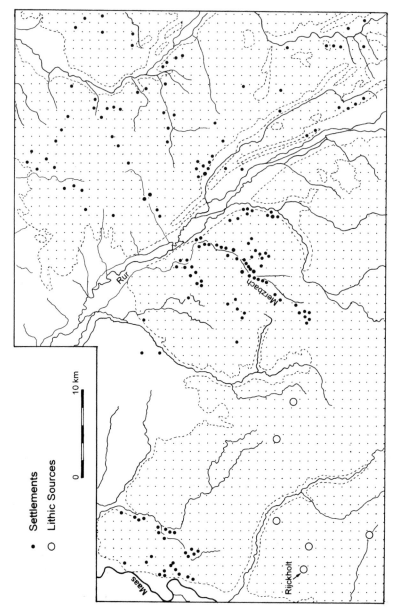

Figure 2.6 The distribution of known LBK settlements and lithic sources in north-west Germany and the south-east Netherlands. The Aldenhovener Platte is centred on the small Merzbach valley. After Zimmermann 1995.

- • Settlements
- ○ Lithic Sources

0   10 km

Maas

Rur

Merzbach

Rijckholt

300 km to the east in southern Poland, but also in varying quantities through time other materials, including Świeciechów flint from some 475 km to the east in Poland, Tomaszów chocolate flint from about 700 km to the north-east in central Poland, Tušimice quartzite from about 145 km to the north-west in Bohemia, and Szentgál radiolarite from over 300 km to the south-east in north-west Hungary (Lech 1990; 1997). The details of this example show how acquisitions and distributions varied through time. This is also evident in the case of the Hienheim region. In the Middle Neolithic phase succeeding the LBK, the extraction of attractive striped tabular chert from deep shafts began, for example at Arnhofen; on-site working was restricted to sites within 20 km of the sources; and finished blades and tools were distributed distances of up to 300 km to the north and north-west. Extraction in this phase has been interpreted as a short-term, seasonal male activity organised from the thirty or so settlements known within a 20-km radius, with distribution beyond this zone aimed partly at immediate neighbours, perhaps kin, and partly over a longer range as means of self-definition by exchange (de Grooth 1997, 94–5).

In nearly all LBK cases, axes and adzes came in from distant places. At Hienheim, amphibolite adzes, of uncertain origin, were the only lithic material to come in from any distance (de Grooth 1997, 93). Among the many case studies of the movement of axes, from the LBK of central and western Europe to the many stone sources exploited in Britain and Ireland, the example of eastern France is particularly useful, since it suggests the regularity of raw material flows, a routine movement between stone sources, settlements from which production was perhaps organised, and areas up to 150 km distant where finished axes ended up (Pétrequin and Jeunesse 1995; Pétrequin 1993). The development of black pelite quartz from a source called Plancher-les-Mines at the southern end of the Vosges, on the north side of the Belfort Gap, is embedded in the wider history of the Neolithic at the southern end of the Rhine, northern and western Switzerland, and eastern France. The first exploitation of pelite in the context of LBK expansion in the region of the southern Rhine and eastern France in the later sixth millennium BC was on a small scale, and distribution was limited; other stone sources were much more in vogue. From *c.* 5000 to 4500 BC use of this source remained limited, while gradually there was a technical shift away from the dominant adze form of the LBK to that of the symmetrically cross-sectioned axe. By the later fifth millennium BC, the scale of production increased, with the first proper quarries. Settlements from which these were worked, to judge by the presence of roughouts and debitage, may have been from 20 to 40 km distant. Distribution, though not yet in great numbers, was up to some 100 km east and west, mainly within the sphere of 'late Rössen culture', but partly into the early Egolzwil group of north-west Switzerland (Pétrequin and Jeunesse 1995, 56–9). By about 4000 BC, the form of these attractive, dark, polished, often long axe blades was predominantly square-sectioned (Pétrequin and Jeunesse 1995, 61–2); it is possible to argue that it took time to unlearn earlier technical working habits, based on familiarity with other stone types, including Alpine rocks (Pétrequin 1993, 52). By now the evidence suggests that settlements concerned with production or at least secondary working of extracted stone were to be found some 20–55 km from sources. Distribution was made for some 150 km east and west. The source seems to lie at this time at the junction of several cultural groups (at least as defined by pottery and other artefacts). Axes certainly seem to have passed, by whatever mechanism of movement was involved, quite freely into the different cultural groups to the east, with over half of axes in the very early fourth millennium BC phase at Hornstaad-Hörnle I on the Bodensee, for example, being from this source (Pétrequin and Jeunesse 1995, 85). From about 3800–3700 BC, extraction of pelite seems to decline (Pétrequin and Jeunesse 1995, 113), and other stone sources take over in importance and popularity, in the case of the eastern Jura region first from the distant southern Alps and then from the immediate east (Pétrequin 1993, 51–2). This seems to coincide with the further technical shift to sleeved axes, that is smaller blades held in an antler sleeve or sheath, in turn held in a wooden haft (Pétrequin 1993, 53–7).

Even if it remains hard to distinguish between down-the-line exchanges, directed exchanges and direct procurement from a distance, here are routine movements at several of the scales noted already in the case of the Nukak, and presumably a great range of socialities, many of them perhaps male. It is not hard to multiply this sense of movement and flow. It has been suggested that salt could have been another resource regularly sought in eastern France (Pétrequin and Jeunesse 1995, 65–6). At least in the quite high-altitude sites of the eastern Jura like those around the small lakes of Chalain and Clairvaux, there was much use of wild cattle, red deer, roe deer and wild boar (Pétrequin 1993, 70; Pétrequin 1989), which again must have required regular hunting trips across a wide range of territory.

Among the Nukak, the fifth dimension of territory described was that of myth. My last example in this chapter therefore is the routine experience of special places and constructions. In the archaeology of western Europe, the literature on the Neolithic often refers to 'monuments' in particular. At this point, however, I want to keep the range of relevant sites and places as wide as possible, from special constructions regularly connected with the disposal and treatment of the dead, and with dealings with the ancestral and supernatural, to other constructions heavily implicated in social negotiations among the living, to natural places imbued with significance by people (Bradley 2000). This will thus cover not only cairns and barrows, but also enclosures, houses and natural places. My question here is the *routine* experience of these varied locations. Much discussion has revolved around their use at special times, but we have thought rather less about everyday settings (Figure 2.7). Clearly these varied. Monuments are not found everywhere, and their presence was presumably recognised as significant in the everyday world. There were sites set just out of sight on hilltops, like the Loughcrew passage graves in eastern Ireland (Fraser 1998), and others located in woodland and perhaps not visible from any distance at all, at least in summer, perhaps like the Windmill Hill and other enclosures (Whittle *et al.* 1999). Many others may, however, have been locally inter-visible, such as long barrows in Cranborne Chase, Dorset (Tilley 1994, 156), and environmental evidence suggests that some long barrows, at least in the region around Avebury, were placed in cleared patches of land (Whittle *et al.* 1993). Monuments were part of landscapes

Figure 2.7 The routine place of monuments: view of the Pembrokeshire coastal landscape, with Carreg Samson. Photo: Vicki Cummings.

to which people had devoted labour and attention. Potentially special constructions were not built in any one area all at once; there was a gradual sedimentation of significance through time. As this process unfolded, people continued to move around their landscapes, passing routinely on other tasks these special places, few of which were absolutely removed from the spheres of regular movement. The example of the western Apache illustrates the morally significant naming of places (Basso 1984), but it is hard to envisage that people experienced special places and constructions only by speech and occasional participation in events such as ritual. Domains of myth, ancestral order, initiation (perhaps part of a landscape distant in the mind) and central social negotiation may have been routinely experienced in part by the active, moving, working body as it went about the patterns of daily life: as points on paths, as nodes of the landscape to be avoided, as part of the 'topographical gossip' by which people often seem to make their way around landscapes (Widlok 1997), or as locations associated with positive and negative emotions, including fear.

Chapter 3

Difficult individuals

The previous chapter has discussed several different dimensions of agency, and gave particular attention to daily life and routines. The details of such basic activities as eating, sleeping, resting, moving and working could constitute what has been called, with reference to life beside the Amazon, 'another type of identity' (Harris 2000, 7). This is the relational and lived side of identity, based in 'what people do in their daily life, their relationships with each other and the environment in which they live', a set of 'elemental interactions and associations' (Harris 2000, 7). I will argue at the end of this book that these daily routines were a source not only of considerable diversity in any one horizon but also a major factor in the slow rate of fundamental long-term change. Their importance, though till now relatively little considered in the interpretation of prehistory, can hardly be overstated. But are they enough on their own? From another perspective, daily life can be seen as only one of the significant dimensions of life to be considered. Reflecting on the Foi of Papua New Guinea, James Weiner has noted that there is always the possibility of contradiction or paradox between the meanings of recurrent practices, though it may be dangerous for these oppositions to be visible in everyday social process. Foi men must mask the fact that women are conceptually dangerous to them, in order to engage in normal sexual activity (J.F. Weiner 1988, 16). Weiner has also underlined how 'the many images of Foi domestic, social and ceremonial activities depicted in myth are no less accurate a rendering of Foi 'everyday life' than an observer's verbal narration of daily activity' (J.F. Weiner 1988, 16).

These analogies are at the heart of the argument of this book, that identity is complex and many-sided, and in a sense therefore resistant to rapid change. Not only are daily routines and attitudes potentially in opposition to each other, they are far from neutral. The varied ways in which daily life was carried forward must have been important, and there is ample evidence that this was the case. The aim of this chapter is now to consider several scales at which the style of daily life could have been expressed. These are the individual, the moral community, and the household; I also discuss the issue of culture. All, including the individual, involve relationships with others. Harris has argued that 'lived identity can be shared amongst many people or only a few, but it is fundamentally intersubjective and connective' (2000, 7). It is consistent with the argument of this book that I see people in the periods I am discussing as formed by all these dimensions.

Individuals

A short history of archaeological individuals

Interpretive prehistory has not done very well by the individual, in part perhaps because of the way in which, at least until recently, theory building has been dissociated from other disciplines. There was very little place for the individual in the long phase of culture history (dominant in Britain from the 1920s to 1950s), and very little sign of broader theoretical underpinning of any kind; it is possible that the model of culture as the determining force was derived from the dominance of 'society', advocated in anthropology by Durkheim in the late nineteenth century and still a powerful influence in the earlier part of the twentieth century (Kuper 1996) when the archaeological culture appeared. There was limited space for individuals in processual archaeology, apart from Big Men, chiefs and other assorted leaders, and even these were hardly treated *qua* individuals, but rather as emblematic of sets of power relations in society, at particular points in trajectories of social evolution. Though the explicit talk was of links to cybernetics and systems theory, it seems as though there was a delayed use of a model of society similar to that advocated by the structural functionalists, dominant in British social anthropology from the 1920s to 1940s. It is ironic to find Evans-Pritchard disavowing a functionalist approach (1956, 320) long before an archaeological variety of functionalism was adopted from the late 1960s onwards.

Individuals did begin to be emphasised as a legitimate dimension of enquiry in the 1980s, as part of post-processualism or interpretive archaeology (e.g. Hodder 1986). In large part, this seems to have been the result of a broad theoretical reaction to the generalising approach of what had come before, rather than a considered view of what can constitute the individual. Post-processual approaches of the 1980s and 1990s tended anyway to be an uneasy mixture of the context-specific, the critical and the deconstructive with the universal and the cross-cultural.[1] Though literary theory had championed the 'death of the individual' (for example as advocated by Roland Barthes) and this is noted in anthropological writing at this time (e.g. M. Strathern 1992a, 77), many early post-processual approaches advocated the presence of the universal individual, largely atomistic and faceless. Even when seen as the knowledgeable actor (for example in Barrett 1994, drawing explicitly on Bourdieu and Giddens), the individual seemed to lack identity, values and motivation (Whittle 1998a; 2001; and recognised retrospectively by Hodder 1999, 136; cf. Brück 2001; Fowler 2000; 2001).

Perhaps we should follow Strathern here (1992a, 75) and see this conceptualisation as inevitably a reconceptualisation of our society at the time. The one exception to the general post-processual conception of individuals lies in gender-conscious approaches. From the papers by Spector (1991) and Tringham (1991) onwards, there has been a concern to offer people with faces and individual identity (continued also in Meskell 1996; 1998). Attention to gender has also in fact led to a broader view of social relations and a concern with the life course of individuals of each and every gender (e.g. Derevenski 2000). There can still be some reservations, however. Spector's lively paper rests on the existence of documentary and oral as well as archaeological evidence, and Tringham's on an imagined soliloquy by a woman as she watches a house burn at one particular – curiously timeless – moment. Analyses of the Early Copper Age cemetery of Tiszapolgár-Basatanya, though sensitive to both (or all?) genders and development through life, are still largely based on literal scoring of the presences and absences of artefacts in the graves (Derevenski 1997; 2000; cf. Chapman 1997a; 2000a; 2000b); it is the scores rather than broader aspects of context and identity which in the end dominate.

Other perspectives

A useful first distinction is between the terms 'individuality' and 'individualism'. These are difficult, and often conflated (Rapport 1996). Individualism is sometimes used in anthropological writing to refer rather disparagingly to the study of particular individuals who may not be representative of a broader group ('methodological individualism': Rapport 1996, 301). It can also be used to refer to the historical variability of 'a particular historico-cultural conceptualisation of the person – the social actor as ostentatiously and conventionally 'distinct', sovereign and autonomous, and as this giving onto his dignity and social value' (Rapport 1997, 6). By contrast, individuality is taken to be 'universally and ubiquitously present', the source of 'agency, consciousness, interpretation and creativity in social and cultural life'; 'the traditional "primitive" who is not self-aware and self-critical, who leads an unexamined life, somehow amalgamated with others, incapable of a sophisticated and conscious elucidation of his cultural practices and social institutions, does not exist' (Rapport 1997, 6). Despite the danger of a confusion of terms, I prefer to keep the distinction between individuality and individualism first advocated by Rapport (1996): between the fact of individual action and consciousness ('the universal nature of human existence whereby it is individuals who possess agency': Rapport 1996, 298) and the way or style in which that may be carried out. In the modern western world, it is a self-aware and autonomous individualism which has dominated, but this conceptualisation need not automatically be reconceptualised for the past with which we are dealing here. It is clear, however, that the post-processual approach has been mainly to emphasise the possession of agency, and even if the single term individuality is to be retained to cover all these dimensions, it is largely a mechanical individuality which is on show.

A further set of examples from ethnographic writing can readily show a variety of ways in which identity in general can be conceived. This unavoidably involves gender, but the primary focus here is not on gender alone. A useful first example is a contrast which has been made between south India and Melanesia (Busby 1997). Gender in south India is fixed and stable, rooted in bodily difference and focused on the capacity for procreation. Relations between husband and wife are seen as a series of balanced exchanges, while relations with children depend on a sense of differently gendered substance. 'Men are related to their children in a male way, through semen and male blood, while women are related to their children in a different, female way, passing on female substance through the womb and breast milk' (Busby 1997, 263); fathers feel closer to sons, and mothers to daughters. The capacity for procreation and nurture is fundamental for male and female gendering, and while these conceptions are different, they are seen to greatest effect in transactions and exchanges between the genders; the person is conceived of as 'internally whole, but with a fluid and permeable boundary' and there are 'substantial connexions between persons who are not bounded individuals of the Western (stereo)type' (Busby 1997, 269). In Melanesia, by contrast, the person is 'a mosaic of male and female substances, *internally* dividing up the body into differently gendered parts' (Busby 1997, 270). It is not so much the obvious and visible difference of sexual organs that matters, more what is done with them. In this sense, gender is performative, and relational, since relationships make persons (Busby 1997, 272–3).

Ideas of substance permeate other cases from Melanesia. The Hua of eastern highland New Guinea have complex gender relations, a good example of Strathern's dictum that there 'there is no single relationship' (M. Strathern 1987, 29). Among them, Meigs (1990) has emphasised a threefold male ideology, of accentuated chauvinism on the one hand, but of envy of women and of complementary interdependence on the other. The dominant metaphor among the Hua is the idea of vital essence or *nu* (Meigs 1984). Vital essence occurs in three states, as a solid, a gas, and particularly as liquid, such as water, blood, urine, sap and water. *Nu* is the source of life, vitality and fertility. Growth is conceived of in terms of transformation from solid to liquid essence; the growth of children depends on parents giving *nu*, which in turn weakens and ages them (Meigs 1984, 121). Male relations with women seem to be based on fear or awe of the power of female *nu*, leading to public denigration but private admiration within the men's house (Meigs 1984, 131). There is similar complexity among the Foi (J.F. Weiner 1988, 41). The Foi male view is that the innate female capacity for menstruation is the source both of sexual regeneration and lethal illness; Foi men can appropriate this capacity by paying bridewealth and by transforming menstrual blood into 'sorcery substance, with which they implement male control of life and death' (J.F. Weiner 1988, 41). Through 'restrictions and regimens', male identity must be achieved.

In both south India and Melanesia, there has been a powerful concept of the 'dividual', connected to others through exchanges of substance, in the former case as a flow from a person but in the latter objectified as part of a person (Busby 1997, 275–6). The major study perhaps has been that of the Mount Hagen people of highland New Guinea (M. Strathern 1988). From the very outset, Strathern is concerned to challenge the appropriateness of a western view of society and the individual for understanding Melanesian perspectives (M. Strathern 1988, 3, 12; for useful commentary, see also Gell 1999). Rather than being seen as unique entities, 'Melanesian persons are as dividually as they are individually conceived. They contain a generalized society within. Indeed, persons are frequently constructed as the plural and composite site of the relationships which produced them. The singular person can be imagined as a social microcosm' (M. Strathern 1988, 13). However, the composite singular person is not to be contrasted with the unity of collective actions, because singular and plural are homologues of each other; 'the bringing together of many persons is just like the bringing together of one' (M. Strathern 1988, 13–14). Part of the conception of the singular person is its partibility, the way in which people are enchained by shared labour, whose products, especially in the context of ceremonial exchange, can be conceived of as parts of persons, 'apprehended as detached from one and absorbed by another' (M. Strathern 1988, 178).

In the case of the Garia of New Guinea (Lawrence 1984), it seems as though individuals themselves can stand at times for the whole society, in ways unfamiliar to a western way of thought, in which the individual on the one hand is normally defined in relation to a wider whole and on the other thought of as autonomous and bounded (M. Strathern 1992a). The Garia had an open form of social organisation, with cognatic kinship reckoned through kin on the side of either parent, and no genealogical boundaries marking off groups. Though some relative boundedness to some rights and memberships can be found, it has also been possible to think of the Garia as conceiving the person as the basis of relationships. '. . . If Garia society were modeled in the encompassing unity of the singular human being, a person would in this sense not be a part of anything else. A multitude of persons would simply magnify the image of one' (M. Strathern 1992a, 81). This homology can extend to a collectivity (however defined and however unbounded) such as cognatic stock. The recurrent internal division of persons into male and female elements can be accommodated by reference to a sense of time and future unions and dissolutions; perspectives can be exchanged for one another, and the part is made from the same material as the whole (M. Strathern 1992a, 83–4).

To offer a little geographical balance, the last example here comes from lowland Amazonia. Among the Jivaroan Achuar, 'being a person is . . . an array or cline of relational configurations, a set of links in a chain of metamorphoses simultaneously open and bounded' (Taylor 1996, 210). The sense of self is based on an image of the body, including its appearance and especially that of the face, and on other people's perception of this image through a web of interaction, feeling (hostile feelings not excluded) and memory. This sense of self, in a shifting and often hostile and violent social setting, is fragile, and can lapse into a state of uncertainty equivalent to sickness (Taylor 1996, 207).

My intention is not to suggest that one or other of these examples could be somehow directly fitted on to the archaeological evidence with which I am concerned; there is sufficient difference among them to make that, in itself, a pointlessly arbitrary exercise. These examples do, however, show considerable complexity in what constitutes identity, gender, and persons and the relations between them. They should challenge any complacency, generated from living in our own world, over assigning the same kind of individuality to each and every situation in the past millennia under discussion here. Individuals, dividuals, persons may have varied, from place to place and through time. The next section offers a possible archaeological example of this.

Individuals on the Great Hungarian Plain: Early Neolithic to Early Copper Age

I have already briefly introduced this area in chapter 1. Here I will use the regional evidence to try to document changes in the way individuals were represented. Though the overall interpretation is difficult, at least it should be clear that individualism in the sense discussed above was not static, timeless or universal. Not only is the archaeological record of the region exceptionally abundant, it also offers an unusual combination: a series of individual burials, and a series of representations of the human form, including the face, through a well-documented sequence, which offers a good sense of changing context (Sherratt 1982a; 1982b; 1983; Chapman 1997b; 1997c).[2]

In the Körös culture, from about 6000–5500 BC, people were dispersed through the river systems of the southern part of the Great Hungarian Plain (and very similar phenomena are to be found in the northern Starčevo culture in the southern part of the Carpathian basin as a whole: see Whittle *et al.* 2002). We do not know whether these were immigrants or indigenous people, although, whatever their descent, they were in a real sense colonisers, since the area seems to have been at best little visited in the preceding millennia. The lifestyle certainly involved a range of new practices, but even if the population migrated in, in a filtered or piecemeal kind of way from the south, it is not clear that the presence of domesticated animals or cereals necessarily engaged people in a wholly sedentary existence. Site stratigraphies are thin, and few substantial structures have been found. The overwhelming majority of sites are found alongside water, in the active river courses, in the alluvial deltas fringing these, and in the older but still wet alluvial deltas and meanders of the late Pleistocene landscape. The vast majority of occupied locations were strung along ridges and levées overlooking water, some of these linear spreads being extensive, but it seems in most cases that the unit of occupation in use at any one time was quite small. We do not yet know whether places were occupied year-round, though some may have been, and we do not know the absolute length of time over which places were used, whether seasonally or permanently. It has been suggested that places became 'timemarks' rather later in this sequence (Chapman 1997c), but it is possible that even short-lived or seasonally occupied locations acquired significant symbolic charge. Though maps of the situation which represent 'sites' as single dots appear to present a populous landscape, it may be that the situation involved a scattered population, with much coming and going, in repetitive and structured ways (as noted also in chapter 2).

Pottery was used in abundance in these locations, from fine-ware bowls to large jars presumably for storage. The larger vessels are quite profusely decorated with incised, impressed and applied decoration, together with surface alterations, but it has been classically difficult to find clear evidence of chronological development in this, and it does not seem that this material culture was being used to mark strong difference, either between sites or areas, or with neighbouring cultural areas (such as the northern Starčevo or Criş cultures, to the south and east respectively). This seems compatible with a landscape of some movement and fluidity. Part of the abundant use of fired clay is a series of anthropomorphic figurines, though we know little of the circumstances in which they were made or used, since they normally occur as fragments in infilled pits and other contexts. Though this circumstance may imply a process of enchainment between people (M. Strathern 1988; Chapman 2000a), and while there are unresolved issues of whether these figurines represent ancestors, spirits, forebears or other known or remembered individuals (Whittle 1996; Bailey 2000), my interest here is in the nature of representation. The great majority are of female form, indicated by modelling and delineation, admittedly often schematic, of large backsides, pubic triangles and breasts. The great majority also have to our eyes rather anonymous, featureless faces, with nose, eyes and sometimes mouth (hair is also sometimes delineated) summarily executed. This may raise the issue of whether masks are being represented (cf. Seip 1999). Many figurines have elongated necks, and variations of this style of 'rod-headed' figurines extend far south into the Balkans and Greece. It has been suggested that such Greek figurines are sexually ambiguous, since in profile they also appear strongly phallic (Kokkinidou and Nikolaidou 1997). This seems to apply also in the Starčevo and Körös cultures (Whittle 1998a, fig. 1). Whatever the figurines may ultimately signify, it is striking that they take human form and that further they seem to offer a fundamental ambiguity to do with female and male gender. By contrast, slightly earlier representations in the region, belonging to local populations in the Danube Gorges, were of a combination of human and fish-like creatures, without sexual characteristics (Srejović 1972; Radovanović 1997; Whittle 1998b).

Burials are also a feature of many sites (Trogmayer 1969; Chapman 1994). These are mainly simple individual graves, some barely cut into the subsoil, with varied body positions, and minimal or no grave goods; some instances of partial bodies are known, and stray bones also occur in occupation deposits and pits. So far, no separate burial grounds have been found, and graves or burials occur mainly on the edges of occupied areas; a couple are known inside burnt houses or structures. It has been suggested that deaths may have been one cause of settlement relocation (Chapman 1994). Strikingly, the majority of Körös culture burials are of women and children. Men were presumably disposed of somewhere out in the landscape.

Can we link these features to obtain some sense of personal identity and self at this time, but at the same time avoiding a characterisation that comes too close to offering what used to be called in social anthropology the personality of a culture (e.g. Benedict 1934; Kuper 1999, 66–7, 124–5)? There is both fluidity and structure in the landscape, comings and goings and yet also places regularly used and some perhaps permanently recognised. There is some sign of gender differentiation in mortuary ritual, and considerable sexual ambiguity in the representation of the human form. Of the possession of individual agency there is no doubt, but we could suggest that individuals themselves had some of these characteristics. The individual may on the one hand have been independent, flexible, partly mobile, able to detach herself or himself from particular situations and relationships and to join others, but on the other hand anonymous in the sense of being able to merge into larger wholes, male and female defined in relation to each other only in certain circumstances, notably the dissolution of death.

Things did not stay the same in the next five hundred years (down to about 5000 BC or soon after), though there was much that is still familiar. For a start the Linear Pottery culture of the Great Plain or AVK[3] extended the distribution of settlement right across the Plain to its northern limits (Kalicz and Makkay 1977), and there is evidence for clearance in the woodlands of the hills beyond (A. Gardner 1999), and for contact with populations in the hills seen in continued raw material exchanges. According to surface survey data, many AVK occupations were more dispersed and perhaps smaller, though basically still strongly riverine. Little more is known in detail of AVK settlement structure than that of the Körös culture. Recent motorway excavations in the north of the Plain have, however, shown the existence of longhouses at Füzesabony-Gubakút (Domboróczki 1997). These are substantial structures up to nearly 30 m long, though they have three main rows of posts rather than the usual five of the classic LBK construction. In another instance revealed by the motorway project nearby, at Mezőkövesd-Mocsolyás, there were also house or structure remains, from 9 by 12 m to 7 by 12 m in extent, defined not by postholes but by spreads of burnt wall daub (Kalicz and Koós 1997). The site at Mezőkövesd-Mocsolyás belongs to the earliest AVK and might be seen as both traditional and transitional, but there is also the possibility that large longhouses were known mainly in the north of the Plain, closer to the area of the classic LBK in Transdanubia and areas to the north. On the basis of present evidence (which includes excavations of much smaller extent than in the northern motorway project), larger buildings only appear to the south in the late AVK Szakálhát phase.

A striking feature of both the Füzesabony-Gubakút and Mezőkövesd-Mocsolyás sites are the abundant anthropomorphic and perhaps zoomorphic figurines (Figure 3.1). These still involve, to our eyes, rather anonymous faces, with triangular heads and schematically modelled eyes, nose and mouth. Some were part of small flat figurines, others certainly part of footed models resembling animals. It is not always clear whether the face on these creatures is human or animal. Other such figurines are known over the broader distribution of the AVK across the Plain, but the considerable majority appear to come from the northern part of the Plain (Kalicz and Makkay 1977, fig. 4). As with other AVK sites, both Füzesabony-Gubakút and Mezőkövesd-Mocsolyás have simple burials. At Füzesabony-Gubakút these were barely cut into the ground, with children most numerous, but with men better represented among the adults than was normally the case in the Körös culture. Beads, including of *Spondylus*, and a pot in one case, constituted the grave goods (Domboróczki 1997). At Mezőkövesd-Mocsolyás, a larger number of burials lay in a semi-circle around the structures, some with beads and bracelets, and in three cases out of 25, a pot (Kalicz and Koós 1997).

Less is known of burial rites in the Szakálhát phase to the south, but another striking development is the appearance of quite large pots with human faces incised and partly modelled on their upper parts. One of the best examples is a group of at least twenty-two such vessels from a (?deliberately) burnt house at Battonya, with

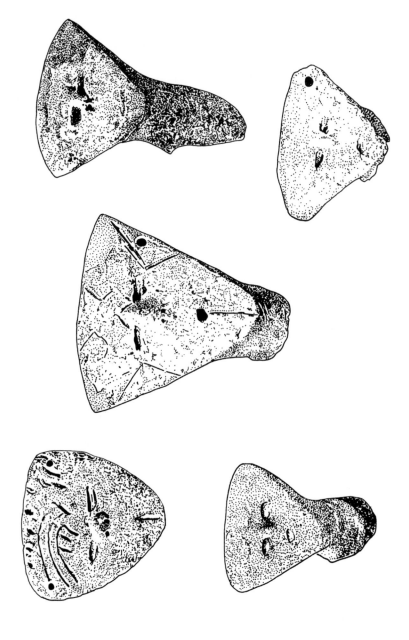

Figure 3./ Representations of human faces in the Neolithic sequence of the Great Hungarian Plain: parts of vessels from the AVK site of Füzesabony-Gubakút. After Domboróczki.

which were also found models of human feet (Goldman 1978). These faces have sharper delineation of eyes, nose and mouth, and some rendering of ears and hair. A prominent M-motif under the face is a recurrent feature, which has been taken as a female signifier (Goldman 1978; Pavlů 1966).

The extent of change compared to the Körös culture is still unclear, but there are intriguing possibilities (to which we will come back also in chapter 6). It is possible that the dispersal and size of AVK occupations indicate a greater degree of short-term sedentism, and this may have been reinforced by the appearance of larger houses, at differing times in different parts of the Plain. As part of this, there was a continued and perhaps heightened interest in human appearance, a possible blurring of human and animal identity, some emphasis on child burials, and at least in the south, some possible attention to gender or sexual difference. Individuals could perhaps still come and go as before, but changing circumstances began to define slightly differing senses of identity, and perhaps vice versa.

In the next five hundred years on the Plain (from c. 5000–4500 BC: the Late Neolithic or Tisza and other cultures), the context was varied. Much research has concentrated on tells or mounds which became now a feature of parts of the landscape. These were in fact, however, not very numerous (Chapman 2000a, 155). They were hardly uniform in either distribution or formation, being more frequent in some eastern parts of the Plain and almost absent in others, and varying in height, extent and rate of formation (Raczky 1987a). Tells varied in character, from some of the lower and broader examples further south, in which there were discernible shifts of focus through time, to the small conical tells of the eastern Herpály group, to the northerly ditched roundel of Csőszhalom, tell-like and with some occupation on the mound, but accompanied by a large open settlement a little distance away (Raczky 1987a; Raczky et al. 1994; 1997a). Some of these sites may have been deliberately planned 'timemarks' which drew on an ideology of deep ancestral time, the aim of a deliberate strategy carried out by limited local interest groups (Chapman 1997b; 1997c), rather than part of a grand plan to manage plains-fringes relationships including flows of goods and cattle (Sherratt 1982a; cf. Shanks and Tilley 1987, 37–41). However, it is also possible that some of the mounds in question were rather more the outcome of social practices than a predetermined effect, the unplanned result of prolonged occupation of one place: in itself hardly a new development. There were also plenty of 'flat' sites in the landscape, from smaller to larger, as at Kisköre-Damm in the upper Tisza valley, a little to the south of Füzesabony (Raczky et al. 1994, color table III; Korek 1989; Chapman 2000a). Well-constructed buildings have been found in greater abundance in this phase, both in tells and flat sites, probably to be connected with a greater degree of permanent occupation. Houses seem not to be markedly differentiated by size or contents (the latter now including rich assemblages of decorated pottery and figurines). Cattle became the most important animal. There were flows of exchange within the plain and with the fringing highland, involving perhaps both animals and material valuables (Sherratt 1982a).

The dead were again present among the living. There are many instances of burials in between (as well as occasionally under) houses. The dead buried in such contexts were generally given only a few more marks of individual identity, largely in the form of necklaces, strings of beads around the middle, and bracelets. In the case of the rather isolated tell at Vésztő-Mágor, south of the Körös river, the number of grave goods appears to have increased in later phases of occupation (Hegedűs and Makkay 1987, 99). This kind of treatment can be seen in both tell and flat sites. The dead were given more careful treatment to the extent that coffins now appear in many instances, for example at Vésztő-Mágor. There are signs of small groups, both within tells as at Öcsod, another isolated tell south of the Körös river (Raczky 1987b), and Vésztő-Mágor, and on flat sites, such as Kisköre-Damm. These could perhaps be seen as family or kin groups but this is difficult to substantiate. There are again adults of both sexes in roughly equal numbers, in many cases with little to strongly differentiate them in terms of grave goods, or body position. In the settlement beside the tell at Polgár-Csőszhalom-dűlő, however, the most northerly on the Plain, men were normally found on their right sides and women on their left, and men's graves can be distinguished by the provision of stone axes, boar mandibles or boar tusk plates, and women's by strings of beads around their middle, as well as in the area of the head, perhaps from having been part of hair ornamentation (Raczky *et al.* 1997a). In the case of Berettyóújfalu-Herpály, by contrast, in the easternmost part of the Plain, the great majority of the burials were of children (Kalicz and Raczky 1984). The overall picture is one of considerable variation.

Anthropomorphic vessels, vessel attachments and figurines were part of a rich material culture. Their forms were now very varied, from the striking sitting figurines (male as well as female) of sites like Hódmezővásárhely-Kökénydomb, Vésztő-Mágor and Szegvár-Tűzköves (Raczky 1987a), some of which are really vessels as well as figurines, to the much more modest small figurines of a site like Berettyóújfalu-Herpály (Kalicz and Raczky 1987, 206–8). Faces are still to our eyes anonymous, and many of the vessels seem to have no head as such, which might have been provided by some organic attachment or addition. There are both identifiably female and male figurines, and some whose sex is ambiguous. It remains dangerous to try to read off identities from these representations, but their very diversity, compared with earlier times, might speak in a general way for a greater sense of individualism.

Neither figurines nor anthropomorphic vessels were placed in graves. It remains unclear in this phase whether they should be seen as ancestors, spirits, forebears or particular individuals. There is perhaps a greater sense of identity being defined in relation to particular places and social groupings, the presence of the dead reinforcing the importance of place. If at least some figurines represented an ancestral domain, there would have been differing presences, of the ancestors and other spirits among the living in the form of material objects, and the known, remembered dead forming a defined community at least in the dissolution of death.

There was both continuity and slow change in this phase. Tells did not emerge overnight, and are barely characteristic of the plain as a whole. Some of their occupants may not have been present on them all the time. People may have attended to their landscapes in very similar ways to their predecessors, though with cattle now becoming the animal of dominant concern. Individuals continued to belong to groups which had a concern for descent and belonging. But things were hardly exactly as before. Individual places were picked out for special occupation (cf. Chapman 1997c), and the business of living in closely spaced houses, even if only for seasons or for short runs of years, must have affected individuals in new ways; the effect, however, at least in specific places and at specific times, may have been to constrain individual action, at a time when figurines and burials might suggest greater individualism. The individual remains partly shadowy – or flexible and mobile – but is also now more tied to particular settings and perhaps roles.

Around the middle of the fifth millennium BC the pattern alters again, and many of those sites with previously prolonged reoccupations were now either abandoned or much less intensively used. From the Early Copper Age Tiszapolgár culture through to the Late Copper Age Baden culture, there seems to have been a long phase again of dispersal of small sites across the landscape. In the Tiszapolgár culture phase (c. 4500–4000 BC), just at the point when certain sites or groups could have created or reinforced preeminence, few tells remained in occupation. The break was not immediate. There were proto-Tiszapolgár burials at Hódmezővásárhely-Gorzsa (Horváth 1987) and Tiszapolgár burials at Vésztő-Mágor. The population seems mainly to have been dispersed once more in scattered small units and the social aggregations represented by the anyway far from common tells were replaced by something else. Now the public collectivity is represented by burial grounds, set apart from settlements or occupations; the classic but probably atypical example is Tiszapolgár-Basatanya itself in the north of the Plain near the Tisza river (Bognár-Kutzián 1963; 1972). Once again, this shift had been prefigured in the preceding phase; some of the burials at Berettyóújfalu-Herpály, for example (Kalicz and Raczky 1987), had been placed at a distance from the tell. While it has been suggested that competing limited interest groups would actively have sought new ways of promoting themselves, and would thus have sought to make displays in this period through mortuary rites separate from occupations (Chapman 1997b), other explanations may apply. The costs of maintaining tell existence may have become too high (cf. Bogucki 1996), in social as well as economic terms. In another context, among the Foi of Papua New Guinea, considerable tension from the demands of close communal living has been recorded, to be contrasted with the greater freedom of more independent existence (J.F. Weiner 1991, 78). The flow of materials and goods through tells and open sites in this period (cf. Sherratt 1982a, fig. 2.5) might have produced tensions at odds with an otherwise communal ethos (cf. Hagen 1999), to be resolved once more by fission among the living. There are burial grounds of varying sizes, the smaller ones perhaps serving more local populations than the largest example, Tiszapolgár-Basatanya itself (Bognár-Kutzián 1963); the northerly position of that site in relation to flows of copper into the plain may have been significant (Sherratt 1982a). While some sites therefore may have had a greater range of artefacts at them, and been longer-lived, there is little other sign of differentiation within the length and breadth of the plain (Bognár-Kutzián 1972). Burial grounds both large and small seem to promote an ideology of commonality, now prolonged among the close community of the dead after its practice among the aggregations of the living on tells and large open sites in the preceding Tisza phase.

Not all Tiszapolgár mortuary rites were identical. Nor was the situation necessarily static. In the Early Copper Age some of the richest sites may have been near or on the edge of the plain, well placed for exploiting movements of copper (Sherratt 1982a). The small group excavated at the Vésztő-Mágor tell to the south of the Körös river were more traditionally furnished than elsewhere, with less variation in grave goods, but still some gender differentiation (Chapman 1997a, 143). From other instances, however, there seems to have been a very widely distributed common way of doing things. A proto-Tiszapolgár female grave at Hódmezővásárhely-Gorzsa, east of the Tisza and north of the Maros (Horváth 1987, fig. 23), was provided with a pot behind the head, abundant beads probably formerly in strings on the legs, hips and neck, and a bracelet on the right arm. By the early Tiszapolgár phase at Polgár-Nagy Kaszárba in the north of the plain (Raczky *et al.* 1997b), there were a male, a female and two child graves (probably part of a larger burial ground) with differentiation by body side and by some of the grave goods, while both the woman and the man were accompanied by many pots. The adult male lay on his right side, with eleven pots by his head and feet. There was the lower jaw of a boar behind his head, as well as stone and bone artefacts, *Spondylus* beads and one copper bead. The adult female lay on her back, again with twelve pots at head and feet, and *Spondylus* beads in the area of the waist, probably from a belt. One of the child burials was of a young girl, on her left side, with four pots at head and waist, a pair of copper bracelets, and scattered *Spondylus* beads. The other child burial lay on its back, and had a pot and a copper bracelet. Even these four examples show traits that recur widely: undecorated pottery (only distinguished across the Plain by broad stylistic zones: Bognár-Kutzián 1972), an emphasis on objects to do with personal adornment and appearance, food remains, token animal remains, and differentiation by age and sex. Tools and weapons occur elsewhere, and there were no figurines in this phase.

Tiszapolgár-Basatanya itself has been the most analysed, since it is well published (including Sherratt 1982a; Meisenheimer 1989; Chapman 1997a; 2000a; 2000b; Derevenski 1997; 2000). Its use ran from the Tiszapolgár phase on into the succeeding Bodrogkeresztúr phase, on into the fourth millennium BC; there were over 150 graves in all, mainly individual inhumations. Women, men and children are represented. The dead were set in rows and their graves were probably individually marked, their positions thereby subsequently respected over long periods of time. Though there is a wide range of grave goods, there is overall no clear sign of major material differentiation between individuals or groupings (the latter explored by Meisenheimer 1989) within the burial ground. There was clearly some emphasis put on gender differences, as emphasised by recent analyses (Chapman 1997a; Derevenski 1997; 2000). These change between the Tiszapolgár and Bodrogkeresztúr phases, though it may be rather artificial to contrast only two such large blocks of time without trying to take account of changes from generation to generation (cf. Meisenheimer 1989). It may be more profitable to look again at the small groups within the cemetery suggested by previous analysis (Meisenheimer 1989), rather than to score the features and contents of individual graves, arranged in two large chronological blocks (and see now Chapman 2000b, concentrating on rows). In Derevenski's accounts (1997, 887; 2000), the various objects in question are linked in the Tiszapolgár phase not only to gender but to age, creating a strong sense of life process, whereas in the Bodrogkeresztúr phase there is a greater emphasis simply on female/male difference (reinforced by the slightly different analysis of Chapman 1997a, 138–43). While there is thus difference, there is hardly, in crude terms, discernible inequality evident in the mortuary rites, since women's graves can be as abundantly furnished with goods as men's, and children (at least in the Tiszapolgár phase when they are more common) seem often to be treated in anticipation of their future development. There seems to be increased emphasis throughout on the dead as though they were living. Thus women, men and children all receive food remains and quite abundant and varied pottery, though relative numbers may vary depending on age and gender (Derevenski 1997, fig. 2), and there are tools and other objects to do with dress and appearance. The last sight of the dead in the grave was of individuals furnished, in ways appropriate to their gender and age, for full, active participation in social life and the maintenance of long established commonality.

In this way, gradual shifts in the nature of individualism have been suggested. The model has been very generalised, and it would take a longer account to explore the extent to which the sense of variation in say the Late Neolithic could be examined as the effect of particular individuals or at least small social groupings, actively seeking to affect their circumstances rather than acting out roles and rules in ways or styles prescribed for them by tradition or custom. It is tempting to apply other models to this attempted case study in individualism. Thus at a general level, the scheme advocated by Mauss is interesting (though difficult) and potentially relevant. Mauss suggested that before the emergence of the Christian-era *personne* and the modern, autonomous *moi*, there had been first a sense of *personnage* followed by the development of *persona* (Mauss 1985; Rapport 1996, 299). *Personnage* was seen as a 'tribal' stage, with individuals holding names and roles within a clan setting, while the *persona* is more independent, with its own civic identity but still no individual inner life. Could all the examples described above be merely *personnages*, or could the figures seen at Tiszapolgár-Basatanya be regarded as *personae*? Mauss was thinking of a different timescale, with *persona* developing in the time of the early state. Especially he was working within the tradition set by Durkheim in which the collective was seen to determine and submerge the individual. It may therefore be more helpful to set this kind of scheme aside as prejudging the issues, and to use the kinds of analogies discussed earlier. Could we see, for example, in the material remains from the sequence on the Great Hungarian Plain anything resembling the difference between the bounded but permeable individual of south India and the partible person and performative identity of Melanesia (cf. Busby 1997)? It might in fact be legitimate to suggest elements of both. The people seen in the burial ground at Tiszapolgár-Basatanya, for example, appear from one perspective to be presented as bounded individuals, with a sense of mortuary treatment appropriate to age and gender (though what was considered or asserted as appropriate may have been far from rigidly fixed). At the same time, the individual may have had a partible dimension, suggested by the non-local objects such as *Spondylus* beads and copper artefacts. On the other hand, although many of the analyses have concentrated on looking closely at individual after individual, the context of belonging to small groupings remains striking (see also Chapman 2000b). There is more that unites in these mortuary rites than separates. Within the group context, there is also a strong sense of asserting at the moment of death a living identity shared by many. Here is the individual, young or old, female or male, presented as ready for social existence, appropriately dressed and recognisable, and able to provide food and drink. Perhaps this could be seen as a performative view of identity, in that the individual was only fully constituted in relation to others, and perhaps this model of relationships was only fully realised as the individual passed on to another world.

It has not been the purpose of this section to choose between the competing possibilities. It has been the aim to argue that what constituted individuals was a far more complex business than most archaeological interpreters have recognised, and that identity was probably varied in any one phase, and far from static through time (see also Brück 2001; Fowler 2000; 2001). In the remainder of the chapter, I want to look more closely at other dimensions of what held individuals together, focusing first on notions of society and culture, which leads to a discussion of the moral community, and then on household.

Society, culture and the moral community

If individuals are elusive, can we not simply stick to the larger entities to which they belonged and which they helped to constitute? Once upon a time, that would hardly have been problematic from a theoretical point of view. Since Durkheim, anthropologists had stressed the notion of the dominant, implicitly bounded collectivity, and went on to debate, for example in the era of the British structural functionalists (Kuper 1996), its internal workings, especially social relationships. Archaeologists at the same time, rather lamely, used the collective concept of the archaeological culture. Badly under-theorised, it nonetheless rather palely reflected some of the features of another major anthropological interest, in culture as pervasive symbolic system (Sahlins 1999; Kuper 1999). In archaeological as in anthropological culture, there were seen to be tradition, institutions and above all boundaries, which it took historical movements of people to disrupt or reform. Society, or culture, depending on one's point of view (Kuper 1999), programmed its individuals, and could be seen as the proper object of study.

Now things are far less certain. It is far too glib to equate anthropological society or culture with archaeological culture, but the anthropological debates on these issues are important. Three examples from these are enough to illustrate the challenges. In his study of the Kachin of highland Burma, Edmund Leach (1954; for detailed commentary see, among others, Kuper 1996; Tambiah 1998) outlined a world of unbounded social relationships in contrast to traditional notions of bounded tribes and ethnic wholes set in the unchanging equilibrium of tradition and culture.

His model, as noted already in chapter 1, was of an open system. Over a long timescale, of some 150 years, Kachin communities were seen to oscillate between more egalitarian (*gumlao*) and more ranked (*gumsa*) political formations. Leach stresses the importance of the difference between ideal and actual behaviour, seeing kinship for example not as a set of fixed rules but as a model to be used and manipulated. As Leach puts it (1954, 8), 'Every individual of a society, each in his own interest, endeavours to exploit the situation as he perceives it and in so doing the collectivity of individuals alters the structure of society itself'.

We have already seen how in her study of Mount Hagen people in Papua New Guinea, Marilyn Strathern (1988) has gone further and challenged the whole notion of society, contrasting our own western expectations with indigenous ways of thinking. The opening two sentences of *The gender of the gift* set the tone: 'It might sound absurd for a social anthropologist to suggest he or she could imagine people having no society. Yet the argument of this book is that however useful the concept of society may be to analysis, we are not going to justify its use by appealing to indigenous counterparts' (M. Strathern 1988, 3). So, while it makes sense to talk variously in terms of sociality, unity, plurality and collective events, these cannot be reduced to collective society. While we see society as what connects individuals and the relationships between them, and individuals as 'conceptually distinct from the relations that bring them together', for Melanesians sociality can be both singular and plural (M. Strathern 1988, 13). Collective actions often give an 'image of unity'. Nonetheless, Strathern is at pains to avoid a different opposition, merely replacing society versus individual, between 'collective life as a unity, while singular persons are composite'. Rather than one dimension dominating or determining the other, the key transformations are homologies and analogies; 'the bringing together of many persons is just like the bringing together of one' (M. Strathern 1988, 13–14). The substance of the book is thereafter concerned not only with contrasts in outsider and insider perception of these possibilities but how they are played out in gender relations and the fields of marriage, work and exchange. This leads (among many other points) to the conclusion that 'collective actions should be seen as one type of sociality, and as one type it therefore coexists with another, namely that sociality evinced in particular, domestic relations. The relation between the two is that of alternation, not hierarchy. The values of one are constantly pitted against the values of the other' (M. Strathern 1988, 319).

In his study of highland Burma, Leach was concerned to break the view that the boundaries of society and culture were the same (1954). In his later study of land tenure among sedentary agriculturalists in Sri Lanka, 'custom' ('what men do, normal men, average men': E. Leach 1961, 298) is also revealed as the outcome of actual behaviour on the ground rather than allegiance to determining and overriding rules (E. Leach 1961). In a long, critical, historical account of the anthropological concept of culture, the difference is sharply set out between a mainly American school of concern with culture as the pervasive collective symbolic discourse, within which social relationships are embedded, and a mainly British school of concern with social relationships, within which culture can be seen as the expression of the style in which these are played out (Kuper 1999). This is not the place to rehearse the historical account, going back to Parsons, Boas and earlier. The important core of the argument is the objection to the use of culture as 'the hyper-referential word', which can somehow replace specific analysis of 'knowledge, or belief, or art, or technology, or tradition, or even of ideology' (Kuper 1999, x). Opposing the view that 'culture is . . . essentially a matter of ideas and values, a collective cast of mind', held in a shared symbolic system, Kuper reflects the view of critics who argue that 'both culture and identity are made up, invented, unstable, discursive fabrications. Every culture is fragmented, internally contested, its boundaries porous' (1999, 239, 247).

Not everyone would agree. Sahlins, for example, has reiterated that culture matters, since 'in all its dimensions, including the social and material, human existence is symbolically constituted, which is to say, culturally ordered' (1999, 400). Even anthropological codgers like Boas and Linton recognised the inventiveness of tradition, and what Boas called 'the lack of specific coherence between various aspects of culture' (quoted by Sahlins 1999, 405). For him, all cultures are hybrid, hybridity being a genealogy not a structure, and sacred symbols (following Durkheim) 'give a people commitment as well as definition . . . a sense of shared existence as well as determinate boundaries' (Sahlins 1999, 411–13). In the same spirit, Taylor has argued for the 'relative continuity of tradition' (1996, 202), making a distinction between spectacular or extreme aspects within a culture and other compartmentalised or complementary perspectives; not everyone need experience the extreme states to be said to be part of a culture (1996, 210). 'Culture may be little more than "a second rate orchestra playing a half remembered tune" without the benefit of a conductor . . ., yet we must still explain how and why everyone remembers the same tune, however inaccurately, and why the level of cacophony in any given 'culture' is in fact surprisingly low' (Taylor 1996, 213).

If in a sense, despite these reservations, both society and culture have gone, or at least have been recast as problematic, where does that leave the notion of collectivity embedded in the archaeological culture? Archaeological culture has remained seriously under-theorised. In the post-processual or interpretive approach, material culture studies have come to replace interest in culture, which was more or less ignored as old hat in processual times. They rest uneasily on the composite base of, on the one hand, a universalised sense of basic grammar (derived ultimately from structuralism), and on the other, a sense of specific context and individual practice. Underpinning ethnoarchaeological studies have been limited in number and extent. Hodder's studies (1982) of the intersection of three tribal/cultural groups near Lake Baringo, Kenya, are now over twenty years old, and anyway dealt with a spatially very small boundary area, largely at one particular moment in time. Not that there have not been many recent illuminating individual studies of particular categories of material culture (as just one example, see A. Jones 2000), but there has been little by way of theorising about archaeological culture as a whole: its boundaries, internal variability and especially the phases in which it changes and reforms. It is symptomatic perhaps that the terms of reference in a recent (very useful) study of metaphor and material culture (Tilley 1999) are distinctly limited. One exception has been to treat culture as though it can be inherited and transmitted like a virus, cultural traits being seen as self-reproducing entities (Cullen 2000). Though this does at least take the issues of wider culture patterning and of culture change seriously, at best it remains only a non-human analogy for the way people act and think, consciously or unconsciously, and at worst it removes any sense of human agency at all.

It is hardly therefore surprising to find the relevance being doubted of a model of widely shared culture for understanding what actually goes on. For example, the setting of the LBK longhouse and its usual material accompaniments, which are broadly similar over wide areas of central and western Europe, have been seen as simply that: a setting within which life was created and lived, a shared material vocabulary, with no common meaning across the LBK distribution (Thomas 1996, 135). But as Hodder has pertinently pointed out (1999, 134), we still have to answer the question of why the setting took a particular, recurrent form.

Rather than posit no common meaning in the widely distributed and shared material culture of the LBK, I would rather raise the question of scales (Figure 3.2). At one scale, action may be a matter of the individual, however constituted, but at another scale, action either by the individual or a collectivity may draw on a much wider frame of reference. Networks and histories are both relevant here. It is possible to model networks in a general or abstract sort of way. For example, Gamble (1999,

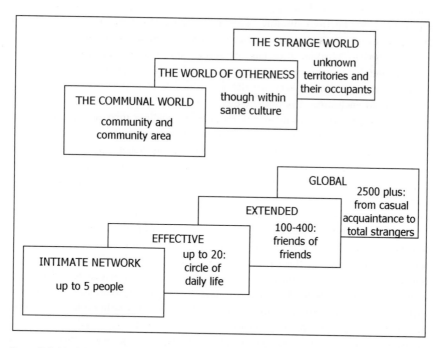

Figure 3.2 Models of networks; above, after Neustupný 1998, and below, after Gamble 1999.

tables 2.8 and 2.9, drawing on a number of sources including Boissevain (1974)) suggests an intimate, face-to-face network of a few people, offering ontological and emotional security; an effective network of up to twenty people, relatives and friends from lineage or residence, which deals with 'the logistics of daily life'; an extended network of 100 to a maximum of 400 people, friends of friends, who can be drawn into the effective network if required, especially through the employment of 'symbolic resources, organized through style and material culture'; and finally, beyond these scales of personal network, a global network, measured in thousands, defined by otherness, and containing casual acquaintances through to total strangers. A similar, though independently derived scheme suggests that communities, groups of families and/or households, up to a maximum of a few such, lived together in community areas and were bound together by close social and emotional ties as well as shared practical imperatives ('a relationship of assistance'). They were set around by a 'world of otherness', which sits between the communal world and the outer strange world, and consists of people and other beings (including the dead) who do not belong to a given community but share artefacts and symbols with it. The world of otherness consists also of overlapping circuits of otherness, and includes through these the 'symbolic systems usually denoted as archaeological cultures' (Neustupný 1998, 10–21).

For all their resonance, these schemes remain very general. They submerge history. Latour offered the dictum that the network is always local (1993), but the nature and history of the network must also affect what goes on at the local point. Cultural uniformity and variability themselves varied considerably. The uniformity of the LBK was far from absolute, with some regional patterning in both styles of house construction and mortuary rites (Coudart 1998; Jeunesse 1997), and more regionalised pottery styles in its later phases. In southern Britain, by contrast, there was considerable variability throughout the fourth millennium BC. There is no exact congruence, for example, between the distributions of pottery styles, cairns and barrows, and enclosures. Each of these can be broken down into local mixtures of style. The ceramic assemblage at any one site is usually a mixture of styles (Cleal 1992); the cairns and barrows within both larger and smaller areas such as the Cotswolds or the upper Kennet valley include a wide range of architectures; and even the ditched enclosures, which have long been seen as having regionalised characteristics (Palmer 1976), can better be seen as much more individualised (A. Barclay 2000). Thomas has referred to this as *bricolage* or a creative play, 'the evocation of particular meanings from a potentially limitless repertoire' (1999, 80, 96). But why should there have been so much uniformity in the one case, and so much variability in the other? The history of specific contexts has to be taken into account. I will develop the argument in chapter 6 that the LBK house was the outcome of a series of fusions, between populations, social formations and ways of thinking about the world. The situation in southern Britain could also now be seen as a series of fusions, but operating in an insular setting in a rather different kind of way. This will also be explored in chapter 6.

Not only does history need to be added to the model of networks, but a sense of the force of what was shared. I have already referred, in chapter 1, to the idea of a moral community or a moral network. This is especially important to counter the ego-centred nature of the networks discussed above (Gamble 1999), in which others exist around 'ego' in widening circles of emotional, practical or logistical, and political support. I want to underline the sense of what the moral community may have expected of smaller groupings and individuals who belonged to it, and thereby the sense of how this affected, constrained and directed what they did, attempted, thought appropriate or felt they could get away with. Two examples already noted in chapter 1 give a further idea of this kind of setting.

In conducting relationships of exchange, it has been argued that the Maneo of eastern Indonesia are concerned for the response of others (Hagen 1999). Exchange among them is complex and important, objects circulating especially as marriage payments. Sociality in the sense of giving attention to others can be seen as an important factor, people being neither under some Maussian imperative always to give and to reciprocate nor guided solely by contingent self-interest. A disposition to generosity and an emphasis on expressing collective virtues by doing things openly have been part of Maneo sociality (Hagen 1999, 366, 372). 'Moral sensibilities inform Maneo efforts to shape perceptions of actions and events precisely as a way to induce responsiveness and to mitigate the appearance of unresponsiveness' (Hagen 1999, 362).

It has also been argued that the emotional correlates of giving and receiving should be considered, through the case study of the Rauto people of coastal southwest New Britain in Melanesia (Maschio 1998). Among them, the gift is something corporate, an important part of collective social time, linking the living and the dead. Identity is acquired through a 'narrative of exchange', which involves and evokes memory, emotion, custom and obligation. The person is contributed to by others, including through gifts; 'persons are created by the gifts of others' (Maschio 1998, 85–6, 96). At the same time, participation in these networks may also involve counter-feelings, of anger, fear of obligation ('This is the road of custom, and it is a difficult road to travel', as one Rauto man put it: Maschio 1998, 86) and vulnerability. Carrying life forward is also a matter of avoiding giving insults, being seen to be too successful or attracting envy (Maschio 1998, 92).

The idea of a moral network is not intended to imply unanimity, and the Rauto example shows the ambivalence, and accompanying emotions, experienced by individual participants. In different contexts, Victor Turner has explored the sense of *communitas* or heightened sociality and transcendent togetherness engendered in rites of passage and pilgrimage (V. Turner 1969). In his examples of procreation/ancestral and installation rites among the Ndembu of Zambia, the liminal phase of the rituals produced a kind of timelessness and inversion of normal states, which promoted an 'anti-structure' of *communitas*. Clearly, this should not stand as a model for all ritual. In other examples, ritual may begin to fail to communicate universally shared values. Among the Iraqw of Tanzania, for example, the ritual authority of male elders depends increasingly on legitimisation by older women, in order to mediate the protest of women as a whole (Snyder 1997). Turner's studies do serve here, however, to show that the ways in which the force of a moral community could be revealed or created are extremely varied.

Community and household

The Rauto number some 2,500 people (Maschio 1998, 85), and the Foi, discussed earlier, some 4,000 people (J.F. Weiner 1991, 6). The number of participants in Ndembu procreation rituals, to judge from the photographs which accompany Turner's text, appears to have been no more than tens of people (V. Turner 1969). It seems unlikely that we could conceive of the LBK, say, as a single, active moral network, given the distance from one side of its distribution to the other. The discussion above has tried to show, however, the importance not only of shifting and unstable senses of what it was to be an individual but of wider relationships and scales of interaction. In the final part of this chapter, I want briefly to give a preliminary, further sense of the archaeological dimensions in which the moral network could be explored; I return to the idea of scales of action and interaction in chapter 6.

The idea of different scales might be articulated through the notion of the 'circuit of otherness' (Neustupný 1998, 20). According to this there are as many circuits as there are communities, individual circuits largely overlapping. Just as the network scheme discussed earlier validated above all the ego or individual person, so this seems to privilege the single scale of the community. It may be better to think of a network formed by concentrations of people, particular communities, and individual households. The archaeological record offers innumerable examples of uneven distributions, and the German term *Siedlungskammer* captures this well, even though its literal translation in English as 'settlement cell' implies something more fixed and mechanistic than I have in mind; settlement concentration may be better.[4] This can easily be illustrated not only by the distribution of LBK settlement (e.g. Bogucki 1988; Lüning 2000), but by groupings of sites among the varied waterside settings of the Körös culture (e.g. Jankovich *et al.* 1989), around particular lakes and other wet places in the Alpine foreland (e.g. Pétrequin 1984), or from valley to valley in central southern England (A. Barclay 2000). We have tended to ignore the significance both of the spaces in between, and the dimensions of settlement concentrations as lived space. Neither was regular. There is much variation within the single example of the LBK. The early sites of Neckenmarkt in easternmost Austria and Strögen in the Horn basin of Lower Austria, for example, can be seen to belong to *Siedlungskammern* of respectively only ten and fourteen sites (Lenneis and Lüning 2001). In the case of the Aldenhovener Platte in north-west Germany, the most intensively investigated single landscape of the LBK, 'sites' consist of varyingly constituted clusters of longhouses strung along smaller watercourses, over a settlement concentration whose total extent might have been at least 40 km in diameter (Lüning and Stehli 1994; Lüning 1997a). Little lay to the south for some 100 km, nor directly to the north, while there was another, smaller settlement concentration some 20 km to the west, that of southern Dutch Limburg, with the flint sources already discussed in chapter 2 in the same general direction at a distance of some 30 km; the next scattered grouping of sites to the east (as the evidence presently appears – the Aldenhovener Platte case classically shows how intensified investigation will change knowledge) is north-east across the Rhine, from Bochum eastwards (Zimmermann 1995). These were small, sometimes very small worlds.

In exceptional cases, it is possible to suggest very small units indeed, as in the rather later examples of the settlements around the isolated lakes Chalain and Clairvaux in the Jura (e.g. Pétrequin 1989). The investigations of the Merzbachtal and other small stream valleys in the Aldenhovener Platte have shown how the concentrations of LBK longhouses could vary even along short stretches of watercourse. This example alone shows how the idea of community must be a flexible one, to which we can add those situations where there may have been traditions and practices of residential mobility or short-lived sedentism, as perhaps in parts of Britain. What was the community in the Merzbachtal: the whole stream valley, particular concentrations of longhouses, or the individual longhouse? The question seems impossible to answer, and its impossibility underscores the importance of a multi-scalar approach.

Houses are the final scale to consider here, since they could be taken to offer the possibility of better understanding of the households to which many individuals might have belonged and from which many communities might have been constituted. But things may not be that simple. There are often either too many houses or too few. And it proves to be as difficult to pin down the household as it is individuals and communities.

As far as structures are concerned, the archaeological record of the Neolithic period in central and western Europe can be seen as either house-rich or house-poor. In house-poor areas and phases, buildings were never completely absent, but are rare and in many instances hard to define. The Körös culture of the Great Hungarian Plain and the northern Starčevo culture west of the Danube are cases in point. Likewise, in western Europe in the fourth and third millennia BC, after the LBK and post-LBK longhouse tradition had lapsed, houses are scarce. In the case of southern Britain, as we have seen, there are good grounds for seeing such substantial buildings as do occur as early in the sequence of the fourth millennium BC (A. Barclay 2000).

By contrast, in house-rich times and places, houses come out of the ground, so to speak, in their hundreds. Not only that, but there appear to be far more than might be expected on any reasonable assumptions about the potential uselife of timber-framed structures. So in many LBK cases, the replacement rate seems unusually rapid. This has been little commented upon, perhaps because of the effort to win reliable site chronologies from difficult horizontal stratigraphies and unhelpful conditions of preservation. On the Aldenhovener Platte, for example, a sequence of fifteen phases can be entertained, covering some 400 years. Langweiler 8, the largest longhouse concentration in the Merzbachtal, was used throughout, except in the last of these phases, normally having no fewer than six longhouses (three in its first and four in its last) (Stehli 1994, fig. 36). That each phase is assigned a new set of structures is also striking; it seems curious that these substantial constructions, heavily built from prime oak, should not on this reckoning have lasted longer than twenty-eight or twenty-nine years. Similar observations can be made at most other longhouse concentrations of any duration. Likewise in the Alpine foreland, rebuilding followed rebuilding, and now that dendrochronology has provided precise reckoning of time, it can be seen that few of the generally small nucleated settlements lasted longer than a generation in any one phase, and often less (and see chapter 6). It is estimated that the houses in site VIII beside the small upland Jura lake of Clairvaux were built in the expectation of no more than ten years of occupation (Pétrequin 1989, 494).

One can plead circumstances of preservation or changes in house construction techniques to explain the lack of visibility in house-poor times, and some of these arguments may be perfectly valid. One can note that lake levels varied, and may have directly necessitated short-term abandonments and therefore subsequent rebuildings. This is certainly a factor on large lakes directly connected to major water flows, but may not apply so forcibly to small lakes and hardly at all to marshy locations. But equally, we should give far more attention to the contexts in which houses were so frequently rebuilt. There seems to be an ideology of renewal at work, an ethos that required continuity to be affirmed and proclaimed in fresh building. In the Alpine foreland, siting a mere few metres distant – a little further from or higher than the water's edge – would have removed the necessity for periodic abandonment and the need for rebuilding. The fact that the same behaviour can be found in the sites not on the larger lakes suggests that there was more to the situation than response to natural fluctuations in water levels.

The pollution of death might be seen as one factor that disrupted the continuity of the household (as noted in the previous chapter). But deaths on their own may not have been potent in this way. There are many burials within LBK settlements (Veit 1996), and burials were also incorporated within the house-rich tells of the Great Hungarian Plain, as we have seen earlier in this chapter. Conversely, there are very few burials or traces of human remains, even infants and children, within the settlements of the Alpine foreland. If deaths were disruptive, these may have been those of prominent household figures, perhaps something equivalent to the married pairs who are the founders of long-lived houses among the Zafimaniry of Madagascar (Bloch 1995b).

This may suggest that for all the physical solidity of the buildings, especially posts, walls and floors, house and household were fragile. The ambiguities of the longhouse community in Amazonia have been described as a series of tensions between competing dominant ideas: unilineal descent, hierarchy, exogamy, virilocality and agnatic residential groups on the one hand, but equality, endogamy and consanguineal residential and territorial groupings on the other (S. Hugh-Jones 1995, 237). The Neolithic house and household might be regarded as alliances of unstable composition, with a potentially shifting membership, and liable to dissolution, provoked not only by the deaths of key members but also by innumerable other kinds of fission. This may also describe much of the character of the basic social grouping in house-poor places. The house was one way of keeping this fragile unity together. The longhouse may have emerged, as I will discuss in more detail in chapter 6, in the particular circumstances of going into the woodlands of central Europe. It was clearly successful as a social institution, seen in its survival (though not without modifications) for a millennium or so. It has even been suggested that something of its possible internal spatial organisation may have been carried on into the smaller house tradition of the Alpine foreland, from the late fifth millennium BC onwards. Pétrequin (1989, 504) has argued that the layout of sites like Clairvaux II (dated between 3470 and 3440 BC), which consist of groupings of separate rectangular buildings, may hark back to the tripartite division of space contained within the single LBK longhouse. Whether or not the functional divisions claimed for the LBK house stand up to future analysis, the general argument is suggestive, and the power of the memory of the longhouse is well seen in the later tradition of the long mound (Bradley 1998a).

There are further complications. The household may itself have been quite varied. Two studies show some of the possibilities for difference under the same kind of roof. Extensive excavation over a number of years at the late LBK[5] site at Cuiry-lès-Chaudardes in the Aisne valley of northern France has produced over thirty houseplans across 6 ha; in five phases of occupation through some 150–200 years, a sequence based on ceramic decoration, there were normally six houses at a time (Ilett et al. 1982; 1986). Residual bone[6] from the pits flanking the houses shows a series of structured differences (Hachem 1995; 1997; 2000). Houses can be divided into two broad categories, a smaller type up to 15 m long with one space or 'room' behind a cross-corridor, and a larger type with two or three such 'rooms' behind the cross-corridor. The bigger buildings have bigger quantities of waste bone. The smaller houses have the largest quantities of wild animals, while the larger buildings have the highest proportions of domesticated animals. There is further difference in the distribution of wild and tame animal species across the settlement, which is maintained through its life (Figure 3.3). Wild boar remains are particularly abundant in the northern part of the settlement, sheep in the western part, and cattle in the eastern part. These patterns have been taken to suggest a degree of specialisation within the settlement, in terms of hunters, sheep herders and cattle herders (Hachem 1997; 2000, 311). Something of the same suggestion has been made with reference to flint production in north-western LBK contexts (Keeley and Cahen 1989).

Bone preservation is normally much worse in LBK contexts than found at Cuiry-lès-Chaudardes and the wider incidence of this kind of pattern is hard to follow. Elsewhere in Europe, for example in the south-east where the faunal evidence is richer, this kind of specialisation is not evident at early dates (e.g. Halstead 1996). There are perhaps other possible interpretations. From the distribution plans (e.g. Hachem 1995, figs 4–8; 1997, figs 14–17), it seems clear that the occupants of most houses used the full range of wild and domestic animals. The highest proportion of game in any one smaller house was just over 40 per cent, while the highest proportion of domesticates was 96 per cent (Hachem 2000, 310). From the fact that bone was preferentially deposited on one side of the buildings (Hachem 1997, fig. 8), it seems that animal bone was being used, either consciously as part of deliberate

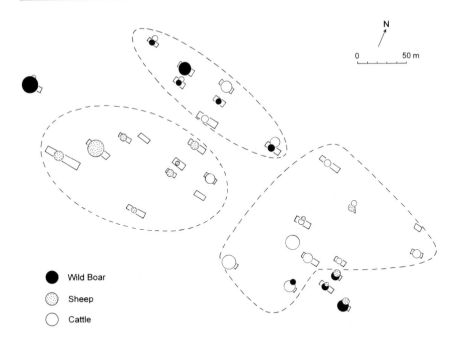

Figure 3.3 Outline distribution of the structured distribution of dominant species at Cuiry-lès-Chaudardes; circle sizes indicate relative abundance. After Hachem 1995.

placings, or unconsciously as part of unthinking routine depositional practices, as a form of display. The incidence of deer and aurochs is widespread but generally low (Hachem 1995, figs 6 and 8). The higher quantities of wild boar (which seem to correlate with the presence of dogs: Hachem 1995, figs 5 and 7) appear in part of the site which might be considered, apart from in the founding phase, as peripheral or on the edge. Was this where it was appropriate to emphasise active hunting, perhaps by younger men? Or were newly founded households placed most appropriately on the edges of the settlement, their occupants ranging more widely in the surrounding woodlands? Cattle were emphasised in the flanking ditches of the larger houses (though these vary in length), and as noted in chapter 2, this could reflect differences in the circumstances of slaughter and consumption in communal feasts or meals, rather than economic specialisation *per se*, either because the larger households were more able to provide such generosity and hospitality, or because the larger houses were used principally or partly for communal gatherings. It is also possible that the differences were generated by varying circumstances through the life of the settlement, over several generations. Within the Aisne valley, it appears that smaller buildings were only built in the longer-lived sites like Cuiry-lès-Chaudardes and Menneville, while shorter-lived and smaller sites like Missy-sur-Aisne had only larger buildings (Hachem 1997, 203). The larger buildings might have housed a number of social units, rather than a single, closed household, whose members acted in perfect unison at all times and through the generations. Variations in the deposition of animal bones may be related in part to the flux and flow of people into and out of the settlement, and to changes in 'household' composition. Variation between the deposited remains of the three main domestic species (cattle, pig and sheep) in the flanking ditches of longhouses can be seen in more detail at Berry-au-Bac (Chemin de la Pêcherie) (Hachem and Auxiette 1995). Here at least, though the sample of buildings is small, there appears far more variation on either side of the larger houses (buildings 200 and 300) than beside the smaller structure 195 (Hachem and Auxiette 1995, figs 67–71). The household was not yet necessarily a fixed or stable institution.

A different sort of relation among houses can be seen in the case of site 3 on the lake of Chalain in the French Jura (Arbogast *et al.* 1995). Here, as in the other sites from this region already discussed, small concentrations of closely grouped houses were built and rebuilt following much the same kind of plan. Two successive levels, VIII and VI, dating to 3200–3170 BC and 3130–3100 BC respectively, have not only good bone preservation but also finds carefully plotted in relation to the houseplans (Figure 3.4). There were four houses available for study in the earlier phase, and three in the younger. These were rectangular buildings of roughly equal size, with raised floors originally holding clay hearths. The hearths were situated in the front portion of the buildings. Much food preparation seems to have taken place immediately in front of the buildings, the entrance being on one of the ends, or in the front portion; waste from a range of kinds of food is found at the front and under the front to middle parts of the buildings (Arbogast *et al.* 1995, fig. 2). Bones would have been subject to scavenging by pigs and dogs, and could also have been moved by localised flooding. Taking the patterns that result at face value, there are again differences between the buildings. In layer VIII in the centre of the house row, building C has a particularly high concentration of bone remains and also some antler working, while its neighbours on one side, buildings B and A, stand out for antler working and a concentration of bear bones respectively. However, while this might imply difference in terms of say household importance or seniority, there are many conjoins and matches among the bones under the houses, suggesting the existence of collective disposal areas (Arbogast *et al.* 1995, figs 12–13). The picture here might be of a single social unit, housed in separate but closely spaced buildings, and operating as a unity, rather than of adjacent but autonomous households.

Some patterns

Many different sorts of situation have been covered in this chapter, which I end by bringing together some correlations. In the case of the Great Hungarian Plain, I suggested that individuals might have been more defined with the appearance of longhouses, and that there was perhaps more individualism still by the time of tell settlements. However, the sharpest definition of the individual came in the Early

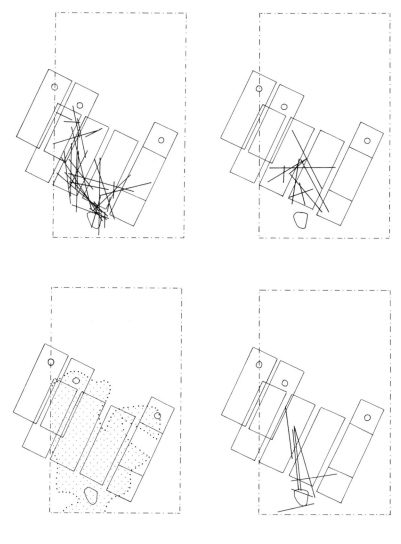

Figure 3.4 Bone distributions across five separate buildings in level VIII, Chalain site 3 (late fourth millennium BC), French Jura. Clockwise from top left: all bones; deer; cattle; and boar; the lines indicate conjoins or matching bones. After Arbogast *et al.* 1995.

Copper Age burial grounds, at a time when there is very little evidence for the nature of houses or households. In the LBK of central and western Europe, substantial, sometimes massive buildings, grouped in varying concentrations but normally free-standing, were accompanied by largely individual burials, either within the settlement or in burial grounds. Judging by the evidence of the Aldenhovener Platte (Lüning and Stehli 1994; Lüning 1997a) and elsewhere, such burial grounds may have served more than one settlement. Where there were closely grouped buildings in the Alpine foreland, we know little of the general mortuary rite. In southern Britain, the evidence is of rare, perhaps specialised, and early buildings, while collectivities are constituted in mortuary deposits of considerable variety, accumulated by differing processes and histories. The ways in which individualism could be seen and in which individuals could be defined in relation to others were diverse. Public rituals of affirmation, like the depositions at causewayed enclosures in southern Britain or the burials in the Early Copper Age cemeteries of the Great Hungarian Plain, were perhaps most pronounced where the residential complex was least defined or most unstable. This leaves the standing of the LBK settlement, so often taken as self-evidently fixed, closed and permanent, as problematic. In all cases, identity is hardly to be found in a single dimension.

Chapter 4

What animals were like

Animals have been treated in many different ways, not only in the past millennia which are the subject of this book but also in the divergent traditions of anthropology and archaeology. When the British Early Agriculture Project, for example, was being formulated in the 1960s and renewed attention was being given to the criteria for domestication and the closeness of man–animal relationships, the overriding concern was for subsistence economics (Higgs and Jarman 1969). By this time, Lévi-Strauss's book on totemism had been translated into English (Lévi-Strauss 1964), and British anthropologists were commenting further on the ways that animals were used in systems of thought (E. Leach 1964; Tambiah 1969; cf. Douglas 1957; 1966). That anthropological tradition continued, with little sign of cross-fertilisation in archaeology, until recently. In adopting a more anthropological approach to animals, some prehistorians have given particular attention to categorisation and symbolism. It is the aim of this chapter to explore both the strengths and weaknesses of this fusion. In particular I will claim the necessity of maintaining a broad approach to animals. I argue that animals were central to the way of life under investigation; they were an inseparable part of how identities were constructed and how the world was seen, but in stressing their symbolic and conceptual importance, it is vital not to lose sight of their physicality, animality and sociality. Animals were a central part of the diversity which this book claims, and another factor in the very slow rate at which fundamental change took place.

A brief contrast between anthropological and archaeological traditions of dealing with animals will help to set the scene. When Lévi-Strauss (1964, 89) declared that animals were important in symbolic schemes not because they are 'good to eat' but because they are 'good to think',[1] he was not really engaged in a detailed discussion of animals as such. The much-quoted phrase emerges from his discussion of Radcliffe-Brown, the British anthropologist in many ways quite alien to the concerns and approaches of Lévi-Strauss but who in a renewed attempt to explain totemism had begun to stress the importance of metaphorical thought (Kuper 1996, 53–6). The principal aim of Lévi-Strauss's *Totemism* was to deconstruct totemism as an anthropological construct, and to use the subject of how 'natural species' were thought about as a way into the universal workings of the human mind, especially the propensity to use analogy and metaphor. Animals, though of course referred to throughout the book, seem in themselves to be taken for granted. Lévi-Strauss dispassionately notes (1964, 57) in Malinowski's treatment of totemism the 'easily verifiable' affinity between people and animals, through the sharing of movement, vocalisation, the expression of emotion, and the possession of body and face. He also underlines the limited explanatory value of a naturalistic approach, praising Evans-Pritchard's discussion of the Nuer, in which the latter had gone no further than suggesting some power of association, for example between the flight of birds and their ability to communicate with the spirits of the sky (Lévi-Strauss 1964, 79).

In real senses, Lévi-Strauss's arguments were little heeded, both over the longer term as structuralism was weighed and found wanting, and in the shorter term as anthropological discussion of animals continued. Much more recently, Willis has noted that totemism itself has far from given up the ghost (1994, 5). But already in the 1960s, other commentators had noted much more complex situations than Lévi-Strauss had appeared to allow. Among the Karam of the New Guinea highlands, for example, a web of categorisations of creatures, from birds to animals such as pigs and dogs, was bound up with sets of cultural and cosmological distinctions among people (Bulmer 1967). Bulmer's starting point was the indigenous classification of the cassowary, for other highland groups a (flightless) bird, but not for the Karam. Rather than explaining this by its 'taxonomic status' or its natural characteristics, Bulmer considered the status of the creature as a prime hunting prey, and from there the importance of the wild, the antithesis between forest and cultivation, conflicts within kinship roles and obligations, and contrasts with dogs and pigs. For the Karam, dogs are notable for their prominent mouths and genitalia, and ambiguous because of origins in the wild forest and of their domesticated co-presence, both helpful and disruptive, among people in settlements and gardens, taking part in hunts on the one hand but on the other hand stealing food, eating filth, killing piglets and breaking open graves. The killing of dogs is hedged with numerous proscriptions and restrictions, and domestic dogs are regarded as the adopted children of their owners (Bulmer 1967, 19). Pigs are regarded as chiefly domestic, filthy but tasty, in a sense like women: dangerous but to be lived with (Bulmer 1967, 20). This treatment seems to share much of Lévi-Strauss's approach but at the same time to go beyond it, in the way that categorisation is rooted in the lived contexts of forest and garden, in the lived roles of men and women, and in the actual characteristics of dogs and pigs.

In a similar way, the relationship of villagers in north-east Thailand to the animal world was presented as complex, expressing 'neither a sense of affinity with animals alone nor a clear-cut distinction and separation from them, but rather a co-existence of both attitudes in varying intensities which create a perpetual tension' (Tambiah 1969, 455). Such attitudes of 'affinity and separation, opposition and integration' are seen at their sharpest in relation to domestic and wild animals, and are bound up with dietary rules and prohibitions, which in turn are related to gender, kinship and household distinctions. The dog, for example, is seen as partly incorporated into human society, and cannot be eaten, but is also considered 'degraded and incestuous' and 'the antithesis of correct human conduct'. Ox and buffalo are positively valued, but are edible, with rules; these include prohibitions on eating their meat at a marriage feast, as a metaphorical statement of the proper rules governing who can marry whom. Wild forest animals are considered inedible, a 'statement of their extreme distance and difference from man', but they have strong metaphorical significance (Tambiah 1969, 455–6). The conclusion that human conduct is not purely intellectual and that 'cultures and social systems are . . . not only thought but *lived*' (Tambiah 1969, 457; emphasis added) rests on a strong sense of specific context.

The classic ethnographies of Evans-Pritchard (1940; 1956) and Lienhardt (1961) on the Nuer and Dinka respectively of east Africa showed long ago the importance of cattle and their fundamental place in systems of value, belief and social relationships (and see discussion in Tilley 1996, 183–4; 1999, 51–2). Further studies have been no less relevant, especially for underlining diversity from situation to situation. Among the Himba of north-western Namibia, cattle are separated into two different categories of value, based on a varying conception of time (Crandall 1998). In the larger set, operating through matrilineal descent and transfer, cattle are a means of gaining wealth and power; they are used in rituals, for example surrounding births, marriages and deaths, but have little symbolic importance as such. The cattle of the other set, controlled patrilineally, are given great symbolic value, but are not much used in rituals or political manoeuvring by men. These and their flesh and milk are sacred, and they are seen both to represent ancestors and to be the possessions of ancestors of the patrilineal descent group in question. It is suggested that the differences can be explained by reference to Himba conceptions of time (Crandall 1998, 109–11). Himba inhabit both a temporal and a timeless world. The stable and permanent world of God and the ancestors exists alongside the transient and changing world of people. Cattle are important for subsistence and for social exchanges, for living, but the most valued animals are those related to the Himba sense of the sacred and immortal.

Another study of cattle in relation to notions of ancestry indicates the ambiguous significance which animals can be ascribed. For the Merina of Madagascar, ancestors are at the heart of existence (Bloch 1985; cf. Bloch 1971). Land and its products are inherited from the ancestors, who are housed on the land in tombs to which the dead will in their turn be taken (Bloch 1985, 635). Descent is 'the merging of the living, the dead and the ancestral land in order to produce an enduring, ideally eternal, entity' (Bloch 1985, 640). Being in the ideal state of the ancestors, however, requires being dead, wholly opposite to the vitality and desirability of existence. In its turn vitality is morally ambiguous, because it is conceptually opposed to ancestorhood and leads to putrefaction. Various myths can be seen to represent speculation about these problems of the nature of existence. Vitality is invested in cattle, and their violent ritual killing is a means to overcome, to get round, the moral ambiguity of this vitality. In actual rituals, an atmosphere of 'violent conquest' prevails, though after the event butchery and cooking seem to take place in a matter-of-fact kind of way (Bloch 1985, 643).

Broader comparative studies have suggested a general shift between hunter-gatherers and farmers in attitudes to animals. Ingold (2000, chapters 4–5) has suggested the general notion of a shift from trust to domination. Hunter-gatherers may be seen as sharing the world with the other creatures that inhabit it; the environment can be seen as 'giving' (following Bird-David 1990). Detailed ethnographies, for example from the north-west coast of America, repeatedly show attitudes of profound respect for animals, and a refusal to create a clear separation between people and animals, or even between animate and inanimate things; creatures had both souls and knowledge akin, or even superior, to that of people (e.g. Hymes 1990). By contrast, pastoralists can be seen as driven by a quite different ethic, of acquisition and domination (Ingold 1980; 2000, chapter 5). Whether this does full justice to the cattle keepers already briefly sketched is an open question. It raises too the question of whether we should take from this kind of comparative study, focused particularly on the worldviews of modern hunter-gatherers, a sharp and instant distinction in attitudes, and simply transfer this to the varied situations of transition in central and western Europe in the sixth to fourth millennia BC. Other documented examples suggest that this may be unwise. Attitudes to the woodland surroundings of rural settlements in Malawi and the wild animals which these contain seem to be ambivalent rather than clear-cut (B. Morris 1995; cf. B. Morris 1998; 2000). From one perspective, the wild creatures of the woodland are conceptually as well as practically opposed to the flow of life in horticultural villages. In these matrilineal communities, the focus is on agriculture and procreation; the woodland can be seen as in part antagonistic to the efforts and aspirations of cultivators (B. Morris 1995, 310). The woodland domain is associated with fierce wild animals, though these are also the source of meat and medicines; hunting is a male activity. Woodland is also the preserve of the spirits of the dead, which makes hunting a conceptually hazardous activity. Wild animals are associated with the spirits of the dead and with affinal (that is, related by marriage) males. Uniting woodland and village is again a sense of time, 'a cyclic conception of life processes' (B. Morris 1995, 310). More detailed accounts show the numbers of occasions on which wild animals or representations of them are used for rituals within the village (B. Morris 1998; 2000). In another central African context, animals as meat are an important medium of exchange and communication between adjacent and symbiotic horticulturalists and foragers (Grinker 1994). The village Lese attach considerable importance to sharing meat between households and kin groups. They do not share meat with the forest Efe, though the latter are expected by the Lese to act as good kin or village members and provide meat for the Lese, for the sake of friendship, loyalty and kinship (Grinker 1994, 155–6). In Lese classification, meat is female, but its acquisition is a male activity. Lese men are involved not only in hunting but also in the creation of clearance and the initiation of gardens, which then become a female preserve. These gendered differences may also be relevant to the conditions in which change was established in central and western Europe from the sixth to the fourth millennia BC.

There is no need at this stage to rehearse the detail of other components of this anthropological tradition (e.g. Willis 1994; Ingold 1988; Manning and Serpell 1994); the difference between this and the dominant archaeological approach, at least until recently, should be very clear. In place of notions of value, belief, categorisation, symbolism, time and gender, the principal concerns in the archaeological field have been practical, economic and evolutionary. Innumerable specialist animal bone reports (to which no disrespect is intended) principally establish species present, and patterns of age and sex, some with detailed attention also to taphonomic process (e.g. Grigson 1999; Halstead 1998), in an effort to reconstruct the site-oriented pattern of the subsistence economy. Bogucki (1993, 492) has noted how easily animals have been considered as products rather than assets, within this dominant model. Specialist reports themselves comparatively rarely discuss the embeddedness of the economy, or its wider social as opposed to practical and economic goals. More reflective papers have sought to investigate the wider implications of particular situations. The shift from the general dominance of sheep and goats in early assemblages from the Carpathian basin to that of cattle in LBK assemblages from the woodlands of central and western Europe has been related to the differences in the underlying ecological conditions (Halstead 1989). A detailed attempt has been made to model possible variations in the practicalities of subsistence in a small settlement of the Alpine foreland (Gross et al. 1990). Here the concern has been to calculate the calorie and protein needs of over twenty people (including children and adults); the possible yields of cereals, animal meat and milk, wild plants, and fish; and labour requirements for cereal cultivation and other tasks. Some of the underlying assumptions can be noted. It is assumed that people were constantly in one place, that the principal element in the subsistence economy was cereal cultivation, and that life was a grim struggle, with very little room for manoeuvre when things went wrong (Gross et al. 1990, 96).[2] Principal constraints were the lack of labour available for cultivating the few hectares required in the model, uncertain climate and weather, and the need to provide winter fodder for animals. Risk was countered by the diversity of resources used, but diversity is seen to hold back technical innovation or experimentation.

This particular model has led to the novel suggestion[3] of economic crash in the thirty-seventh and thirty-sixth centuries BC in the Alpine foreland of northern and western Switzerland (Schibler, Jacomet et al. 1997). In sites at the head of Lake Zürich (e.g. Schibler, Hüster-Plogmann et al. 1997), and westwards and south-westwards on the other large glacial lakes, occupation levels of this date show a continuation of existing patterns of domestic animal use, but also suggest an increase in the hunting of game, principally red deer (as measured by counts of bones per square metre of excavated sites), an increase in wild plant collecting, a shift to larger fish, and a probable decline in the amount of cereal cultivation (Schibler, Jacomet et al. 1997). This coincides with good evidence for a colder climate, seen in tree ring evidence and manifested also in higher lake levels (and some reduction in the number of visible lake-edge sites). It is supposed that the principal effect would have been shorter, colder and wetter growing seasons. Given the assumptions of an economy already at the limits of sustainability, the suggested response was to survive by resorting to hunting, gathering and fishing on a far greater scale than would normally have been the case. I will examine this suggested scenario in more detail later in this chapter, and explore a possible alternative explanation. Here the potential value, as well as the general character and assumptions, of this kind of model can be emphasised, for it could lead to a 'thick description' of the conditions and realities of lived existence, and to a detailed account of a specific historical trend.

The establishment of difference and change seems to be the underlying goal of much research on animals. A particularly influential model, that of the secondary products revolution (Sherratt 1981), has operated at a much higher level of generalisation than the Alpine foreland model just discussed above.[4] As is too well known to need detailed repetition, the model proposed a series of innovations subsequent to a primary Neolithic economy which concentrated on primary products, such as cereals and meat. 'Secondary products' were the traction power of animals harnessed for use with wheeled vehicles and ploughs, their milk and wool, and in due course the fermentation of grapes and barley to produce alcoholic drinks (Sherratt 1987). The model has been commented on many times (e.g. Bogucki 1993; Chapman 1982; Whittle 1985). It treats too much together, in the search for broad historical pattern. It may have correctly predicted the introduction of wheeled vehicles (Bakker et al. 1999) but the effect of these may have been very limited: more like small hand-carts than massive waggons, on the evidence of the Alpine foreland. The date of the introduction of the plough remains uncertain, and again its effect may not have been an instant shift to extensive cultivation. Milking may have been introduced earlier than predicted, as is beginning to be tested in Britain by the development of techniques for the identification of lipids in pottery (Richard Evershed, pers. comm.; cf. Halstead 1998; Balasse et al. 2000). Fermented drinks may likewise have been made by a variety of means, from the start of the Neolithic if not earlier. These will persist as issues for technical debate. The assumption that intensification and specialisation were to be expected within general patterns of change, with innovation accepted from far-distant sources, remains in need of emphasis, and I will come back to questions of change briefly in chapter 7.

Perhaps following the lead of collected papers such as Ingold (1988) and Willis (1994), a more recent trend within archaeological writing on animals has been to draw much more explicitly on the anthropological literature, to examine the categorisation of animals and associated symbolism. The character of these arguments has varied. Discussing the Late Mesolithic of southern Scandinavia, Tilley (1996, 62–5) drew attention to the frequent occurrence in graves and other contexts of red deer bones and antler and artefacts made from these materials, and argued convincingly for considerable symbolic importance. He also noted, drawing explicitly on Lévi-Strauss and others, the ambiguity of animals, on the one hand different from but on the other hand similar to people in their basic anatomy and behaviour, as the reason for their use as appropriate metaphorical media (Tilley 1996, 63). The argument, however, in large measure rests on the natural characteristics of the species that could be presumed to have made them symbolically appropriate, especially their sociality and affective behaviour, but also their fertility and vitality. The claimed 'natural basis for drawing analogies' (such as red deer=herd=clan=territory, red deer=sociability=sharing=

kinship, and red deer=hunting blood=vitality and fertility=social reproduction) may be plausible enough (Tilley 1996, 65), but it is not a position, as we have seen, that Lévi-Strauss himself would have supported. In the Early and Middle Neolithic of southern Scandinavia, votive deposits (in wet places and elsewhere) suggest clearly that cattle replaced red deer as the dominant animal symbol, with blows to the animal head indicating the kind of killing, perhaps sacrificial; cattle became 'emotional subjects of desire' (Tilley 1996, 184), at the heart of a domesticated world turned against and opposed to the previously life-giving and benevolent forest (Tilley 1996, 111–12; 183–4). In this case, however, there is little or no discussion of the natural characteristics of cattle (or their possible ambiguity), and the underlying symbolic logic is ascribed to the 'production and provision of food' (Tilley 1996, 111), with wider analogies drawn from the Nuer and Dinka cases as described by Evans-Pritchard and Lienhardt (Tilley 1996, 183–4).

A naturalistic position has also been set out by Andrew Jones (1998) in discussion of the Orkney islands. The main argument is that animal remains were frequently placed in both domestic and other contexts, for example cattle bones in the outer walls of houses at Skara Brae, in such a way as to draw in and represent the surrounding landscape; animals help to constitute the experience of place (A. Jones 1998, 303). In perhaps the most striking example, it is noted how on the south side of the small island of Rousay, long known for its concentration of chambered cairns, cattle remains are associated with constructions on the lower slopes such as Midhowe, which also contains disarticulated human remains in segmented spaces, while deer remains are found in the higher placed cairns such as Knowe of Ramsay and Knowe of Yarso, where amongst other human remains there are skulls. The view is that deer as upland animals are appropriately placed on the higher parts of this landscape (A. Jones 1998, 315–17).

A less universalised view of red deer has been argued by Sharples (2000), in the context of the British Neolithic as a whole and Orkney in particular, where there are good reasons to suppose that deer may have been introduced to the islands and carefully managed. Here the argument is for an ambiguous status for this species, in the Orkney context deliberately introduced but probably never domesticated as such, but neither wholly wild, and in the wider British context perhaps partially subject to prohibitions on consumption, given the low numbers in most Neolithic assemblages (Sharples 2000, 113–14). There are also cases on the Orkneys where red deer appear to have been slaughtered, consumed and deposited in special circumstances close to settlements (Sharples 2000, 110–12). Given these observations, as well as bearing in mind the position of Lévi-Strauss, it might be legitimate to consider other interpretations of the Rousay situation noted above. It might be more important metaphorically than is allowed in a straightforward representation of the landscape and the place of creatures in it, that cattle and humans are bound closely together as some kind of indissoluble collective, while the human spirit or soul, as suggested by the skull, is associated with the ambiguous category of (half-)wild red deer. We will come back again to the significance of deer and other game in early Neolithic contexts elsewhere later in this chapter.

In the context of a wider discussion of metaphor, Tilley (1999, 52–4) has also drawn attention to Melanesian ethnography on the symbolic importance of pigs. He highlights, to illustrate the 'pre-eminent ritual significance' of pigs throughout the region, the particular case of the northern Vanuata islands (in this case as documented by Layard 1942), where boars with tusks so long that they formed circles were prime sacrificial animals and items of exchange; tusks were a measurement of time, an exchangeable valuable, a means of male advancement and both a metonym of and metaphor for male identity. This is an interesting case study, but there is little discussion here of the pigs as pigs; the focus is on their tusks and on male agency. In other Melanesian cases, for example among the highland Karam already noted (Bulmer 1967), the behaviour of pigs is part of the basis for their symbolic status, while among the Tsembaga people of highland New Guinea it seems to be the facts of their reproductive fertility, growth and desirable taste that make pigs the central focus of the ritual cycle (Rappaport 1968). In the Mount Hagen case, the indigenous view is that products are created by multiple means; neither husband nor wife can claim sole ownership of land and its products (M. Strathern 1988, 162–3). Food given to pigs by wives is grown on land belonging to husbands' clans, cleared by men and planted by women; 'sole "ownership" is claimed by the husband only vis-à-vis other husbands, in the sphere of ceremonial exchange' (M. Strathern 1988, 163). In the Vanuatu case, using these observations, there may be much more to the significance of pigs than male agency alone.

A final example of more recent archaeological discussions takes us back to cattle (Parker Pearson 2000). Starting from the universal symbolic importance of food (cf. Gosden and Hather 1999), Parker Pearson examines the economic and symbolic importance of cattle among the Tandroy people of southern Madagascar. Cattle are central to the Tandroy (Figure 4.1). They are part of a way of life that is at once sedentary and mobile. They help to define male identity. They are accumulated for wealth, exchanged at marriages, and sacrificed at funerals, to open 'the channels of communication with all the ancestors' (Parker Pearson 2000, 225). Cattle, however, are not part of normal diet, their consumption being restricted to ritual events, especially connected with funerals, when sheep and goats are also sacrificed; who may or may not share helps to define kinship relationships. Regular diet is provided by a variety of cultivated plants, imported rice (regarded as more or less sacred), chickens and guinea fowl; cow's milk is available only for a short period in the wet season, and sheep and goats are not milked. Many wild animals are taboo, or eaten away from settlements. Cattle bucrania are deposited at ancestral tombs, but there is little else in the deposition of animal bones around settlements that would indicate their importance as ritually sacred. Many bones in the refuse of a given settlement are from animals not raised there. Much bone is fragmented and destroyed by dogs.

This ethnoarchaeological study manages to combine anthropological concerns for the social, symbolic and sacred with archaeological interest in diet, subsistence, patterns of residence and taphonomy. It begins perhaps to indicate the scale of the challenge involved in better understanding of the place of animals. On the one hand, much of the anthropological evidence reviewed so far has been fragmented: cattle

Figure 4.1 Tandroy cattle, southern Madagascar. Top: on the move; middle: entering a mortuary ceremony; bottom: transformed into meat after sacrifice during mortuary rites. Photos: Mike Parker Pearson.

here, pigs there (some treated as objects of value, others as ambiguous, related in part to their behaviour), sheep rarely present (except in the last example), and hardly ever all together at the same time. Most attention is given in these accounts to the definition of social relationships and the workings of sacred imperatives, and relatively little to the flow of life as constituted in part by animals and their behaviour. On the other hand, much of the archaeological literature has concentrated on species by species descriptions, seeking purely economic explanations within an evolutionary framework and a logic of self-sufficient, sedentary existence. What has been reviewed so far shows both opportunities and difficulties. The rest of this chapter attempts to reinforce a sense of how closely people and animals were bound together both in their daily lives and in domains of sacred significance. I want to restate the ubiquity and physicality of animals, explore the varying human social-ities involved in their tending, review the probable closeness of the bonds between people and animals, and emphasise the intimacy of the ways in which animals were used as social and symbolic assets. My contention is that this relationship was part of a considerable diversity and sometimes ambiguity of identity, and is also another important indicator of slow, long-term change.

Physicality, intimacy and sociality

People in the millennia which are the principal focus of this book lived in a world full of animals. The emphasis on colonisation and domestication in much of the literature encourages us perhaps to forget the diversity of this natural situation. Whether people regularly hunted and consumed wild animals or not, they must have regularly encountered wild animals as well as their domesticates. In fact, there is evidence over wide areas that hunting was a significant activity, especially but not exclusively in early phases of the Neolithic. A considerable range of game is documented from the Körös culture, from red deer and aurochs down to badger and hare, along with fish and birds (Bökönyi 1974; 1992; Takács 1992), Wild animals were still important in the Tisza culture of the earlier fifth millennium BC, and at least two tell sites, Berettyóújfalu-Herpály and Csőszhalom, have remarkably high percentages (Bökönyi 1974; Bartosiewicz 1999; Schwartz 1998). The range of wild species still strongly recalls the much earlier situation in the Körös culture. Bökönyi (1974, 111–12) argued that this was a phase of intensive local domestication of cattle, but it is possible that there was still relatively little difference between aurochs and 'domestic cattle', as seems also to have been the case earlier in the Körös culture (Bökönyi 1974, 110). Even in Tiszapolgár culture burials of the later fourth millennium BC, wild animals in the form of boars' tusks, red deer antler and teeth, and aurochs and other bones were a regular accompaniment of the dead, along with remains of domesticates and a range of other artefacts (Chapman 1997a; 2000b; Derevenski 1997; 2000).

Poor preservation of bone has long been a problem in the area of the LBK; many assemblages of animal bone are depressingly small, as from Bylany (Clason 1968). An earlier picture was of the numerical dominance of domesticates (Müller 1964),

but this has gradually changed. Though game seems at face value overall less important than domesticates, the amounts of wild species vary across the extent of the
LBK, being more common in more southerly areas and in earlier phases (e.g. Döhle
1993; Hachem 1995; 1997; 1999; Kreuz 1990; Pucher 1987; 1998; Uerpmann and
Uerpmann 1997; Jeunesse and Arbogast 1997). In a sample of ten earliest LBK
sites, the percentages of wild species varied considerably, ranging to over half in
some but decreasing to less than a quarter in others; the numbers and relative
proportions of the domesticates also varied from site to site (Uerpmann and
Uerpmann 1997, fig. 3). A wider study also found a tendency for higher frequencies
of wild animals in early sites within a given area (Hachem 1999); these also, from
detailed studies in the Aisne valley, seem to occur in longer-lasting sites and beside
smaller buildings (Hachem 1995; 1997; 1999), to which we will return below. In
the fifth millennium BC, comparisons suggest that the amounts of game declined in
domestic contexts in the broad area between middle and upper Rhine and upper
Danube, though wild animals as represented by antlers, teeth and tusks remained
important in mortuary ritual (Jeunesse and Arbogast 1997). In Hinkelstein and
Grossgartach group (that is early post-LBK) graves from Trebur, Hessen, adults were
lain extended, with things placed up and down their corpses. As well as pots and
stone artefacts, there were sides of beef represented by deposits of cattle ribs, and
some sheep and pig bones; the wild is represented here by a belt of red deer teeth
(Spatz 1997, figs 7–10).

In the Alpine foreland from the later fifth into the mid fourth millennium BC, red
deer were of equal and at times greater importance compared to cattle and other
domesticates (Figure 4.2) (Gross *et al.* 1990, fig. 4; Schibler, Hüster-Plogmann *et al.*
1997). The hypothesis of economic crash in the thirty-seventh and thirty-sixth
centuries BC has already been noted above. It seems to be the case that the amounts
of domesticates did *not* decline, nor did the character of the settlements in terms of
layout or buildings or other artefactual deposition change. It might be argued that
the suggested trends are simply the product of variation in the conditions of
preservation, including varying lake levels. It might be argued, if that were not the
case, that increased densities of red deer bones indicate longer periods of occupation,
or shifts in the seasonality of occupation, in what was not yet necessarily a fully
sedentary system. If climatic conditions did become colder, from a 'dwelling
perspective' people may have only intensified what they already frequently practised,
responding to the changing pattern of weather. Deer hunting was an old activity in
this region. Some Mesolithic sites, like Schötz 7 in the Wauwilermoos, were clearly
camps focused on the exploitation of red deer (Wyss 1979); deer are also among the
remains at their Neolithic successors in the same immediate locality, such as
Egolzwil 3 and the slightly later Egolzwil 5 (Vogt 1951; Wyss 1976). At Egolzwil
5, domesticates outnumbered wild game, but only by the order of three or two to
one. Only if the whole system is modelled as near the limits of sustainability does
the crash hypothesis need to apply; the evidence rather may suggest the continuing
importance of the wild over centuries alongside the introduction of domesticated
animals and cereal cultivation.

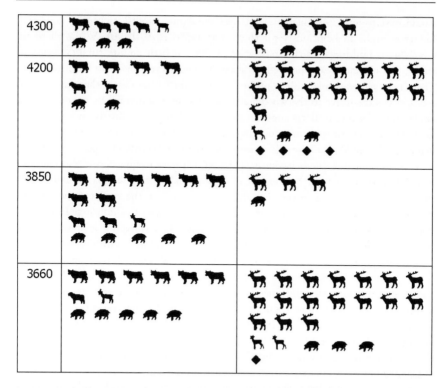

Figure 4.2 Outline scheme of the main trends in animal representation on Zürichsee sites, northern Switzerland, 4300–3350 BC. The diamonds indicate various other wild animals. After Schibler and Jacomet 1999.

These examples should be sufficient to establish the extent of contact with wild animals, even though this clearly varied from place to place and through time. Regular encounters with wild animals as well as tending to domestic ones must have taken people into every part of their environment, unless we see hunting as purely defensive in relation to gardens and plots where cereals were cultivated (Uerpmann 1977). Given the other witnesses to human movement, given by lithic and other evidence, restriction to the confines of residence and its associated clearances seems extremely unlikely. There is some direct evidence for the grazing of sheep and goats away from settlements, in the form of prickles of Rosaceae, probably blackberry, preserved in their fossilised droppings at the Horgen culture site of Horgen Scheller on Lake Zürich, dated to just before 3000 BC (Akeret and Jacomet 1997; Ebersbach *et al.* 1999). Assuming again no taphonomic distortions, these have been taken as indicating grazing on woodland edges, clearances or clearings, and hedges, in winter and spring; the sample recovered and examined gave no indication of summer grazing. Given this absence, these animals may have been even further afield in the summer months. It has regularly been assumed that cattle in the Alpine foreland would have to have been kept indoors over the winter months, with leaf and other fodder brought in laboriously for them (e.g. Gross *et al*. 1990). While there are clearly some buildings which served as stalls, there is little architectural evidence for stalling on a major scale, or even sufficient to house even the most minimal herd. There is as yet no comparable coprolite evidence for cattle. Given that aurochs and red deer could survive in the woodlands during winter, untended by people, it may be far more economical to suppose that most domestic animals in the Alpine foreland did most of their own foraging in winter. If assisted and tended to varying degrees, this would also have taken people far out into their landscapes.

The range of probable behaviours of the wild species in question is also relevant. Red deer and boar might be thought of as potentially more serious natural raiders than roe deer or aurochs; given that all regularly occur in the various bone assemblages, it seems unlikely that they are all the result of defensive hunting. In fact, we know little of the conditions in which aurochs flourished, though it is presumed that they preferred river meadow woodlands, light deciduous forest with rich understorey and natural grassland and marshes, compared to red deer which may have been tolerant of more densely wooded conditions (Hüster-Plogmann *et al*. 1999; Steppan 1999). In addition, all wild species may have been subject to some degree of disturbance by people and their domestic animals. In the case of Zealand and southern Sweden, aurochs appear to have disappeared already before the Neolithic, and by the Middle Neolithic on Fyn (Aaris-Sørensen 1999). This too may indicate the likelihood that many wild animal remains in Neolithic contexts were the result of planned forays at a distance from settlements and camps.

Two implications follow. The relative importance of wild and domestic animals is normally discussed in terms of percentages of bones present (that is, having survived a range of taphonomic and depositional processes) in settlements and occupations. This may tend to under-represent the importance of wild animals, if these were more likely to have been consumed out in the landscape (cf. Parker Pearson 2000, 230). These percentages also fundamentally under-play the time spent out in the landscape, either engaged in other activities, or in planned hunting trips. Tending domestic animals might have been a more constant commitment, but hunting could have been more expensive in terms of concentrated time. Even say 10 or 20 per cent of wild animal bones, normally assigned a minor role without further discussion, may stand for a very significant form of activity. Secondly, it would seem from all these arguments that people, whether they were indigenous or incomers, had a very detailed knowledge of the animals in the environments in which they lived. The ubiquitous physicality of these abundant natural symbols was a constant part of people's surroundings; it is hard to imagine life in this period without constant reference not only to the presence of animals, but their form, movement, sound, colour, smell and taste.

How animals were categorised should be an open question. The overriding tendency has been to assume a sharp distinction between wild and tame. Given this distinction (whether or not the accompanying morphological or other criteria are immediately clear: Higgs and Jarman 1969), the focus normally shifts automatically to the suitability and use of domesticates, but if the distinction between wild and tame was blurred, other possibilities come into the picture. In terms of what may have fostered fear, envy and admiration (Lévi-Strauss 1964, 89), there may have been little to separate wild and domestic. Both, in measures varying by species, had consciousness, faces and voices; sociality and emotions; physical attributes such as strength, speed, fertility, virility and vitality; and a pattern of growth much slower than that of plants and more akin to that of people (Ingold 2000, 86). Animals could have been classified in various ways, such as by the taste of their meat, or the environmental niches or ranges that they occupied, or their sociality, or their size. There is some evidence to suggest that sociality and size were important. Throughout the sequences with which we are concerned it is combinations of cattle, pigs, sheep and goats which were the important domesticates, with red deer of especial importance in earlier times (cf. Jarman 1972). More solitary or dispersed animals may have been less significant, not only because more elusive, but also because less social. Circumstantial evidence may suggest that size was a more important criterion of categorisation. In the long term, cattle replaced red deer in many parts of central and western Europe. As we have already seen, in the Alpine foreland from the later fifth into the mid fourth millennium BC, red deer were of equal and at times greater importance compared to cattle and other domesticates (Gross et al. 1990, fig. 4; Schibler, Hüster-Plogmann et al. 1997). For the earliest LBK, when there were also significant numbers of wild animals in bone assemblages, it has been suggested that grouping by large and small size helps to produce more regionally coherent patterns of use than enumeration simply by species (Uerpmann and Uerpmann 1997). In fact, there seems little need to expect regional patterning, but the suggested four groupings of wild and domestic cattle, wild ungulates except wild cattle, middle-sized 'domestic artiodactyles' (sheep, goat and pig), and others, are useful. Earlier still in the Körös culture, sheep and goats were the species represented by the most bones. They were, however, only part of a spectrum of species, from large to small. Taken together, red deer, aurochs and domesticated cattle (with rarer wild asses and even rarer horses) in fact represent a more abundant grouping, and there are anyway good grounds for doubting a sharp distinction between aurochs and domesticated cattle in this phase, since measurements of long bones and horn cores overlap (Bökönyi 1974). Sheep and goats may have been adopted in part because they filled a gap in the size range, between large animals on the one hand and much smaller game on the other, and competing as it were only with pigs and roe deer. The latter are more solitary, though their densities can be high in favourable conditions, while pigs seem not to have been kept in great numbers on the Great Hungarian Plain, perhaps because they were less suited to the partly wet and partly open conditions.

Novelty may also have played a part. Sheep and goats might have been adopted in the Carpathian basin simply because they had been used further south-east at earlier times, at least if indigenous people were directly involved in new practices (Figure 4.3). Unlike cattle and pigs, sheep and goats have had a less glamorous ethnographic press. There are, however, suggestive examples. Sheep are a significant sacrificial animal for the Tandroy people of southern Madagascar, after cattle (Parker

Figure 4.3 Excavation in 2000 at Ecsegfalva 23 on the Great Hungarian Plain, with shepherd, sheep and dog in attendance. Photo: author.

Pearson 2000, 225). Among pastoralists in western Mongolia sheep's tibiae represented patrilineal descent or genealogical descent, and were particularly important
in communications between people and ancestors (Szynkiewicz 1994). The taste of
sheep, their appearance (whether or not fleeces were shorter- rather than longer-
haired at this stage), the sound of their voices, and even the style of their physical
motion, could have made these animals a novelty in their right at this early date. If
they were milked, this might have been easier than with cattle (cf. Halstead 1998).
Their slaughter would have produced, as noted already, smaller and handier quantities of meat for consumption. Despite supposed ecological barriers or constraints, it
seems clear that some effort was made in earliest LBK contexts to keep herds of
sheep and goats (Uerpmann and Uerpmann 1997).

   People were bound closely to animals, both wild and domestic, on a daily basis.
Animals may have guided, in a real physical sense, many of the routines of daily life
(see chapter 2). It has been argued that the shift from hunting to husbandry represents a shift from trust to domination (Ingold 2000, chapters 4–5). A parallel
argument has been the creation at the start of the Neolithic of the *domus*, opposed to
the *agrios*, or wild (Hodder 1990). In turn, both arguments could be seen as attempt-
ing to invoke the historical moment when culture and nature were separated and
treated as different categories. But in many instances, such a rigid distinction between
nature and culture is hard to maintain (e.g. M. Strathern 1980; Descola 1992).
Ingold (2000, chapter 5) has listed a series of examples (from the Amazon and
Colombia to Mali and Mount Hagen in Papua New Guinea) in which horticulturalists maintain a respectful attitude to their surroundings. For the Achuar of the
Upper Amazon, for example, the garden is not opposed to the forest, for the forest is
itself like a huge garden (Descola 1994); Hageners do not oppose planting and the
domestic realm to wild nature, but the realm of people to what lies outside human
care and sociability (M. Strathern 1980; Ingold 2000, 83). For the millennia under
discussion here, especially in the early phases of the establishment of new practices, I
suggest a similar range of attitudes to animals: varied and ambiguous.

   If people were frequently of indigenous descent, and encountered, used and thought
about wild animals regularly, it seems plausible that attitudes of respect and trust,
found frequently in ethnographic descriptions (e.g. for north-west coast America,
Hymes 1990; De Laguna 1990; Kennedy and Bouchard 1990), would have endured
towards animals in general. This is certainly also compatible with the closeness and
intimacy of the likely relationship with domestic animals. We know little of the scale
of herds, though possible maximum figures (e.g. Dahl and Hjort 1976) allow for the
possibility that people knew each of their animals individually. Speculatively, there
may also have been feelings of guilt in regard to animals, for altering an older
relationship through domestication (cf. Eliade 1968). The suggestion that red deer in
Britain may have had an ambiguous status (Sharples 2000) has already been noted. In
areas such as this, and in those parts of central Europe where wild animals seem to
have been less numerically important (Döhle 1993; Jeunesse and Arbogast 1997), it
could be that wild animals were left alone as a mark of continuing respect, to
compensate for the changing nature of the relationship with domesticates.

Animals were not only an ever-present natural symbol, but their tending constituted people themselves as social symbols. The socialities of husbandry have been
comparatively little commented upon in the archaeological literature. Looking after
cattle among the Nuer and Dinka was at the core of male identity (Evans-Pritchard
1940; Lienhardt 1961). Among the Tandroy, 'men and women own cattle but only
boys and men take them to pastures, bring them home to the cattle pens, castrate
them, kill them, and exchange them with other men' (Parker Pearson 2000, 221–2).
The life of Tandroy cattle boys can be removed from the rest of the domestic sphere for
months at a time, but there has been little further comment on the socialities involved
even in this. The practice of combating risk by placing animals with kin and other
allies is widespread (Parker Pearson 2000, 224; Halstead 1999; Dahl and Hjort 1976;
Dahl 1979). Animals being herded at a distance from settlements would still have
embodied numerous relationships, and the herders would have stood for these links as
well. Presumably cattle, pigs, sheep and goats ranged at varying distances from
settlements. Tending them may have been a year-round occupation, despite the
frequent arguments for the necessity of providing winter fodder in the Alpine foreland.
Speculatively, cattle keeping could have taken herders further afield for longer periods
of the year. Cattle may therefore have been associated with a tension between
solitariness and extreme commonality, when people and herds came together and
slaughter and large-scale consumption took place. Sheep and goats, at least on the
evidence of Horgen Scheller (Akeret and Jacomet 1997), might have browsed closer to
settlements, and their tending and their consumption, as already suggested, might
both have been associated with a more constant, domestic sociality. Pigs have been
closely tended in the past (e.g. Halpern 1999), and could also have been associated
with close control around the domestic sphere of houses and gardens. In some areas at
least, such as the Alpine foreland or the Carpathian basin, the frequency of hunting
might suggest a group rather than an individual activity, and in this instance again
there may have been a tension between solitary time in the woodland and the
sociability of return. We can remember here the Foi men who spend much of their
time in the gregarious life of the communal longhouse thinking about their hunting
forays in the bush (J.F. Weiner 1991, 35; and see chapter 2 here). The particular
importance given to red deer and then cattle may reside partly in the facts of sociality
('good to be with' and 'good to be seen with'), and not be reducible either to their
natural or ascribed symbolism ('good to think') or their taste ('good to eat').

Thinking animals

I have tried so far to emphasise the physical immediacy of animals in people's lives,
as well as the varied ways in which they might have been classified and treated,
including with reference to their own and human sociality. I want now to consider
further how animals may have been treated as symbols. As I have already considered
the household scale in the last chapter, with reference to variations in animal
keeping, I will concentrate in this section on more public arenas. In both cases, I
argue that the nature of activity and the selections made speak for a close connection

with animals as food, while the scale of activity indicates the involvement of smaller rather than larger social groups; though animals were regularly transformed into bones which operated as metaphor and metonym, the intimacy of the context may normally have brought to this sphere something of their living physicality and the close lived relationship between people and animals. Later on, I will underline this by comparing household and other situations with the way natural creatures were treated in contemporary late forager communities; the appearance of domesticates may have intensified the ways in which late Mesolithic hunter-gatherers represented creatures important to them.

Public arenas

In the example of Jura households (at the end of chapter 3), it might be argued that the patterns of bone deposition were simply the result of repeated routines. In that case, one could suggest either that people were barely conscious of the symbolisms involved, or, as I prefer, that these were deeply embedded in daily life. In the case of longhouses in the Aisne valley and elsewhere, the same possibilities may apply. There is also the question of timescale. It is not certain over what period of time such bone deposits formed in the relatively shallow flanking ditches in question. One suggestion is that flanking ditches, at least on loess soils, would have filled in very quickly by natural erosional processes (Stäuble 1990; Uerpmann and Uerpmann 1997, 574). In this case, the use of animals as symbols would have been a feature especially of the foundation of a household, and this may have become embedded as memory in the routine use of the physical structure.

Neither kind of reservation seems to apply to the deposits made in the ditches of enclosures. Much of the best evidence comes from the fourth millennium BC, when such arenas were widely distributed through many parts of western Europe, from central-western France to southern Scandinavia, with important examples also in the Rhineland, as well as in southern Britain (Whittle 1996; Andersen 1997; Oswald et al. 2001). Like so much else, these are very diverse, but there is a persistent, recurrent and widespread tradition of deliberate deposition in ditches as well as in associated pits. Unless one were to go back to the very first interpretations of enclosure ditches as occupation areas, this practice must indicate deliberate and conscious deposition in arenas that by many other criteria (Bradley 1998a) can be marked out as special. Few examples show a single foundation deposit only, and repeated (though of course varied) depositions are much more common. The character of individual deposits, however, is often small-scale and intimate. The first interpreters such as Curwen in southern Britain (see Oswald et al. 2001) were right to the extent that these are transformations of material important in the domestic sphere, and re-presented in the more public space of arenas at a scale recalling that of the former.

Though in total the numbers of animal bones at many of these enclosures can be impressive, representing potentially hundreds if not thousands of animals even at individual sites, the individual act of deposition often involved a far smaller set of symbols. Three recently published sites from southern Britain can serve as good examples. At Windmill Hill, it seems clear that deposition varied within and between the three ditch circuits (Whittle *et al.* 1999), and it is dangerous to over-generalise, but there were recurrent finds in all three circuits, not only of linear spreads of material but also of concentrated deposits, set in ditch terminals and at intervals within the individual ditch segments. These proved to be very varied in terms of composition and history as measured by the degree of fragmentation (Grigson 1999), but the selection of the partial remains of a number of animals for inclusion in individual deposits was recurrent. The placed deposit 630, from above the primary fill of the inner ditch (Whittle *et al.* 1999, fig. 97; Grigson 1999), shows various fragmented cattle bones and skull fragments, the latter probably from the same animal. There was also a sheep/goat tibia, and part of the femur of a young human was found inserted in the shaft of an ox humerus. Other placed deposits have the partial remains of cow, sheep/goat, pig and sometimes dog. More complete remains, possible examples of 'conspicuous non-consumption' (Grigson 1999, 229), are much less common. Sherds of weathered pottery also add to the impression of selection and transformation; many of these deposits may not have gone straight into the ground following the acts of slaughter, butchery and eating which the bones partially represent. It may be that the selections made acted metonymically, so that the token amount deposited could have stood for a much larger whole, basically beyond meaningful quantification, but the recurrent individuality of the placed deposits is striking and surely significant in its own right.

At Etton, the scale of excavation allowed an even more extensive view of patterns of deposition around the enclosure (Pryor 1998). From the low-lying situation and the evidence for flooding, it is extremely unlikely that people were permanently at the site. There is evidence, however, from ditch segment 1 in the south-west part of the enclosure for the keeping of livestock, in the form of enhanced phosphate levels and remains of dung-feeding insects (Pryor 1998, 355). As at Windmill Hill and other sites of this kind, animal bone constituted a regular presence in the ditch segments of the enclosure, more or less right around the enclosure, and in the phases of successive recutting and filling of the ditch segments. The densities were not even. Animal bone and other material was used to enhance the significance of ditch terminals, and presumably thereby that of entrances. The quantities of bone other-wise vary from segment to segment without any obvious correlation with the length of each segment. What does seem striking is the tendency for different species to dominate segment by segment (recalling, in a general way, practices seen beside Aisne longhouses), in phase 1A in the western arc for example (Pryor 1998, fig. 107; Armour-Chelu 1998) cattle in segments 1, 2 and 5, sheep in segment 3, and pigs and sheep in segment 4, and in the eastern arc pig in segment 10 but cattle in segments 11 and 12 (Figure 4.4). In the eastern arc in phase 1A, in segments 6 and 7, there were deposits placed at intervals along the base of the ditches of a kind not found elsewhere, including complete pots, human and animal skulls, animal bones and antler; other segments in this eastern arc in this phase had been backfilled with gravel and topsoil dug from them. In this phase and in 1B, perhaps in contrast to the more continuous deposits of phase 1C, it is recognised as possible that these were

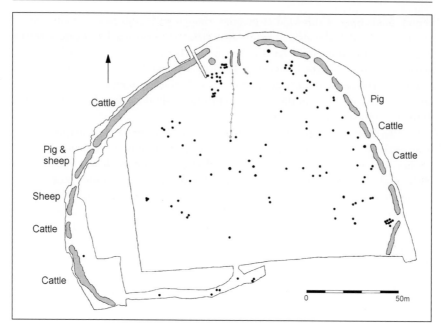

Figure 4.4 Outline trends in the dominant depositions of animal bone in the phase 1A ditch segments at Etton. The ditch segments are numbered 1–14 clockwise from the lower left. After Pryor 1998.

individual events separated in time (Pryor 1998, 358). Small pits, mainly from the northern and eastern parts of the interior of the enclosure, had dark, charcoal-stained fillings, many burnt flints, some sherds and well-burnt animal bone; some had an individual item at their top such as a polished stone axe. One possibility is that these represent funerary rites for individuals (Pryor 1998, 354), and deposition in adjacent ditch segments and pits might have been complementary, though the pits cannot be closely tied to the sequence of the ditch. Once again, when examined in detail, the scale of action is intimate and personal, and animals were involved as a fundamental presence.

There is no sense in insisting on uniformity of practice. The scale of the Etton excavation has reinforced the impression of considerable complexity. The phase 1C deposits of animal bone were more continuous and might be seen as having been deposited in the 1C recut as a single larger-scale event, because of their continuous spread along the ditch (Pryor 1998, 358). This was, however, at a time when the layout *qua* continuous circuit had somewhat degenerated (Pryor 1998, fig. 115), and the detail of individual segments, such as number 10, may not in fact require a single act of deposition. In this instance (Pryor 1998, fig. 39), though not necessarily in all others of this phase, one could as well suggest series of very small token depositions, reduced in scale but maintaining a previously established way of doing things. Something of this kind of practice, though with perhaps a partially shifted emphasis on wild animals and exotic materials, was continued in phase 2 of the enclosure, with earlier and later deposits in pits, both cut into the top of the ditch and in the interior (Pryor 1998, 360). In ditch segment 12 a pit contained remains of two aurochs skulls above a short plank, as well as other animal bone and pottery, while the later pit F385 in the interior held a horse skull and red deer antler (Pryor 1998, figs 49 and 118).

Finally, from the more restricted excavations at Maiden Castle (Sharples 1991), another set of variations is evident. Finds in the primary fills of the inner and outer ditches were very sparse. In a subsequent phase, the outer ditch was infilled with chalk, probably at the same time as a series of 'middens' rich in animal bone, sherds and other material were deposited in the inner ditch (Sharples 1991, 253). It has been argued that most of this material was the result of domestic activity, carried out within or otherwise immediately adjacent to the enclosure (Sharples 1991, 254), but it is at least as likely, not least from the placing of remains in lenses in the partially filled ditch (Sharples 1991, 51 and fig. 49), that this was special activity involving gathering, the killing and consumption of animals, and other tasks, in an arena defined as unusual by its layout, associations and earlier history, and once again within a small-scale social setting.

There is no need to force every example into the same mould. At a similar date across the Channel in northern France at Boury-en-Vexin, Oise, for example, an impressive and concentrated array of cattle and sheep bone may speak for conspicuous consumption on a considerable scale (Méniel 1984; 1987). There, as well as ditch segments with animal bone in more familiar kinds of deposit, there was one segment with a concentration of cattle joints and some near-complete skeletons, as well as sheep joints and partial skeletons. It is also easy artificially to separate the enclosures from other activity in surrounding landscapes. The acts of slaughter and consumption represented in the isolated Coneybury pit near Stonehenge, for example, involving a few cattle and roe deer (Maltby 1990), might not have been greatly different in kind from those seen in enclosures; the chain of connection is seen in this example in the partial representation of carcasses destined for use elsewhere. I have referred in this discussion to the separate headings of household settings and public arenas, but the two may in fact have been partly interchangeable. In the southern British case, as already noted, the evidence for buildings remains equivocal and regionally patchy (Darvill 1996); there are also good arguments for seeing many of such larger buildings as have been found as belonging to the early part of the Neolithic sequence (A. Barclay 2000). In Ireland, the number of quite substantial rectangular buildings from the early part of the sequence continues to increase (Cooney 2000). Here there were varied contemporary monuments, though not in all areas, and the 'house' may have been only one of a series of arenas or settings in which important social interaction was transacted.

It is easy too to separate enclosures of the kind discussed above from the earlier tradition of longhouse life. While many of the known LBK enclosures belong to the late phases of the culture, and in the case of Langweiler 8 on the Aldenhovener

Platte the enclosure seems to formalise the space between longhouses and then take this over as longhouses lapsed (Lüning and Stehli 1994), there are now other examples where enclosure and longhouses were more clearly contemporary. Vaihingen in south-west Germany is a case in point, the history of the ditch overlapping that of the longhouses; each share in the history of the site, notably here linked by the presence of human burials in the ditch, in pits and graves alongside it, and in the ditches or pits flanking longhouses (Krause 1997). There is so far little published information on the animal remains from Vaihingen. At Menneville in the Aisne valley in northern France a large oval enclosure formed by a single-circuit ditch with individual segments of varying length surrounded a late LBK settlement with houses; the chronological relationship between enclosure and houses remains uncertain (Hachem et al. 1998). Some houses were close to the ditch, and most of the ditch segments contained little 'domestic waste'. It is possible that the enclosure came after the settlement had been abandoned, or fell in phases of disuse. The settlement is notable for a number of burials, alongside buildings. There were also burials in some ditch segments, and outside its south-east edge, corresponding to a gap in the enclosure ditch (Hachem et al. 1998, fig. 4). The latter were adult and child burials, while those inside the settlement were mainly children. These contained normal grave goods in the form of ornaments and artefacts, including pots. Burials in the ditch were slightly different. Single burials had ochre and ornaments, but no pottery; one had a cattle horn core and rib. Three multiple burials contained the remains of children only. Their remains were in considerable disarray and there were no ornaments, ochre or complete pots (though there were sherds). Animal bone was, however, much more prominent. In segment 273, the remains of a minimum of four cattle and four sheep/goats accompanied two children (Figure 4.5). In segment 189, a double child burial followed a single one, and cattle and sheep/goat bones are again present. In segment 188, the partial remains of seven children are found in three groups, possibly deposited at the same time, and again accompanied by cattle and sheep/goat bones. Unlike in the settlement contexts of the region, the animal bone was far less fragmented. At a later stage in the ditch fills of segments 188 and 189 more or less above the earlier burials were found cattle skulls, probable commemorative deposits (Hachem et al. 1998, 136). In this case it is plausible enough that the main visible activity was funerary ceremony of some kind (Hachem et al. 1998, 138), but these were not quite of the regular kind. In the absence of a detailed site chronology it is unwise to be dogmatic, but the setting seems to provide already, contemporary with or just after the end of longhouse settlement, many of the themes which continue in later enclosures of the kind already discussed. There are familiar contrasts, such as between the more open and extensive setting of the ditch circuit and the individual longhouses which it contained or commemorated, or between the scale of the ditch circuit as a whole and the more intimate depositional events in individual segments. It is no surprise at all that animals should take their place alongside children in this context as contrasting symbols of fertility and the future, commonality and shared pasts, and abundance and the concerns of particular social groupings.

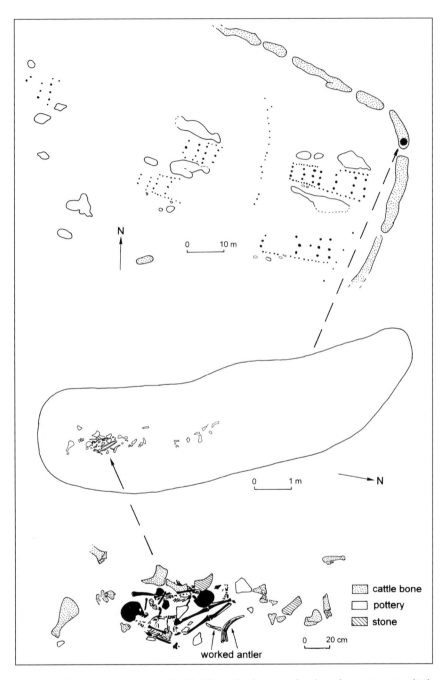

Figure 4.5 Remains of children (in black), cattle bone and other depositions in ditch segment 273 of the late LBK enclosure at Menneville, northern France. After Hachem *et al.* 1998.

Mythic dimensions

I have argued so far that a rationalised, abstract and distanced view of animals is limiting. Animals were complex symbols, and as such an important component of fluid senses of identity. I have also stressed, in trying to reach a sense of what animals were like in early agricultural communities, the continued significance of wild creatures. As well as binding people very closely to most parts of their landscape, wild creatures may have been one vehicle for the continuation of older attitudes of respect for and closeness to the partners of a unified world. In the final section of this chapter, I want to consider the possible mythic dimensions of animals a little further (and I take this general theme further in chapter 5). I will suggest that as well as having an important role in representing such themes as routines and physical existence, sociality, abundance and fertility, domesticated animals may have had in part a significant mythical role. But this may not have been quite as in earlier times. I will also argue that there is some evidence for shifts in how hunter-gatherer populations represented creatures in the phase of contact and transition, perhaps affected by new practices and attitudes.

The literature on the place of animals and creatures in general in the myths, especially the creation myths, of hunter-gatherer people is certainly abundant, and can be seen as part of a broad set of relationships that have been characterised as based on trust (Ingold 2000, chapter 4). The example is given by Eliade (1968, 194–5) of the Aboriginal Karadjeri origin myth of two brothers who walk, talk and name things, to bring the world into existence; they emerge from the earth first as dingos, before turning into human giants and later transforming themselves into giant snakes. On the other side of the world, on the north-west coast of America, particular animals seem often to have stood for particular stories and specific traits and virtues, though myth need not be seen as fixed or static (Hymes 1990). The Nuu-chah-nulth of Vancouver Island respected animals as equals or even superior beings, and thought that animals had once been humans (Arima 1983; G.F. MacDonald 1981; other references in Whittle 2000c). For the Tikigaq people of Point Hope, Alaska, a central myth was that the point itself, jutting out into the strait up and down which migrated the whales important to their existence, had itself once been a whale. The death of the primal whale, at the hands of a primal shamanic harpooner, made what followed possible, and the whale lived on as the point, part body and part spirit (Lowenstein 1993).

By contrast, the example has already been given earlier in this chapter of how sacred Himba cattle serve as a means of access to the ancestors and represent them, but they are not in themselves the ancestors (Crandall 1998). Among the Nuer, the ancestors of clans were thought of as having possessed cattle herds (Evans-Pritchard 1956, 258), but there is no evidence that cattle themselves, whatever their other importance, were venerated or regarded as guardian spirits (Evans-Pritchard 1956, 249). Could this different sort of emphasis seen in the ethnographies of some cattle keepers be transferred also to the archaeological situations under discussion? Most of the relevant archaeological examples discussed so far have been to do with animals transformed after slaughter, butchery and consumption into bones and deposited as such in various ways in different contexts. These bones may have stood for a very wide range of notions, as has been argued, but a mythic dimension is not immediately apparent. There may be some partial exceptions. Cattle skulls were used as commemorative symbols in the ditch at Menneville (Hachem *et al.* 1998). Later, a close association with a funerary or ancestral tradition is seen in the presence of cattle skulls under southern British long barrows, either on their own as at Beckhampton Road (Ashbee *et al.* 1979) or with human remains as at Fussell's Lodge (Ashbee 1966). Since cattle skulls also occur in the ditches of contemporary enclosures, as at Windmill Hill (Whittle *et al.* 1999), there may have been some blurring of distinctions between previously separate categories. Cattle slaughtered and deposited in wet places in southern Scandinavia might be another example of animals given special treatment in their own right, but on the one hand these could also be seen as sacrifices mediating between the human and spirit world (Tilley 1996, 184) and on the other hand animal remains have often been found to accompany human remains in similar contexts (Bennike 1999). It is again ambiguous whether animals were the principal focus.

The final way in which the possible mythic dimension of domesticated animals might be revealed is in representations of creatures in the phase of contact between indigenous people and new populations and practices. Two principal examples suggest themselves, from either end of the geographical range considered in this book. In the Danube Gorges, an indigenous population had existed if not flourished since at least the beginning of the Holocene. A tradition of building and burial reached its peak in the later seventh millennium BC, just at the period when other populations, which used pottery and domesticates including principally sheep and goats, had begun to appear in the wider region (Radovanović 1996; Garašanin and Radovanović 2001; cf. Whittle 1998b; Whittle *et al.* 2002). Indigenous people hunted many different kinds of animals and fished in the Danube. Remains of creatures from this range were incorporated centrally into built structures and burials. The chronology is complex and practices varied through time (Radovanović 1996) but a few brief examples from Lepenski Vir serve to remind us of the ubiquity of animal remains among the living and dead. A-settings of stone beside the central focus of the hearth mimic animal and/or human jaws, and there were deposits of fishbone regularly on the west side of hearths, with red deer parts on the stone platforms at the back of the hearths. Antlers were deposited with some burials. In one burial from Lepenski Vir 1,[5] the extended skeleton of an adult man had the cranium of a woman on its left shoulder, an auroch skull on the right shoulder, and a deer skull by the right hand, with its antlers nearby (Radovanović 1996, fig. 4.3). Decorated boulders were first given abstract motifs, but in later phases (from Radovanović's area phase 4, of the later seventh millennium BC) became, in our terms, semi-representational, with faces that appear part-human and part-fish. These were normally placed within structures, at the back, front and sides of hearths. The most monumental and figurative belong to a concentration in house XLIV at the beginning of Lepenski Vir II (Radovanović 1996, 157, and fig. 3.62). Srejović (1972, 122) identified those creatures with faces as deities or as mythic and ancestral fishy beings of the river. Radovanović (1997) made two important further connections. She suggested first that the creatures in question can specifically be identified as or linked to sturgeon, from details of the scaly ridges on backs and the top of their heads. Such beluga can reach a length of 4–5 m. These are migratory, and came up the Danube each year. In the later levels of Lepenski Vir, no bones of such large fish have been found. The second connection lies in the fact that the majority of the later burials of Lepenski Vir lie parallel to the river (Radovanović 1996, 187, 224), facing downstream, suggesting that the dead were placed so as to look down the river for the annual return of the ancestral fish.

One more connection might be added. The argument is circumstantial, based on context and the suggested chronology of development. Though the Gorges phenomenon began before the appearance of a new way of life in the wider region, its most accentuated features belong to the likely phase of contact with a changing outside world. In this sense, much of what happened in the Gorges was a reaction to what was happening elsewhere. It might be argued that such a reaction was an attempt to maintain and heighten indigenous identity in the face of the threat of new practices (Whittle 1996), but it is also becoming clear, not least from the fact that pottery occurred even in lower levels at Lepenski Vir, that this did not happen in isolation (Garašanin and Radovanović 2001; Borić 1999; Cook *et al.* 2002; Whittle *et al.* 2002). There was presumably therefore a degree of knowledge within the Gorges network of new practices elsewhere, and more or less contemporary sites can be found within a range of about 100 km. Though Srejović and Radovanović have drawn attention to the fish-like creatures, no one has directly questioned why fish should have taken this central role, other than by stressing the obviously important and carefully placed position of Lepenski Vir (and other sites) by the river. May it be that this was in some kind of opposition to the importance of domesticated animals among the new practices in the changing world around the Gorges? The contrasts could hardly have been greater, between sheep and goats, visible, audible, often on the move, living in herds, and profanely killed on a regular basis by their human keepers, and beluga, sensed as much as easily seen in the river, under the water, difficult of access, awe-inspiring, and normally left alone by people. The beluga, to follow Srejović and Radovanović, may have had or acquired a mythic dimension, resting in part on their annual return. Sheep and goats too may have had a place in stories and origin or creation myths as creatures not from the region. What countered them was not only red deer or aurochs, from the region, but something also from the outside.

This example is of course problematic. My argument assumes that the decorated boulders had an overwhelmingly central importance, whereas it could be countered that these were only one part of a varied and rapidly changing worldview. It is also hard to bring beluga and sheep and goats directly into comparison from the actual archaeological evidence. My second example is also problematic, but may provide a more immediate juxtaposition. I have suggested elsewhere that the striking Mané Rutual-type motif found on a small series of decorated menhirs in coastal Brittany, which has previously been interpreted as an axe, an axe-plough or a plough, could be in fact a representation of a whale (Whittle 2000c). Such menhirs could belong to the beginning of the Neolithic in Brittany, perhaps in the later fifth millennium BC (Figure 4.6). There is no need to repeat the whole argument here, but some points can be restated. The alternatives of axe, axe-plough or plough are not convincing, since this is a semi-representational style, especially as seen in the combined example of the originally joining pieces found separately in La Table des Marchand and Gavrinis. The distribution is coastal. A newly discovered decorated menhir, inland from Nantes, has an abstract motif (Scarre and Raux 2000). The motif is often large, especially on the Grand Menhir Brisé and La Table des Marchand-Gavrinis examples. It seems, at least in those cases, to have been designed to impress, and in the latter example is larger than the other things represented on the menhir. The general layout and relative proportions of the motif can be taken to resemble a whale, though admittedly the recurrent loop on the top side is hard to explain as a dorsal fin or even a spout.

What is of particular interest in the context of this broader discussion is the juxtaposition on the La Table des Marchand-Gavrinis example of the Mané Rutual motif with two four-legged animals, a possible crook, a definite (as well as smaller) axe, and two small crescentic motifs. Though small, these crescents could nonetheless be significant, perhaps part of a symbolism of sky, earth and underworld (Boujot et al. 1998). The scene has been taken (Kinnes and Hibbs 1989, 163; Bailloud et al. 1995) as a unified representation of central features of an agricultural way of life, with plough (the Mané Rutual motif) and corn (the crook motif) as well as a cow and a sheep (on the basis of differences in the representation of the two sets of horns). If the whale or some other interpretation is allowed, a different picture emerges. The whale is going one way, the animals and the axe (as defined by the direction of its blade) another. It is as though, in a way similar to that suggested in the context of the Danube Gorges, different creatures from two worlds have been brought together. In the indigenous context, as seen in the burial settings in the middens of Téviec and Hoëdic, red deer were particularly significant, their antlers placed above some burials and their teeth used as ornaments; stable isotopic analysis of human bone from Téviec and Hoëdic suggests an important role for marine resources in the diet (Schulting 1998; Schulting and Richards 2001). Even if the whale motif is rejected, it is hard to deny to the decorated menhirs not only a symbolic but also a mythic dimension, and the presence of the four-legged animals in such a context is just as important.

What might the various motifs have stood for? Our response must depend in part on a view of who is most likely to have put up and decorated these impressive constructions. One plausible answer, though there are many uncertainties not least with the chronology, is that the menhirs were put up by an essentially indigenous population in contact with new practices and perhaps incoming people. Another possibility is that they were part of an alternative ideology brought in from the outside (Sherratt 1995b). If we took the former view, the various motifs could stand for a series of ideas or figures: for sea and land and, remembering the small crescents,

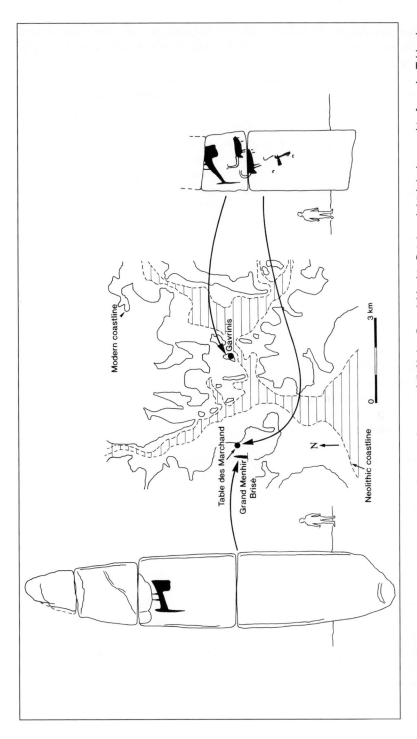

Figure 4.6 Mythic representations? Location and restored views of (left) Le Grand Menhir Brisé and (right) the menhir from La Table des Marchand and Gavrinis. After Whittle 2000c.

perhaps also sky; for old and new; for wild and tame; and for natural and cultural. We might see these as elements of a single myth, perhaps something to do with the coming of domesticated animals, or, following James Weiner (see chapters 1 and 5), as a succession of metaphors, contrasting by turns the permanence of the whale and the sea, the arrival of domesticated animals and human control, and the enduring forces of sky and even an underworld. As Weiner has noted in relation to the Foi, many interpretations could emerge from such a succession, and it is hardly necessary to insist on a single meaning. Finally, as is well known, many menhirs seem to have been dismantled or broken, some to be incorporated into other, different constructions. These included much more abstract traditions of decoration (Shee Twohig 1981). Though a case has been made for 'remembering by forgetting' (Bradley 2002, 36–41) it is as though the mythic force of menhirs had deliberately to be broken.

Two other pieces of evidence, finally, more certainly from phases of contact, also point to the impact that domesticated cattle may have had among indigenous people in north-west Europe. In front of the south façade of the primary phase of the long cairn of Er Grah, close to where the Grand Menhir Brisé originally stood and where the La Table des Marchand-Gavrinis menhir, as well as other smaller ones now recognised only by stone holes, may also have stood, a pair of domesticated cattle were found in a pit (Tresset and Vigne, forthcoming; Anne Tresset, pers. comm.; cf. Tresset 2000). Radiocarbon determinations suggest a date in the late sixth and early fifth millennia BC, presumably a context belonging to the Late Mesolithic though conceivably also to the earliest Neolithic of the region. There is no other certain sign from the middens of Téviec and Hoëdic, dated to approximately the same time, for use of domesticates in the indigenous context. It may be significant, if the Er Grah deposit is an indigenous one, that these animals were not consumed. Rather, they may have been sacrificed as something both new and conceptually powerful. Even further afield, something similar may have taken place on the south-west coast of Ireland. At Ferriter's Cove, in a later fifth millennium BC context of probably mobile existence, with short stays seen in a series of thin layers and very slight structures, a few cattle bones were found; a sheep's tooth also found could not be certainly dated (Woodman et al. 1999). There is no evidence for indigenous cattle in early post-glacial Ireland. Given the date (though note reservations connected to a possible marine reservoir effect: Tresset 2000, 27), and assuming that these were not remains of aurochs brought over from western Britain, these were probably domesticated animals from the mainland of continental north-west Europe. Since the remains consist of only seven pieces from leg and foot, it is not clear whether these animals were brought over alive, and it might perhaps be just as likely that a preserved joint, or even bones themselves, were brought back from a long-range boat trip. It is also significant that the experience was not quickly repeated. Among a population living by sea fishing and by hunting wild pig, domesticates were still not adopted for some centuries. Perhaps, in this kind of context, the consolidation of change required a more sustained exposure to myth and story, as well as to a different practical logic.

Chapter 5

Looking back

My discussion so far has been about the complexity, not to say messiness, of existence, as seen in what constitutes daily routines, the characterisation of individuals and their relationships to larger groupings, the moral community framed by values and intentions, and the ties between people and animals. In exploring what carries life forward, I have so far said little about one important dimension: the past. The argument of this chapter is that looking back is a central part of the identities of people in the period examined in this book. Looking back is present in the routines of daily life as well as in the special times and places to which archaeologists have given most attention; indeed what is remembered at special times of heightened, often collective, self-awareness may often (though far from always) draw on the central features of daily life. Memory can perhaps better be thought of as an open-ended series of rememberings, which resist neat classification. In all spheres, remembering is as likely to be fluid, dynamic and creative as fixed, static and closed. Different ways of remembering may help us, perhaps uniquely, to understand different scales of interaction among people and varying dimensions of self-consciousness. The pervasive presence of the past in the present may have created a history of histories, whose power is relevant to what I see as the slow development of long-term change.

Three initial examples will help to define both the importance and the diversity of ways of remembering.

Remembering at work

The first example takes us back to the Foi of highland New Guinea. The identity of Foi men is cast as complementary to that of women, and *vice versa*. Men's routine tasks include responsibility for initiating clearance, plantings and construction, and hunting and trading. There is plenty of routine, daily activity, in gardens and about the house in the longhouse settlement (J.F. Weiner 1988, 43–6). Time is also spent in bush houses and in hunting areas, where men hunt, fish and forage (J.F. Weiner 1991, 34). During the 'stylised and complex sociality' of longhouse existence (J.F. Weiner 1991, 5), men reflect on their days out in the hunting areas; at the heart of longhouse existence with its emphasis on the values of 'gregariousness, competitiveness and confrontation' (J.F. Weiner 1991, 8), there is remembering of a more fragmented and separate dimension of social existence. Men remember in other ways. They actively seek contact with ghosts, the disembodied but still powerful souls of the departed, through dreams, partly in association with particular, named places in the landscape (J.F. Weiner 1991, 2). Men also remember the dead in their performances of memorial song poems, linking again names and places. It is women, however, through their primary association with death, who compose these memorial song poems in the first place (J.F. Weiner 1991, 2–5).

Place is also central to the rememberings of my second example. Among the western Apache, Basso (1984) has outlined major categories of speech, including ordinary talk, prayer and narrative or story, the latter in turn divisible into myth, historical tale, saga and gossip. These have differing temporalities and locations, not least in the fact that myths and sagas may take hours to tell. Historical tales are closely linked to named places in the landscape. They are about people 'who suffer misfortune as the consequence of actions that violate Apache standards for acceptable social behavior', asserting a sense of shared morality and identity (Basso 1984, 35–6). The rememberings in question are both generalised and from far back in time, but are to do with individual people, and are linked directly to specific parts or features of the landscape. It is these which act as the prompt for remembering, stalking people with their moral presence.

In yet another setting, among the Jivaro of Amazonian Ecuador, both remembering and forgetting are important (Taylor 1993; 1996). Jivaroan sociality can be seen as 'affective memory', or the 'condensation and memory of the affective moods built up by daily interaction in nurturing, sharing and working' (Taylor 1996, 206). This is also a fragile state, easily disturbed by shifts in social alliances and feuding. Along with many other people of Amazonia, the Jivaro have no ancestor cults, and practise both simple funerary rites and shallow genealogical memory. Forgetting the dead involves transforming them into something quite different, whose otherness helps to define values and relationships among the living. Through concepts of continuity of soul and singularity of face and name, the dead remain important as the source of identity and destiny of the living, for if one person does not die, someone else cannot be born, but according to these conceptions they must be transformed from specific memories as alive to a mental representation as deceased (Taylor 1993, 655) and be reduced to an 'abstract singularity'. The death of men may cause houses to be abandoned, with bodies left in them or elsewhere to hasten the dissolution of the corpse. Separation and erasure are here central concepts, but the deceased appear to remain a potent force. 'Being nowhere in particular . . . [the dead] are, potentially, everywhere all the time' (Taylor 1993, 653).

Cumulative selections

'Memory is cumulative selection', wrote Anne Michaels in her poem 'Miner's Pond'. Although Bloch has denied that there is a generalised need for people to remember the past (1998, 81), it is hard to envisage life being carried forward without very varied senses of looking back. Debate about the character of memory goes as far back as Aristotle, and already almost a century ago Bergson (1911; quoted in Stewart 1999) struck a promising note in noting that 'there is no perception which is not full of memories. With the immediate and present data of our senses, we mingle a thousand details out of our past experience.' Not uncharacteristically, archaeologists until very recently have largely ignored explicit discussion of memory, though making heavy implicit use of it in concepts such as culture, monumentality and tradition. The wider literature on memory is impressively large, but it has many strands to it, and there is overall a tendency to seek rigidly to classify memory, as though it were a single phenomenon or a single faculty. This section seeks briefly to outline a case for selective and creative diversity, and I will then use that perspective to examine the importance of memory in action in daily life, in myth, in the development of monumentality, and finally in connection to concepts of ancestry and descent.

Much discussion of memory seems to be characterised by dualistic classification: oral versus written; individual versus collective or social (Halbwachs 1925; 1950; Coser 1992; Fentress and Wickham 1992; D. Middleton and Edwards 1990); habitual versus conscious (Connerton 1989); involuntary versus voluntary (Leslie 1999); inscribed (and dynamic) versus incorporated (and static) (Connerton 1989); and autobiographical versus semantic (Bloch 1998, chapter 8). All these distinctions, and others, are important, but the point here is that it is hardly possible to retain them within a single concept or phenomenon. Connerton (1989) was among the first to draw attention to the importance of bodily performance in distinguishing incorporated from inscribed practices. For him, performative, ritualised enactment is one of the key ways in which societies remember, commemorative ceremonies being indeed perhaps one of the most convincing demonstrations of the existence of social memory (Connerton 1989, 4). Certain things can only be expressed in ritual, and ritual form demands participation, rather than the mere listening to, say, narrated myth (Connerton 1989, 54); and by comparison with myth, the structure of rituals is claimed to have significantly less potential for variance (Connerton 1989, 57). While these and other observations have led to renewed attention being given to the bodily and material dimensions of remembering (cf. Kwint et al. 1999), they overplay distinctions. Texts or inscribed practices may themselves become fossilised, and ritual may be creative and innovative as well as fragmented and interrupted. To take part in ritual is not necessarily to accept it; while rituals may engender communitas (V. Turner 1969), they may also be contested (e.g. Snyder 1997). Ritual may itself depend on varying kinds of remembering, and can hardly therefore be used to justify the distinction of a particular kind of memory.

The collective and selective dimensions of remembering were perhaps first stressed by Halbwachs (Coser 1992). Halbwachs argued that memory can function only in a collective context, and that collective memory is always selective. As Middleton and Edwards have put it (1990, 1), 'remembering and forgetting are integral with social practices that carry with them, in important ways, a culturally evolved legacy of conduct and invention, both material and social, central to the conduct of daily life'. In fact, the examples used by Halbwachs are quite limited, drawn from studies of pilgrims and of families with differing class perspectives. It is no surprise that Halbwachs was a 'second generation Durkheimian' (Coser 1992, 1), and to avoid the individual being seen as a mere automaton, others sympathetic to his general approach have preferred the term social memory to that of collective memory (Fentress and Wickham 1992, ix).

It is therefore now timely to broaden the approach to rememberings. The example of the Foi shows that the nature of the collectivity involved may vary. The example of the Jivaro demonstrates the importance of forgetting, as is also seen in other situations (Küchler 1987; Battaglia 1990; Forty and Küchler 1999). The Tiv of northern Nigeria were obsessed with genealogical descent, but in a way that involved considerable selection of those relationships which were to be remembered (Bohannan 1952). Bloch (1998, especially chapters 7–8) has shown in studies of Madagascar not only how rememberings can be highly selective, but how they take different forms within the same society, from exemplary tales with moral value (recalling the example of the western Apache quoted above) to mythic representations and more literal accounts based on sincerity but lacking the authority of exemplary tales. There is thus a variety of ways, oral and non-oral, of evoking the past. He concludes:

> Adult humans construct a multiplicity of narratives of different types appropriate to different contexts and this very multiplicity ensures that their knowledge is not bounded by the narrative characteristics of any one of them. Narratives talk in different ways about what is known. They are not knowledge itself.
>
> (Bloch 1998, 110)

In some situations, the distinction between autobiographical and semantic memory may become blurred, and what is remembered may be the previous instance of recall rather than the original event (Bloch 1998, 126).

Bloch among others has recognised the importance of material objects and places, from the weave of hats (Bloch 1998, 109) to notions of the house and its constituent and changing constructional elements and decoration (Bloch 1998, chapters 2 and 6; Bloch 1995a). Recent studies of the materiality of memory in historical situations (e.g. Forty and Küchler 1999; Kwint *et al*. 1999) have focused on memorials, both lasting and ephemeral, and objects, from souvenirs and toys to banners and photographs. There is a tension, however, in this emerging enterprise. On the one hand, memories and associations should not be simply projected on to objects as passive recipients, without giving attention to the inherent qualities and properties of objects and material forms themselves. On the other hand, this may imply both a kind of essentialism and a self-contained agency (Pollard 2001; Gell 1998). The way out of this dilemma may be not only to suggest compromise solutions, such that objects are 'active in the manner of objects not in the manner of people' (Gosden 2001, 164), but also to stress again the multiplicity of ways in which material forms may evoke and be used to evoke remembering. The near-obligatory references to Proust (especially to his biscuit), seen in so many recent papers, draw on the force of remembering, but downplay the individuality of the writer's situation and experience.

Bloch has been one of the few authors interested in the possibility of bringing together the observations of psychologists, concerned with the observation of the workings of memory in the individual brain, and the wider insights of anthropologists, historians and others concerned with memory in social fields. He has noted (1998, 115) the difficulties of such a reconciliation, since much psychological observation is of very short-term memory tasks in artificial, experimental conditions. Despite this perhaps unavoidable limitation, there have been important developments, especially in the field of neuroimaging (e.g. Foster 1999). The emergence of the technique of functional magnetic resonance imaging (fMRI) has allowed insight into how the brain actually operates during the performance of memory tasks. Many tasks tested so far have indeed been short-term, but there are signs too of interest in long-term memory encoding processes (e.g. Mayes and Montaldi 1999). Without going into detail, the most interesting feature for our purposes here is that it seems that different parts of the brain are involved in the whole suite of memory tasks. There appears to be no neurophysiological basis for the existence of a single seat or faculty of memory. A textbook review of memory offers the threefold division of sensory memory, short-term or working memory, and long-term memory, and concludes that 'memory does not comprise a single unitary system, but rather an array of interacting systems, each capable of encoding or registering information, storing it, and making it available by retrieval' (Baddeley 1999, 19).

This should encourage us to think in terms of diverse rememberings and uses of the past rather than of a single faculty of memory. Seventy years ago the psychologist Bartlett carried out a famous series of tests of short-term or working memory, focused on the recall of written texts. He found that there was considerable deviation in the re-tellings of his readers. More or less a contemporary of Halbwachs, Bartlett's results pointed in a rather different direction.[1] Two conclusions are particularly worth quoting in full:

> Remembering is not the re-excitation of innumerable fixed, lifeless and fragmentary traces. It is an imaginative reconstruction, or construction, built out of the relation of our attitude towards a whole active mass of organised past reactions or experience, and to a little outstanding detail which commonly appears in image or in language form. It is thus hardly ever really exact, even in the most rudimentary cases of rote recapitulation, and it is not at all important that it should be so.
>
> (Bartlett 1932, 213)

and, the final sentences of his book:

> I have never regarded memory as a faculty, as a reaction narrowed and ringed round, containing all its peculiarities and all their explanations within itself. I have regarded it rather as one achievement in the line of the ceaseless struggle to master and enjoy a world full of variety and rapid change. Memory, and all

the life of images and words which goes with it, is one with the age-old acquisition of the distance senses, and with that development of constructive imagination and constructive thought wherein at length we find the most complete
release from the narrowness of presented time and place.

(Bartlett 1932, 314)

With such a range of creative rememberings in mind, I now look at number of
further situations and styles in which looking back was at work.

The range of rememberings in daily life

My first example goes back to the Körös culture on the Hungarian Plain in the first
half of the sixth millennium BC. It makes use especially of observations from my
own recent excavations at Ecsegfalva 23, in the Berettyó valley, near the northern
limits of the Körös culture distribution,[2] but could as well apply to other sites and
situations in the region investigated by others (e.g. Makkay 1992; cf. Chapman
2000a). I will include similar reflections on LBK daily life in the next chapter, as I
try to give a sense of how daily routines, different kinds of looking back, and a
history of histories were all enmeshed.

Like most Körös sites, Ecsegfalva 23 was by water, in this case neither on the edge
of the older terraces of the Pleistocene river system nor along the edges of the Holocene
valley, but at one point in the loop of a great meander of late Pleistocene origin which
was a still-water lake by this period. There is no obvious reason why people should
have chosen this particular spot for occupation out of a whole series of other higher and
drier ridges or levées; in the succeeding phase, the spot was avoided and the next ridge
taken up. Perhaps its initial choice was in a sense random, or connected to very
particular or contingent events. But once used, it appears that the locale remained in
use, since a 30-cm occupation deposit built up over a period of time probably to be
measured in generations. It remains to be established from further analysis of the finds
whether this was a seasonal or permanent occupation, or a base used episodically at
varying temporal scales. There may have been practical reasons in an uncertain
environment, prone perhaps to flooding, whose effects in a flat landscape would have
been considerable, why knowledge of what happened or was likely to happen in a
given spot was desirable. Movement structured around recognised locales may also
have been based on memory of the first land-taking. It is not clear whether the Körös
population consisted of people from the south, or of indigenous people from the hills
and other zones surrounding the Plain, or a fusion of both strands. In all cases, they can
be regarded as incomers to a previously little used region. This may not have been, at
least initially, a large population, and repetition of occupation may have been
important in establishing a sense of order and security in a new setting.

The occupation of Ecsegfalva 23, and of many other sites like it, was carried forward
in a cycle of actions that partly involved looking back. This was a relatively small
occupation, so that the remembrance already discussed was played out partly among a
human group of modest size, but partly with reference to a wider population. The

stratified occupation deposit seems to be the result of repeated, concentrated activities, in what I believe was a cycle of building, use, deliberate burning, abandonment and reoccupation. Perhaps both memory and anticipation were features of this cycle, letting go of and retaking the place on the one hand, and looking forward, in periods of more intense socialisation, to gatherings and even feastings. Pottery is very abundant, though complete vessels are rare. Analysis of former contents suggests that vessels may not have been much used, which in turn opens the possibility that much pottery was made for particular, short-lived events. That it was broken could be due not so much to the material enchainments envisaged by Chapman (2000a), as either the circumstances of abandonment or the desire for closure after gatherings. The material residues, whatever the process, would certainly have given a distinctive texture or layering to the occupation surface. The other feature of the accumulating surface, certainly as excavated and presumably as experienced during the occupation, was a considerable quantity of burnt daub fragments. These were the remains of what I believe were relatively flimsy and short-lived structures, some perhaps buildings for dwelling, others perhaps more akin to shelters or stores. The extent of material accumulations might in some way have been in inverse relation to the length of occupation. There is certainly a striking contrast between on the one hand the material abundance and flimsy structures of the Körös culture and on the other the more restrained assemblages and yet more massive buildings of the LBK. There is much analysis still to do of the remains from this one site alone, to say nothing of the wider phenomenon (cf. Shaffer 1999), but it may well be that here as elsewhere in the wider region of south-east Europe many structures were deliberately burned at the end of their use (Stevanovic 1997). If so, this is another kind of closure, and people would have walked daily over a surface textured by memories of the past in the form of sherds and daub. Indeed they may have deliberately have concentrated such material effects in single locales in order to confine or channel rememberings. Much of what has been suggested as typical of the Late Neolithic tells of the Hungarian Plain in terms of an ideology of deep ancestral time (e.g. Chapman 1997c; 2000a) can in fact be seen as already present in the Körös culture.

Life was carried forward not only by special events and gatherings. Dwelling here consisted of a wide range of activities. Alongside fishing, hunting, fowling, shellfish collection and small-scale cultivation of cereals (whether at the site or elsewhere), people gave much attention to animal herding, especially of sheep and goats. Much of this activity may have been concentrated in the early summer, and tending to sheep grazing and folding, and perhaps from time to time in the season of late spring or early summer floodings moving animals away from the danger of high water level rises, seems to have been a major rhythm in the flow of life. Sheep and goats may, contrary to some suggestions, have done reasonably well in the environments of the Plain. Because sheep and goats were practically ubiquitous across Europe in the Neolithic, although in varying quantities, it is easy perhaps to take them for granted (see also chapter 4). In the context of the Plain, a contrary suggestion can be made. Whether their herders were from the south, or indigenous people from the broader region, these animals must have been recognised as exotic, deriving from elsewhere to the south. People here regularly encountered a very wide range of other fauna (even though these were probably less important in strict terms of calorific intake), and everything points to a wide knowledge of their environment and extensive movement through it. Sheep and goats would have been strikingly different to other, local fauna in terms of appearance, form and sound, and perhaps also in terms of innate behaviour, smell and taste. Much of daily life may have been structured around tending to these animals, whose very character, however, may have carried potent connotations of different times, oriented to the south, and connecting people even in remote and briefly occupied locales with a much wider network of remembrance.

There must have been other senses of orientation. There is a stark contrast between the abundance of locally made pottery and the paucity of stone tools, in the form of fine-grained rocks, obsidian and limno-quartzite. The former may have come from anywhere on the highland fringes of the Carpathian basin, and the latter two from the north-east and north respectively, at distances of 150–200 km (Starnini 2000). As analysis of other assemblages has already shown, obsidian probably travelled already in relatively small preformed cores, and was subsequently worked right down to very small dimensions, and clearly not often casually discarded (Starnini 2000). It seems hard to argue that this material and the objects made from it, and by extension the routine tasks performed with it, would not have evoked memory of their ultimately distant procurement, either negotiated with forager populations to the north of the Körös culture or acquired directly after long expeditions by people of the Körös culture themselves.

In other Körös culture sites so far investigated, the remains of rather more women and children have been found than of men, deposited in a variety of ways (Chapman 1994; Trogmayer 1969). The evidence from the small-scale excavations so far at Ecsegfalva 23 conforms to this picture, with an adult female burial on one periphery of the site, a child skull deposit on another, and child bones from the main occupation deposit, possibly disturbed from earlier burials. Where then were the men disposed of? Were they merely given separate rites somewhere out in the landscape, to date outside the reach of regular archaeological investigations, marking perhaps the greater range of movement in their lives, or were they in fact deliberately forgotten after death, to free them from the bonds of the living, or to liberate the living from the burden of their remembrance? In this case, there is so far no easy answer. In the Körös culture situation at least, there was perhaps no single dominant form of remembering; being and identity were constituted through many kinds of remembrance. It is difficult to confine these to actual or verifiable memories, as the earlier quotations from Bartlett suggested would be impossible, and personal, episodic memories slide, easily perhaps in some cases, into imagined and mythical realms. It is to myth that I now turn.

Myth

It may seem a considerable leap from memories to myth, but I want to consider them both in the context of looking back, of making reference to a past or the past, which is often sharply defined but also timeless. Myth is important, though rarely explicitly considered by archaeologists. It is powerful, widespread, deals with themes of recurrent if not central importance, is often or perhaps normally public, and it straddles the distinction made by Connerton (1989) between inscribed and incorporated performances. It often takes the form of narrative, delivered in words to an audience. Connerton sees the delivery of a myth as structurally different from the performance of a ritual; 'to recite a myth is not necessarily to accept it' (1989, 54). However, I have already noted difficulties with this view of ritual, and the bodily aspect of the performance of myth, or some myths in some settings, should not be overlooked. It involves a speaker and an audience, standing or sitting in perhaps prescribed postures and in a defined physical setting.

Connerton has called both ritual and myth 'collective symbolic texts' (1989, 53). There is uncertainty, however, about just what sort of collective symbolic texts these may be. James Weiner (1994; 1995) has outlined two possible positions. The majority view, expressed in different ways by both functionalists as far back as Malinowski and structuralists including notably Lévi-Strauss, has been that myth serves to 'unify and coordinate the worldview and morality of a community' (J.F. Weiner 1994, 388). It obviously does so in different ways, for the functionalists by directly linking the content of myth with social practice, to offer accounts of origins, while for the structuralists by explaining the conceptual underpinning of the social world, but in both cases ultimately providing kinds of charter for what can be seen in any present situation (J.F. Weiner 1994, 388–9). The differences between these variations, however, may be extreme. Lévi-Strauss classically analysed myth, in his four volumes of *Mythologiques*, in relation to other myths, as analysis of the form of classification. Weiner has elsewhere (1988, 12, 155) stressed the concentration by Lévi-Strauss on the structure of signs rather than on the metaphoric content of myths. On the other hand, it is possible to see myth as simply another version of language in a world in which culture and convention are not pre-given, such that all utterances including myth are potentially subversive, since they differentiate the world anew:

> Each [mythical] story provides an insight, an oblique and novel perspective that disabuses us from the normal, everyday habit of taking our world, our descriptions of it, our way of acting in it, and our beliefs as true, natural and self-evident.
>
> (J.F. Weiner 1994, 387)

Whether the second position, challenging though it is, can be applied to all myth remains to be seen. Indeed, one of the problems in discussions of this kind is that, once again, a wide range of tellings and lookings back are lumped into a single, universal form. There are certainly indigenous distinctions between kinds of narrative. The western Apache, as we have seen, distinguish between ordinary talk, prayer and narrative or story, the latter divided on the basis of time and purpose into gossip, historical tale, saga and myth. Myths deal with events that occurred 'in the beginning', 'to explain and reaffirm the complex processes by which the known world came into existence', and they are performed only by medicine men and medicine women (Basso 1994, 34). Here already is regularity and convention. The Foi and Daribi of New Guinea also make distinctions between kinds of tales, stories, moral tales and origin myths (J.F. Weiner 1988, 150–1; Wagner 1978). Among the Foi, the context in which myths are performed appears also hedged about by convention, and although there are many myths (J.F. Weiner 1988, *passim*), their style is strongly recurrent. More variation and creativity, in fact, may reside in magical spells owned by individuals and in memorial songs for particular people (J.F. Weiner 1988); but while connected to myth, these are not myths themselves.

Two interesting examples, the Lugbara and the Foi, may help to illustrate the relevance of this discussion to the themes of this chapter. The Lugbara lived across the Congo–Uganda border (J. Middleton 1960). A society described as composed of tribes, clans, territorial sections and lineages can be seen at different levels, from the linking relations of authority of those who hold statuses in these 'units', to the immediate world of family and inner lineage, which regularly conceives the surrounding world as hostile (J. Middleton 1960, 230 and 236). The wider social network is conceived of in terms of clans, and clans are conceived of in terms of myth (J. Middleton 1960, 231). These go back in a line of descent from ancestors recognised in genealogies, which may often change (J. Middleton 1960, 12), to the founders of clans, who were the sons of a pair of hero-ancestors, who were the descendants of a line of siblings put on earth by God the creator (Figure 5.1). The scheme slides from genealogy to myth, and from human figures to not-quite-human figures such as the hero-ancestors and their predecessors. In the intimate world of the family and lineage, genealogy is a principal focus of concern, men especially manipulating the cult of the dead as the means to authority. Lineages are the agnatic (or uterine) core of a territorial section, and the means to think of that as unchanging, whereas in reality there is change all the time within and between lineages and territorial sections (J. Middleton 1960, 7–13).

Middleton stressed that such a scheme was never related to him as a single narrative (1960, 232), and it was certainly flexible enough to include the historical appearance of Europeans, their strangeness represented in the fact that they walked upside down, as the people of the myths in the time before the hero-ancestors also did (J. Middleton 1970, 39). Myths ranged from the first creator to the two hero-ancestors. They often took the form of narratives of sequences of events, connecting listeners in the present with understanding of how their landscape had been shaped (J. Middleton 1970, 39), and were performed with considerable drama and energy (J. Middleton 1970, 38). The myths often have a fragmented quality, and there is much that requires a mythopoeic rather than a literal approach (Middleton 1970, 37). But in Middleton's accounts, these myths were extremely important, being a means by which Lugbara made sense of many basic features of their present society: 'statements about social relations that the Lugbara saw as being so important that they had to be stated symbolically and mythopoeically' (J. Middleton 1970, 38).

In his detailed account of Foi mythology, Weiner (1988) offers an overlapping interpretation, though with much greater attention to the relation of one myth to

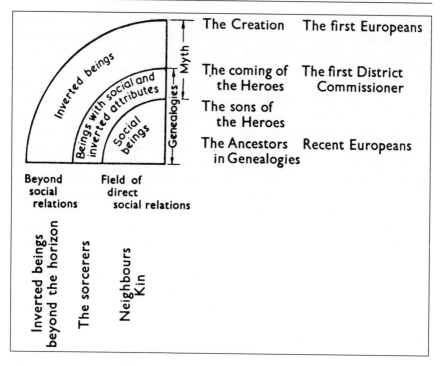

The Creation   The first Europeans

The coming of   The first District
the Heroes   Commissioner

The sons of
the Heroes

The Ancestors   Recent Europeans
in Genealogies

Figure 5.1 Lugbara (central Africa) categories of social space and time. From Middleton 1960, by permission of the International African Institute.

another. Myths are for public narration in the communal setting of the longhouse (J.F. Weiner 1988, 13, 296). They cover a great range of subjects, usually providing narrative sequences in a timeless past, or vaguely in the beginning, in which representative figures work through a series of encounters and problems. The myth of the heart of the pearl shell (J.F. Weiner 1988, 279–82) concerns the search of a young man for possession of the literal heart of the pearl shell, whose importance in exchange relations however resides in its movement or flow between and among people. Weiner sees Foi mythology as a linkage between their key conceptual analogies (J.F. Weiner 1988, 5), as 'the poetic or aesthetic revelation . . . of fundamental paradoxes' (J.F. Weiner 1988, 16), and as providing the cosmological and moral closures that ordinary life does not permit (J.F. Weiner 1988, 16); 'myth provides a transient, fleeting, and incomplete structure for those people whose reality it encompasses' (J.F. Weiner 1988, 16–17). It operates, by obviation or alternating substitution or contrast, as a 'series of successively embedded metaphors' (J.F. Weiner 1988, 285), open therefore to many interpretations and meanings, and in this sense fluid and potentially subversive (J.F. Weiner 1988, 289; 1995, xx).

    If myths reveal 'what is fundamental to Foi conceptualizations of morality, intention, consequence, agency, and personhood' (J.F. Weiner 1988, 149), can we see anything of their operation in the archaeological evidence for Neolithic central and western Europe? At first sight, the outlook is bleak. Both Middleton and Weiner could listen, as field anthropologists, to the narration of myths and indigenous commentaries (including in the case of Middleton the instruction to shut his notebook and feel the force of the mythological vision: J. Middleton 1970, 37). But there are features of the archaeological record which I believe we can think of in mythical terms, and it is even possible that there is an informative pattern or structure to their distribution and sequence.

There is abundant evidence to suggest the working of memory. The often quoted link between longhouse and long mound is a case in point. Given the chronology of the fifth millennium BC, and the demonstrable juxtapositions or proximities in situations such as north-central Poland, where Sarnowo is not far from Brześć Kujawski, and now the demonstrable direct overlays of long enclosures over long houses at Balloy in the Yonne valley of the Paris basin (Mordant 1997), it is possible to argue for extended memories of some kind as the medium in which the transference or transformation of ideas was made. In the case of enclosures, this becomes more difficult. There are far fewer enclosures in the fifth millennium BC in the western part of Europe than there were in the later part of the LBK; the weight of the distributions of Stichbandkeramik and Lengyel enclosures is further east, from Bavaria eastwards (summarised in Whittle 1996). It is probable that enclosures in southern Britain do not belong to the earliest Neolithic (and therefore start in the early centuries of the fourth millennium BC), and yet the concept can still plausibly be seen as going as far back as the fifth or even sixth millennium BC continental antecedents; there are also more local and contemporary possible sources of the practice (discussed in Whittle et al. 1999). In this case it is more than likely that direct memories had transmuted into tales, sagas or myths, and without further distinguishing between these (see above), I suggest that the idea of enclosures was transmitted in the realm of myth. Indeed, Bradley (1998a, 82) has discussed southern British enclosures as mythical settlements which hark back to the world left many generations before. Having already discussed some of the decorated menhirs of Brittany in the last chapter, I want now to consider the so-called portal dolmens of the Irish Sea area, and *Spondylus* shells in the LBK. These further examples also raise the possibility of significant change through time.

Portal dolmens

Portal dolmens are widespread in the Irish Sea area, especially in eastern and northern parts of Ireland and in western parts of Wales and south-west England. They are characterised by substantial capstones of varied shapes. Some are thick and rounded, while others are thinner but often spectacularly tilted; all are supported by uprights forming a more or less rectangular, simple chamber (Figure 5.2). It is plausible to see many of these as early in their regional sequences (Cooney 2000; Bradley 1998b; Tilley and Bennett 2001; Cummings and Whittle, forthcoming), though this is not the place for detailed discussion. Bradley (1998a; 1998b; 2000)

Figure 5.2 Pentre Ifan, Pembrokeshire, with Carn Ingli and the sea behind. Photo: Vicki Cummings.

and Tilley and Bennett (2001) have already discussed with reference to south-west England how these constructions appear to draw on and mimic features of the natural landscape such as tors and hilltops. Bradley (2000, 109–10) has drawn attention to how the building of monuments can add new meaning to already significant natural places. Tilley and Bennett have developed this point, to suggest that 'in elevating large stones, these people were emulating the work of a super-ancestral past' and 'the dolmens . . . were the tors dismantled and put back together again to resemble their original form' (2001, 345). Further:

> West Penwith is one of the few places in Britain from which the sun can be seen to have a watery death and birth at important points in the solar calendar . . . elemental cosmological themes of fire, water, stone, birth, death and the regeneration of life, may have had a particular resonance and symbolic power.
>
> (Tilley and Bennett 2001, 336)

In turn I want to suggest a further, specifically mythical dimension to these constructions. Whether dolmens resemble tors or *vice versa*, I believe there is more to the relationship than imitation or emulation. Construction involves transformation. Three features help to support this claim. Some portal dolmens have pits below their chambers (Cummings 2001), and these constructions therefore involve more than just the recreation of a tor or hill. Though it has often been supposed otherwise, there is little evidence for the original presence of surrounding and concealing cairns, and there is good evidence in some cases for deliberately and carefully built platforms of smaller stones, from which the uprights appear to emerge. Thirdly, most capstones have a slope or tilt, formed either by the form of their upper sides or by the whole stone being literally tilted, sometimes dramatically. In several striking examples this arrangement mimics locally visible hilltops, such as the convincing link between Pentre Ifan and Carn Ingli in south-west Wales (Tilley 1994; Cummings 2001). In some cases, the link may be to a general resemblance to tors, as argued for Chun Quoit in West Penwith (Tilley and Bennett 2001, 346). In yet others, there may be no such reference, and it is possible therefore that the tilt has a significance of its own. This might be referred to some feature of daily life in forager or early farming existence, such as tents, but it may be more plausible to think of what the raised stones actually stood for. Archaeological language and convention predispose us to call these stones 'capstones' or 'roofstones', but this is far too general, and misses what the architecture emphasises, that the stones have been raised.

Where there is a probable link between raised stones and tors or hills, it is plausible to think of the mythical agency of those natural features themselves. Mountains were a prominent feature of Lugbara mythology, for example, being a reference point or starting point in stories about creation and human origins (J. Middleton 1970, 36–9). In far western North America, mountains can be seen as male in relation to female locations with rock art (D.S. Whitley 1998). Tors and hills in the landscapes of the Irish Sea zone could be seen in this light as having a significance of their own, and there is thus a potential dialogue between natural places and built constructions, perhaps even an 'obviation' or alternation in Wagner's and Weiner's terms. The raised stones of portal dolmens might also, in conjunction with pits and platforms, have had a more general metaphorical or mythical significance. They could be seen as a version of creation, in which the earth was raised to the sky, or an account of how earth and sky were once joined. One Lugbara myth was about a time when people could move between the earth and the sky via a rope, a tree, and a tower; when these gave way, people were scattered over the earth into their present locations and social groupings in the world (J. Middleton 1970, 36).

Spondylus *shells*

My final, brief example concerns *Spondylus* shells. Their origin in the east Mediterranean or Black Sea and their broad distribution far to the north-west are well known (Willms 1985). They appear not to be a marked feature of the earliest Neolithic of south-east Europe, but they appear in central Europe first with the LBK (and then far from everywhere or in regular quantities). The chains of exchange then extend from central Europe back into a cultural world for which there is little other evidence of connection; presumably a general orientation to the east or south-east was recognised. So although resembling many other objects or materials, in that they were acquired from a distance, perhaps beyond direct knowledge, *Spondylus* shells may have had an unusually mysterious quality. They might be taken as a material token of belief in the LBK world of a mythic origin in the south-east. This may be mirrored also in the general orientation of LBK longhouses (Bradley 2001; 2002). Neither need reflect the precise history of LBK origins, which as we shall see in the next chapter may have been more a matter of events and fusions in the territory between the Danube and the eastern end of the Alps. *Spondylus* was regularly transformed into bracelets and beads, but it also frequently survived its long journeys and histories with surprisingly little modification. In the case of the LBK cemetery at Aiterhofen in Bavaria (Nieszery 1995), both women's and men's graves contained variously beads and bracelets, while some men's graves also contained *Spondylus* shells with a distinctive V-shape cut out of them (Figure 5.3). It looks as though these items were a more prominent feature of the graves of less mature adults, as though by the time men had reached seniority, they had normally passed on these potent objects (Hofmann 2001), of perhaps mythic origin. This suggestion recalls the flow at the core of the Foi myth noted above about the heart of the pearl shell (J.F. Weiner 1998).

A history of histories?

Colin Renfrew (1976) once related the appearance of megalithic construction in what can be called Atlantic Europe to a shortage of land; after expansion to the west, populations had nowhere else to go and were forced to regulate their relationships by ritual constructions. A different perspective is possible in the light of this discussion of myth. The nature of myth may have changed during the course of the history of transmission to the west. People in the Körös culture may have referred to the south in aspects of their material culture and perhaps in their choice of sheep and goats as a preferred animal, as argued above. People in the LBK may have had a sense of being oriented to the east or south-east, imbued on a daily basis by the physical orientation of their longhouses and reinforced by the occasional acquisition of objects or materials such as *Spondylus*. By the time of fifth-millennium menhirs and fourth-millennium portal dolmens, these earlier reference points had themselves passed into mythic status, both rivalling perhaps and fusing with the mythologies of indigenous populations.

There are frequent references to the way in which new features can be incorporated into belief systems and mythologies. The arrival of Europeans, for example, was incorporated into Lugbara cosmology and categorisation (Figure 5.1) (J. Middleton 1960, fig. 9). In a generalising discussion of their religion and metaphysics, Guenther (1999, 426) has suggested that 'hunter-gatherers regard nature as pervasively animated with moral, mystical and mythical significance', and notes the prevalence among them of shamanism as a way of 'entering and conceptualizing such a universe and . . . relating to, channeling and transforming its beings and forces for the benefit of humans'. Ecstasy and transformation pervade shamanic ritual, cosmology and cosmogony; mythical beings from the past such as the Trickster enable and also subvert creation, in a layered and temporally fluid universe (Guenther 1999, 427–30). In description of a specific hunter-gatherer group, the Nyaka of southern India, Bird-David (1999, 259–60) has noted belief in the co-existence alongside themselves

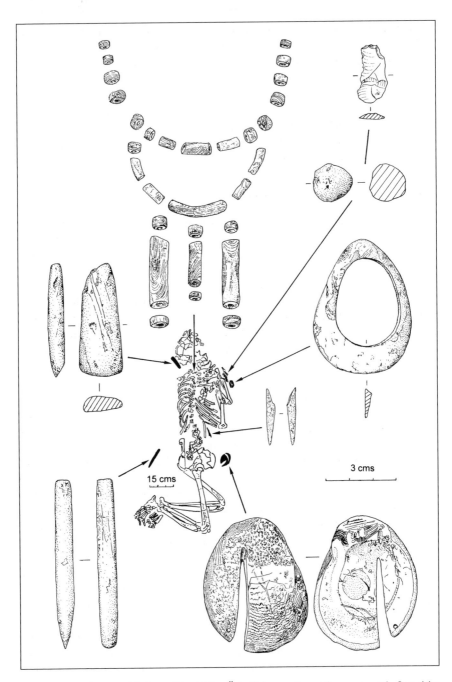

Figure 5.3 Man's grave 28, from Aiterhöfen-Ödmühle, southern Germany, with *Spondylus* beads, bracelet and notched shell, stone tools, bone point and flint artefacts. After Nieszery 1995.

of non-human persons including the deceased, former inhabitants of their area but of different identity, mythical ancestors, naturalistic spirits and non-Nyaka deities including Hindu ones. Contact is kept with these both simply by being in the forest and by annual rituals of possession.

Recurrent themes in the archaeologies discussed here have included longhouses, the communal space between longhouses, animals both wild and tame, sky and earth, and axes, shells and other objects. The creativity and profusion of monumental contruction may therefore owe much to a history of histories, in an intensifying, proliferating and fusing mythic realm.

Monuments and remembering

The recent literature on monuments is considerable (e.g. Bradley 1993; 1998a; Edmonds 1999; Thomas 1999; Tilley 1994; 1999) and has brought many new insights into the character and meaning of monumental constructions of a very wide variety. They stand for this or that idea, their conceptualisation enables other views of the world, and they shape human experience and link it to other realms in profound ways. What is still missing from many accounts, however, is a sense of their temporality. How and at what intervals did they come into existence? This brief discussion is about the temporal rhythms that may be seen in some monuments, particularly as an insight into the way in which rememberings in general may have been played out. Earlier discussion in chapter 2 about routines in the taskscape can also be noted.

Final monumentality is often preceded by modest beginnings. For every monument that went on to be embellished, there may have been other constructions, much harder to recognise, which were short-lived or even ephemeral. In the area around Avebury in north Wiltshire, for example, it is striking how many of the investigated monuments have unspectacular starts. The West Kennet long barrow might have begun as a small sarsen and earth mound, the Horslip long barrow as a series of intercutting pits, the Beckhampton Road long barrow as a setting of sarsen stones and bone deposits, and Millbarrow as a small timber structure (Piggott 1962; Ashbee *et al.* 1979; Whittle 1994). There are both renewal and selection. Continued construction may also be piecemeal. We think easily from a modern architectural perspective of the completed project, but it is possible that the sequence of building was often much more protracted, with successive stages as significant in their own right as the final form. Chambers in some barrows may have been freestanding for a while. There are hints of this at Hazleton, itself overlying a place made significant by occupation or middening (Saville 1990), and new radiocarbon dates from the West Kennet long barrow also allow this possibility.[3] In the case of Wayland's Smithy long barrow (Whittle 1991), there are also indications from new radiocarbon dates that the second, more elaborate version of the monument was effected in stages, the stone chambers freestanding for a while within the trapezoidal area defined by the stone kerb, but with the mound taking much longer to fill in.[4] It has been customary to refer to barrows 1 and 2 here, but really the whole sequence right from its start can be extended into a whole series of punctuated events. The same perspective could also be applied without difficulty to the Windmill Hill enclosure (Whittle *et al*. 1999).

Can we get any closer to the circumstances which triggered particular events and renewals? The need is all the more acute in those cases when the apparent span of remembering is considerable. I have already referred to the chronology of the enclosure idea. The case of barrows with transepted chambers is another example. There are circumstantial and typological arguments for seeing these as relatively late in regional sequences of construction. New dates from Wayland's Smithy along with those from other monuments more or less confirm this view. From this a different perspective emerges. An idea, a way of doing things, was kept in memory for a very long time, over centuries, or a significantly old and rare practice was revived, after a considerable interval. There may be a powerful combination of timelessness and specific circumstance. Ritual tradition may exist in its own time, transmitted from generation to generation in stories and myth, to be enacted at intervals felt to be propitious, or simply contingent upon the actions and intentions of particular individuals. There may also be an important element of creativity in the renewal of tradition.

None of this need be surprising. It is compatible with the earlier discussion of the creative and selective nature of rememberings, and the ways in which these are woven into daily life and into different temporalities. We do not find it problematic that longhouses in the LBK evidently had very varied biographies, some surviving longer or being built and extended in more elaborate forms than others (see Bradley 2001). It is easy to envisage – at least in a general fashion – histories of individuals, marriages, households and alliances, sequences of growth and decline, and runs of success and failure. But while successive longhouses were the product of particular circumstances, their renewal also honoured an idea, of social formation and continuity. Perhaps this kind of perspective needs to be taken to the study of monuments, to bring a sense of the particularities of lived existence to a realm partly characterised by its abstractions.

Remembered forebears: the multiplicity of ancestors

One of the abstractions which I have so far discussed very little is that of ancestry and descent, which I will use as a final example of selective remembering. Even a few examples from the considerable range of practice recorded by ethnographic fieldwork should reinforce a sense of unease with the simplistic way in which ancestry and descent are often treated in current archaeological interpretation. Kopytoff's discussion (1971) of practice among the Suku of Congo is instructive. It is convenient to quote his summary of the sub-Saharan context:

> Ancestors are vested with mystical powers and authority. They retain a functional role in the world of the living, specifically in the life of their living kinsmen . . . African kin-groups are often described as communities of both the living and the dead. The relation of the ancestors to their living kinsmen has

been described as ambivalent, as both punitive and benevolent and sometimes even as capricious. In general, ancestral benevolence is assured through propitiation and sacrifice; neglect is believed to bring about punishment. Ancestors are intimately involved with the welfare of their kin-group but they are not linked in the same way to every member of that group. The linkage is structured through the elders of the kin-group, and the elders' authority is related to their close link to the ancestors.

(Kopytoff 1971, 129)

Not only are the ancestors not the generally benevolent force imagined in much of the archaeological literature, it becomes clear in the case of the Suku, and of other people in the region, that the key distinction is not between the living and the dead but between elders and non-elders. The Suku setting is the corporate matrilineage (Kopytoff 1971, 130). In this, juniors owe respect to seniors, and older seniors, or living elders, look to the dead for guidance and help in times of crisis; of necessity the dead must be approached differently from the living (Kopytoff 1971, 133). Contact is formalised, but the setting of contact appears to be less so: at the graves of people older than their supplicants, or at the intersection of paths; there are no separate or special burial grounds (Kopytoff 1971, 130). Kopytoff concluded (1971, 140) that 'the term "ancestor" sets up a dichotomy where there is a continuum . . . African "ancestors" are more mundane and less mystical than the dead who are objects of "worship" should be in Western eyes'.

Among the Lugbara, mythology and genealogy elide. The scope and content of their mythology have already been described above. The wider social network is conceived of in terms of clans, and clans are conceived of in terms of myth, as noted above; but 'clans are dispersed and are not corporate groups' (J. Middleton 1960, 7). The smaller and segmented descent groups are lineages of varying scope. Within the Lugbara lineage different kinds of ancestors are recognised (J. Middleton 1960, 32–4).[5] On the one hand there are all forebears, including on occasion the living, who form a collectivity in which individuals are not important; the dead are the focus of ritual sacrifice, since they send sickness to the living, and collective shrines are set for them. On the other hand there are individual forebears, who are recognised as direct and significant ancestors (or 'ghosts' in the terminology which Middleton adopts) by agnatic descendants, with whom they are in personal and responsible contact, through the provision of individual shrines. The living make offerings to the varying categories of dead at shrines, since the dead may send sickness to express displeasure with actions seen to weaken or disunite the lineage. The shrine and the cult of the dead become the focus of central values to do with lineage and kinship (J. Middleton 1960, 34–5).

Lugbara shrines are varied and powerful, though they often take the form of simple arrangements of stones, and they are situated in a range of settings from within the settlement to outside it (Figure 5.4). Although ancestry as defined here is so important in Lugbara life, there appears to be no rite of collective burial as described for parts of Madagascar (e.g. Bloch 1971; Mack 1986). The world of the dead lies 'somewhere beneath the surface of the world' (J. Middleton 1982, 150).

Figure 5.4 Simple but powerful stones: a lineage shrine of the Lugbara, placed in the bush. The nearer part is a house for lineage ghosts, and the farther setting, an old grinding stone, is a fertility shrine. From Middleton 1960, by permission of the International African Institute.

The dead are feared as well as revered (J. Middleton 1960, 201; 1982), and as so often elsewhere, funerals are occasions for gatherings, licence, and the important business of realignment (J. Middleton 1960, 202–4; 1982). The dominant rite seems to be individual inhumation, within houses, compounds and elsewhere, and some elders are given burial trees, figs planted at the head of their graves, which become sacred and are referred to in the same term which is translated as collective ancestor (J. Middleton 1960, 66; 1982).

Among the Tiv of northern Nigeria, a belief in genealogy was at the heart of social relationships (Bohannan 1952). 'To know things Tiv one must know Tiv genealogies' (Bohannan 1952, 301), as these were a constant topic of casual and serious discussion, relevant to kinship, marriage, settlement, ritual and other aspects of social existence. While the general belief was that all the many Tiv were descended from one man, Tiv himself, through fourteen to seventeen generations, the more constant concern with descent was played out in the more immediate setting of the lineage and territorial segment, consisting of some 200–1,300 people. In that context, 'three fathers' is the normal range of individual genealogical memory of particular ancestors, beyond which more anonymous ancestors provide a genealogical charter to link back to Tiv (Bohannan 1952, 313). Both genealogy and more general ancestry can be seen as charters, to validate present social relationships, which in turn prove the genealogies (Bohannan 1952, 312, 315). The key criterion is consistency. Genealogies are learnt according to context, need and the accidents of personal contact among kinsmen; the resulting 'ramifications of personal geneal-ogical knowledge . . . vary enormously from one individual to another' (Bohannan 1952, 303). They also change and develop through the course of individual lives. Differences in genealogical knowledge can be seen in the expanding awareness of 10-year-olds, youths of 15, and young men of 25. In Bohannan's account (1952, 304):

> A man over 25 feels that he ought to be able to place every adult male in his minimal lineage in terms of living fathers, in terms of compounds, and in terms of segments-within-the hut. Within his own segment-within-the-hut he can give a fairly complete genealogy in the male line. He is most unlikely to know his father's father's sisters, their marriage guardians, marriage exchanges, and so forth. Many Tiv acquire no more genealogical knowledge. Old men who know no more than this are called 'those of little importance'.

From listening to discussions at moots, inquests and funerals, ambitious men of early middle age can learn much more, and may go on to be recognised as geneal-ogical experts in older age (Bohannan 1952, 304), and 'it is the political leader who is credited with the greatest knowledge of genealogical data in all their ramific-ations' (Bohannan 1952, 307).

Mortuary practices on Madagascar have been much cited as a point of comparison in the British literature on Neolithic ancestral traditions (cf. J. Whitley 2002). As a specific instance of the process of secondary burial (Hertz 1960), the *famidihana* rites at collective tombs of the Merina of central Madagascar (Bloch 1971) have had particularly strong impact. The details suggest a more complex situation. The Merina tombs are or were often placed as a symbol of endurance well away from the foci of daily life (Bloch 1971, 105, 114), the choice of location being further contingent, depending in part on self-interest and practicality (Bloch 1971, 120–2). Some of the groups involved with tomb use may be or have been patrician (Bloch 1971, 45), but defining such groups as permanent corporate descent groups is problematic, since individual choices and circumstances lead to considerable variation and flux (Bloch 1971, 114–20). At a more general level, while there is a descent group ideology, it is hard to capture any fixed sense of descent groups on the ground (Bloch 1971, 216–22).

The Merina tombs themselves often accumulated a collectivity of dead, some of the dead going straight to them and others after temporary burial elsewhere. The occasion of fresh depositions is often the setting for *famidihana*, brief removals, re-wrappings and parades of corpses, which may be much more to do with personal and emotional links with the individual dead, and the conquering of the fear of death, than with the importance as such of undifferentiated ancestors (Bloch 1971, 168–71), important though these *razana* are as an organising principle and even as the basis of moral behaviour (Bloch 1971, 67).

If the 'constant invoking of the ancestors and ancestral practice' (Mack 1986, 17) is widespread, it seems to be because the idea of the ancestors is here linked with the concept of what is 'morally desirable or appropriate in social relations' (Mack 1986, 64). Other beings are recognised, from a creator or god, to the Vazimba or original inhabitants, legendary figures and 'secondary divinities', but it is the ancestors who are the most frequent point and concept of reference (Mack 1986, 64), permeating daily routine as well as guiding special occasions, and converting cattle, for example, from 'mere beasts into a channel of communication' with this other dimension (Mack 1986, 66; cf. Parker Pearson 2000). Studies of groups in Madagascar other than the Merina (e.g. Mack 1986; Parker Pearson 1992) also make it clear how much variation there is to be found, even given the comparatively short known history of human occupation on the island. Burial practices, which are one domain in which the ancestors are encountered, created or invoked, are very varied, involving different modes, techniques and sequences of deposition. Tombs and memorial places vary in their visibility or relative concealment (Mack 1986, 81). Within the practice of secondary burial, there are differing sequences: among the coastal Betsimisaraka and southerly neighbours the retention of the body, collection of materials of decomposition, and then separate burial of these and the skeleton; among the Merina and Betsileo in the centre of the island the speedy burial of the body, unseen decomposition, and then exhumation of bones and their placing in an ancestral tomb (Mack 1986, 72). Bloch has also noted much variation within Merina practice (1971, 155–8). Underlying a wide variety of primary and secondary burials, however, may be a recurrent concern with impurity and pollution (Mack 1986, 70).

Difficulties and possibilities

Ancestors have been much in evidence in the British archaeological literature over the last few years, operating as legitimators of present position and standing for corporate identity. They have not, however, been much discussed in their own right, and are in danger of being over-used (J. Whitley 2002). Ancestors can be defined quite simply, if broadly, as any forebears who are remembered (Bloch 1994). It has been argued that 'claims of communication between the dead and their descendants are universal' (Steadman et al. 1996, 63), though it is unlikely that this is in fact the case. Dealings with forebears, however, are extremely varied (e.g. Bloch 1994; Newell 1976), and my examples and discussion here aim above all to re-introduce a sense of the possible diversities back into archaeological interpretation, linking these in turn to the spectrum of rememberings already considered.

   The simple models of ancestry and descent in use in much of the archaeological literature seem to derive partly from our understanding of our own modern world and partly from the historically limited models which have been anthropology's response to the diversities found in the field (Kuper 1988; M. Strathern 1992b). Two linked archaeological interpretations have been dominant. First, there are generalised or anonymous ancestors, often linked to what have been called 'corporate descent groups' and acting as legitimators of resource control for them in processual and neo-Marxist theory (I. Morris 1991; Meillassoux 1972). In the collective deposits of many western European monuments from the fifth to the third millennium, many bodies have by one process or another been transformed into disarticulated, incomplete and broken remains, which it has been found convenient to connect with Hertz's notion of secondary burial (1960) and in turn with a transformation from living individual to anonymous but powerful ancestor. These collective emphases are then often seen to be replaced at some stage, normally in the third or second millennium BC depending on region, by more closed and individualised systems of descent, focused more on genealogy and specifically remembered individuals. Last (1998a) has given a powerful account of a possible genealogical history in the sequence of burials in a mound at Barnack in the Welland valley.

There are many difficulties with this set of views, and some can be explicitly noted. To filter both anthropological and archaeological observation through the lens of our own world is limiting. The three variables of the Saxe/Goldstein hypothesis – corporate descent groups, scarce resources and formal disposal areas – are only very loosely defined, and even as such do not occur universally together (I. Morris 1991). While the transformation of skeletal remains in archaeological deposits from the fifth to the third millennium BC is certainly a fact, and perhaps an important motif, it is by no means clear in many specific cases that secondary burial as such was the rite in question; *in situ* transformations, disturbance by succeeding depositions, and circulation of remains are all competing possibilities. The Merina example indicates the difference between descent group and descent group ideology. The Lugbara and Tiv examples suggest that generalised ancestry and specific genealogies can be part of a single spectrum of reference to the past. Among the Merina, ancestry may be as much a moral principle as a system of reckoning descent, and here as elsewhere much of immediate concern is to do with relations with remembered individuals, and dealing with other powerful notions such as impurity and the fear of death. Ancestors and systems of descent can be seen as ideologies, open to selective use depending on context, and as ideals often departed from in practice, just as 'kinship-based societies' rely on endless fictions about kinship and operate on the basis of residence and alliance as well as of kinship (Kuper 1988; Scheffler 1966; 1985).

Finally, descent group need not necessarily denote closed descent group. For a start, while many peoples in Africa, for example, do represent their groups as strictly patrilineal or matrilineal, they also in fact recruit from the outside and show considerable flexibility in practice (Scheffler 1985, 9; Kuper 1988). Secondly, other people can be represented as members of 'nonunilineal, ambilineal or cognatic descent groups' (Scheffler 1985, 10; 1966). Unless only unilineally bounded groups are to be called descent groups at all, cognatic groups present particularly interesting possibilities for thinking about the possibilities of forms of descent in the Neolithic. Scheffler has defined (1966, 544) cognatic descent-constructs as 'those in which sex of the linking kinsman at each step is immaterial for the tracing of the continuum [of relatedness] and the continuum itself is significant'. Whereas many African societies conceptualise or claim to conceptualise relationships, rights, obligations and membership in terms of a distinction between lineages and local groups, in highland New Guinea the groupings overlap (Scheffler 1985, 11).

There is no magic formula to be won from the difficult and contested ground of the anthropological literature. It is possible, however, to stress a much greater range of possibilities, an overlap or even conflict between differing concepts which may have been operating simultaneously, and at the same time some kind of linkage between the selective rememberings of descent and the rememberings which permeated everyday existence. People could be seen as having used both genealogy and a more generalised sense of ancestry, one or the other tending to be the dominant metaphor depending on context but neither fully describing actual practice. Members may have been recruited from male and female lines, and from outside any 'closed group', even if at times there is a projection of an idea of restricted belonging.

This might apply as well to LBK cemeteries as to the later constructions with collective deposits of human remains. Both cemetery of individual graves and monumental construction with collective human remains may have evoked or been associated with a number of differing principles or concepts. LBK grave may evoke LBK house, and graves as a collective may evoke the community of the living as well as its past (cf. Bradley 1998a, 46–8). That membership of the household was to some extent open, or open to recruitment from the outside, may be suggested by the strontium isotope analysis of burials from Flomborn and Schwetzingen, in this case interpreted as indicating that women of regional highland origin came into Rhine valley settlements (Price et al. 2001).

In the case of the collective deposits in the monumental and other constructions from the fifth to the third millennium BC, the interpretation in both early and indeed more recent descriptions of the human remains themselves is frequently in terms of close physical resemblances suggesting a more or less closed family relationship. This has never really been adequately tested against an explicit set of expectations or challenged, and it may be that researchers have been predisposed to see a family relationship because the notion of family is the currency of the modern world (cf. M. Strathern 1992b). On the other hand, the language of very recent interpretations in the British literature has been in terms of 'the ancestors', some of my own accounts included (e.g. Whittle 1996, chapter 1). A number of contrasts could perhaps now be offered. The formation of many (but there is no need to insist on all) collective deposits may have been the result of successive depositions of whole corpses, with subsequent disturbance, breakage, disarticulation, re-arrangement, and even circulation and removal. Interpretation has concentrated on the end result rather than the process of formation. That may speak much more for the immediacy of individual deaths, grief, funeral ceremonies and a marking of specific relationships which we can consider genealogical, than for ancestral veneration. Placings and groupings by age, sex or gender, and position within a construction (nearer to or further from the entrance, left or right, and so on: cf. Shanks and Tilley 1982; Thomas 1988), could also speak far more for an intense interest in the *persona* of particular individuals than in the generalities of 'the ancestors'. The body itself may have been an important metaphor (Fowler 2000), linked to the further metaphor of transformation (Whittle et al. 1999). It has also been argued that the dissolution of articulation was an important concept in such practices in eastern Britain, referencing relationships with others and marking the 'temporality of dying' (Lucas 1996, 104).

In arguing for the general possibility and plausibility of open descent groups, it is important to keep closed descent groups in mind. There are architectural arrangements which seem to demand a sense of contrast or opposition. Segmentation and bilaterality in chamber layouts have too often been treated in the long British literature as a matter of disembodied architectural evolution, on the path to greater or lesser spatial complexity. The lateral chambered Cotswold-Severn long cairns are a good case in point. It can be shown that there are general contrasts in the nature of the deposition of human bone between these and the other main two Cotswold-Severn architectural variants (Thomas 1988). But what are we to make of the often striking placing of chambers back to back, closely set but each accessible only from its own long side of the cairn, as at Hazleton or Ascott-under-Wychwood? Are these something to do with the mythical dimensions of group history or the territorial allegiances of the living, or could they also suggest demarcation in terms of membership?

In the Lugbara case described earlier, genealogy and ancestry were part of a single conceptual scheme, and in practice the Tiv remembered only those forebears and ancestors as suited the contingent situation. In the same way, it can be suggested that concepts of ancestry were themselves open to transformation from the sixth to the fourth and third millennia BC. A sense of beginnings and general descent may have been embedded in the patterns of daily routine in the LBK, reinforced by material exchanges or acquisitions from the east or south-east. Parts of the LBK house have been suggested as shrines (Bradley 2001), and in any case the Lugbara case indicates the general possibility of very small settings and even trees having considerable significance. Descent may have been partly tracked through the house, and it seems that there were different categories of remembered forebears as represented in settlement burials and cemetery burials. In the changing world of north-west Europe from the late fifth millennium onwards, there must also have been much variability. Memory, held especially in my view in myth and story, seems to have connected these two worlds, enabling the longhouse–long mound and enclosure links which have already been discussed. But though connected to long rememberings in this way, each was the setting for rather different kinds of interaction: on the one hand the playing out of ideas of relationship, in large part perhaps genealogical, but connected also to notions of transformation, and on the other hand the celebration of an intense sociality and new materiality. Ancestors in the general sense implied by much of the recent British literature may have come only gradually into the picture. Many early constructions may have had little to do with 'the ancestors'. Many early constructions in southern Britain begin in a modest way, becoming monumentalised only at the end of their sequence. By contrast in western Britain and in Ireland, there were monumental if compact constructions potentially from an early date. It is hard to see a long history in the construction of portal dolmens and related monuments. These seem to have nothing directly to do with the longhouse memory, and may be related much more plausibly to indigenous ideas about the relationship of people to their landscape and its mythical history, and to their routine and other movements in the landscape (Bradley 2000; Tilley and Bennett 2001; Cummings 2001). Rather than generalised human ancestors, such constructions may have referred much more to the realm of myth, first inhabitants, spirits and creators.

The complexity of the situation should be underlined. If constructions such as portal dolmens were indeed early in western areas,[6] why did they appear here and why at this time? Their hypothetically early date might be connected in some way to the other signs of early contact between Ireland and north-west France, such as in the movement of domestic cattle in the form of bones, meat or even live animals, but it could also be an indication of some kind of indigenous reaction or response to changes afoot also in southern and eastern Britain, where an element of intrusive population still cannot be excluded. In turn, monumentality in southern and eastern Britain may have been influenced by the prior existence of constructions of powerful renown to the west.

In complex histories such as these, with remembering in general a creative, selective and contingent process, not everything need have been held in memory simultaneously or revealed all at once. In discussing the issue of whether any people really lack a durational or linear sense of time, as well as having a concept of static or cyclical time, Bloch has referred to evidence from Bali, and to 'the long conversation that is Balinese society', in which 'at some time, one notion of time is used, and others, another . . .' (1977, 284). He suggested that static or cyclical time was something most often expressed in ritual contexts, whereas linear, durational time was encountered in the practical spheres of agriculture, village and politics. The contrasts suggested by the archaeology under discussion here may be more blurred, but there are powerful general notions of partiality, fragmentation, contrast, and overlap in the long conversations which might have brought a 'Neolithic' world into being.

My discussions in this chapter have been both comparative and general, and in the next chapter I will try both to pull together the different strands so far considered separately, and to link these to more detailed treatment of specific archaeological situations.

Chapter 6

Lives

As we saw in chapter 3, the anthropologist Adam Kuper concluded his review of the concept of culture with the view that this can always be broken down, that we have multiple identities, and that culture could be thought of as a public discourse, which can be broken down into limitless constituent parts (Kuper 1999, 246). Likewise the anthropologist Maurice Bloch has referred to the 'the long conversation that is Balinese society', in which 'at some time, one notion of time is used, and others, another' (Bloch 1977, 284). Archaeologists wrestling with the relationship between 'agency' and 'structure' and the satisfactory definition of these terms may have much to learn from this kind of approach to identity and action in the world. One recent insightful account of the variation in depositional practice in LBK settlements characterised the LBK as emerging 'between structure and agency', somewhere between 'shared principles and individual histories and local solutions', and suggested that the 'locus of that dialectic is the house' (Last 1998b, 19). Another recent account has also examined the scope for agency in the LBK, using Habermas's concept of *Lebenswelt* and Bourdieu's notion of doxa, to examine whether change was simply unimaginable or whether orthodoxy was promoted by the suppression of change (Sommer 2001). There is a welcome attempt to examine issues of uniformity and diversity in different material practices through the history of the LBK, and in terms of controlled, negotiable and neutral 'sectors', but the conclusion (e.g. Sommer 2001, fig. 3) remains a generalising contrast between houseplans, lithics, pottery and domesticates.

So far in this book I have tried to illustrate, through a combination of ethnographic and archaeological examples, the actuality of multiple identities, of long conversations and public and private discourses, of the messiness of existence with its mesh of routines, individualism, shared values, life courses, rememberings and intentionalities. I have looked at a complex array of dimensions, from learning about the world and bodily engagement with it through such basic routines as sleeping, eating or moving, and such basic features as the postures in which the body is held, to the at times fluid notions of identity that may go far beyond the physical individual, involving also a network of loyalties, affiliations, allegiances and values. I have also tried to show the importance of animals in the construction of identity and people's understanding of the world, and I have argued that multiple kinds of remembering, regularly selective and creative, help to orientate people in the world not only with reference to grander schemes of beginnings and descent but also in relation to how daily lives were carried forward. I have not said as much directly as I could about material culture or the materiality of existence, but this is implied throughout.

This should all indicate the scope for breaking down 'lumped' concepts such as culture, agency and structure. There is little need for the kind of theoretical abstraction that characterises so much of recent debate, and the archaeological record (if this term is allowable in a neutral sense) should of itself in fact encourage and enable a much more fragmented and complex approach to interpretation. As John Robb (1999, 7) has argued, 'top-down cultural analysis tends to portray cultural systems as deceptively logical and unrealistically consistent'. In this chapter therefore, I want to try to give a further sense of the complexity of things in actual situations. I have chosen the LBK, the early Neolithic of the Alpine foreland, and the early Neolithic of southern England in contrast to that of western Britain. I have already drawn on these in earlier chapters. I would like to have included the early Neolithic Körös culture of the Great Hungarian Plain here, but I have already discussed this at some length in previous chapters. I do not have the opportunity here for either the extended synthesis or the detailed treatment of individual settings, contexts and situations which would be desirable. Rather I want to try to give some sense in each brief example of the layerings of existence and of the histories to which these belong. In this regard, the Körös culture, or rather the history of people in the southern part of the Tisza drainage basin between 6000 and 5500 BC, is in various ways part of the history of the emergence and thereby the character of the LBK, or rather the history of the multiple existences of longhouse people through the woodlands and river valleys of central and western Europe. For reasons of practicality it is hard to avoid using these generalising labels, and my accounts will not easily avoid a generalising tone, but it is easy to see how dangerous this can be. I have chosen the three case studies to illustrate differences between situations, but one may also reflect on the extent of variation within each situation and on the degree to which experience was shared across existences which we normally choose to represent as different.

Longhouse lives

The very way in which the evidence for the LBK comes to us encourages generalisation. The partialities of survival and research promote this. Some of the biggest and best studied faunal assemblages are in the Paris basin (Hachem 1995; 1997; 1999; 2000); the Aldenhovener Platte remains the most extensively investigated and published landscape (Lüning and Stehli 1994; Lüning 1997a); and some of the best published burial grounds, such as Aiterhofen (Nieszery 1995; cf. Jeunesse 1997), have come in recent years from southern Bavaria, with far better preservation of the human remains than from the better contextualised examples of the Aldenhovener Platte or Elsloo in Dutch Limburg. With the floor levels of longhouses almost without exception gone, the widespread similarities in house plans, pot styles, stone tools and grave rites encourage us to think in terms of some kind of network, not only extensive but active and interconnected throughout its total distribution. Other studies have already shown how regional or local practices can in fact be seen throughout (e.g. Modderman 1988; Coudart 1998; Veit 1996; Orschiedt 1998; Zimmermann 1995; de Grooth 1997; Last 1998b), underlining the already quoted dictum of Bruno Latour (1993, 117) that 'the network is always local'. The emphasis here, with space restricted and with individual case studies anyway easily available to readers, is on suggesting ways in which multiple, layered identities could be thought about within the realms of the LBK.

History is the first dimension to reflect upon. We are still not sure when the LBK came into existence and it need not be the case that all its later constituent elements somehow came simultaneously into being. The development of the rather simple pottery that characterises the *älteste* LBK, for example, might have either preceded or followed the emergence of longhouses. My interest here is principally in those longhouses. It is normally estimated that these were in existence by 5500 BC, with suggestions that they could go back to 5600 BC (e.g. Sommer 2001, 250; Stäuble 1995); evidence from the site of Brunn II just outside Vienna could even take this back a little earlier (Peter Stadler, pers. comm.). It has also been suggested that this first phase was prolonged, lasting up to four hundred years (Sommer 2001, 254; cf. Price *et al.* 2001, fig. 1). Sites of the *älteste* LBK have been found scattered across the area from north-west Hungary to the middle Rhine (Gronenborn 1999, fig. 1). By now quite familiar lines of argument suggest a choice between colonisation from somewhere in northern Hungary and acculturation of the indigenous population (summarised with references in Sommer 2001, 251–4). The case for the appropriate conditions for a major colonisation is not overwhelming (Whittle 1996, chapter 6). Both faunal assemblages with their strong presence of wild animals (Uerpmann and Uerpmann 1997) and lithic assemblages with strong similarities in point technology (Mateiciucová 2001) indicate the possibility of major continuities with indigenous practice. Lithic materials like the radiolarite from the northern Hungarian source of Szentgál or flint from the Dutch Limburg source of Rijkholt-St Geertruid were moved widely through the *älteste* LBK sphere, and both sources had been used previously in the Mesolithic (Gronenborn 1997). The simplicity of *älteste* LBK pottery is compatible with imitation of ceramic styles to the south-east. On the other hand, genetic evidence allows for an element of incoming population, which might be dateable to this period (Sykes 1999). Gronenborn in particular (1999) has argued for interactions and fusions especially on the western edge of the *älteste* LBK distribution, between incoming LBK populations (of whatever origin) and other populations using La Hoguette and Limburg pottery. The continued reality of such fusions seems to be reinforced by the recent strontium isotope analyses of the burial grounds at Flomborn and Schwetzingen in the middle Rhine in the middle or Flomborn phase of the LBK (Price *et al.* 2001).

The general argument for a fusion of populations could now be extended, and the longhouse may have a particular role in this process. Since Hungarian archaeologists have long debated the role of the local Szatmár group in the emergence of the AVK or local Plain variant of the LBK (Kalicz and Makkay 1977), it is possible that the LBK emerged in the area of the Körös culture east of the Tisza river on the Great Hungarian Plain. It is perhaps far more likely in the present state of evidence that the LBK emergence is to be located somewhere within the area bounded by the Danube as it makes its great turn, the eastern end of the Alps and the Drava river to the south. Here there is evidence for small, scattered Starčevo-Körös populations, up to and level with Lake Balaton (e.g. Kalicz et al. 1998; Bánffy 2000), and further survey and excavation will presumably produce more sites of the kind seen at Szentgyörgyvölgy-Pityerdomb, where two single-phase structures up to 14.5 m long defined by posts and bedding trenches were found (Bánffy 2000). There is, however, little immediately local evidence for a Mesolithic presence, and in this regard the situation west of the Danube is comparable with the contemporary one east of the Tisza. There is little evidence for direct Mesolithic–Neolithic contact, and rather than any kind of frontier there was a limit to the Körös distribution and a zone to its north largely empty of a regular Mesolithic presence; the southward movement of obsidian, however, shows interaction across or through this zone.

Whichever of these two areas – west of the Danube or east of the Tisza, or indeed both – saw the emergence of the LBK, we can perhaps begin better to define the context in which this took place. This was not obviously one of major increases of population on either side of an unstable frontier; the situation may rather be to do with contact between low-density populations. In this setting, the appearance of the first longhouses is of particular interest (Figure 6.1). Post-framed structures in the northern Starčevo and Körös cultures were neither particularly common nor substantial, examples rarely exceeding 10 m in length (Lenneis 1997); though there are exceptions, many Körös structures may have been quite short-lived shelters, consisting largely of walls framed by bundles of reeds and covered by daub, with only a very light post or stake frame. Many of these seem to have been burnt at the end of their use. The longhouse is much bigger, though it is not clear whether any of those belonging to the *älteste* LBK much exceed 20 m. At Bruchenbrücken, Friedberg, for example, from the western part of the distribution (Lüning 1997b), houses were little more than 16–17 m long, and defined by outer bedding trenches and few internal postholes, though these were definitely arranged in cross-rows of three (Stäuble 1997). In other cases, many more internal posts have been found (Stäuble 1997, 67; Neth 1999, fig. 72). The longhouse could have been created for the first time by a larger group coming together and deciding, say, to double the size of a conventional structure, to take in more people or to make visible and more enduring a union or fusion between people of differing identities and pasts.

If there is anything in this speculation, it could suggest that the longhouse itself had a powerfully symbolic history *from the outset*. The idea was widely copied by people as far west as the Rhine, though there also seems to be quite a lot of variability in these *älteste* LBK houses, and given that there may have been varied constituents of this population, the house as fusion may have been accepted from the outset as a form promoting the integration of people of varying identity. The

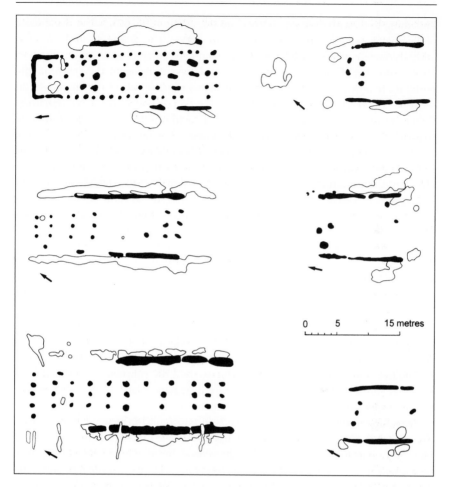

Figure 6.1 House plans of the *älteste* LBK (arrows indicate north). Clockwise from top left: Miskovice; Bruckenbrücken; Gerlingen; Bruckenbrücken; Rosdorf; and Bylany. After Hampel.

sequence at Bruchenbrücken seems to have been quite a long one, and as far as can be seen the practice was of replacement by rebuilding rather than by burning. Visible continuity was perhaps part of this emergent history.

If the *älteste* LBK phase did last for a longer rather than shorter time, the implication would be that subsequent developments were more accelerated or intensified. Two features are of particular interest, both suggestive of the possibility that the developing house structure itself served to go on evoking a powerful past. In the houses which emerged after the *älteste* phase (Modderman 1988), the Y-configuration in the centre of larger houses might also be a reference to the past; the first of these settings had probably appeared in the *älteste* phase (Neth 1999, fig. 72). It might be something to do with doorways in the long sides (Veit 1996, 62), but in the absence of floorplans this is classically difficult to prove. The arrangement seems too arbitrary merely to fit or facilitate arrangements for entrance and exit. It seems to offer a complex of possible symbolisms. It draws attention to the centre of the building. It provides an orientation, normally to the east side of the longhouses in question. It appears to emphasise above all the central post of the Y-configuration. Could this draw on cosmological principles, or could it refer in some way to simpler structures such as tents, older than the longhouse, but not forgotten? In turn, the Y-configuration passed out of fashion in later LBK building (Modderman 1988), but in both phases the idea of tripartite compartmentalisation was important. This has normally been interpreted in more or less functional terms, though in differing ways, from central basic living unit, with granary and stall as additions (Modderman 1988), to control of women in rear portions furthest from the entrance (Hodder 1990), or the use of the northern, sometimes planked portion as a mortuary shrine (Bradley 2001). One argument for the use of the southern or south-eastern part of the longhouse as granary has been the doubling of posts in some instances in this portion (Modderman 1988). But this doubling of posts is not universally present (Coudart 1998). Perhaps what was important was the symbolic representation of a union of differences. Whether or not architectural compartmentalisation exactly mirrored the social composition of the inhabitants of a particular longhouse, the codified building practice could have served to evoke a history of bringing different ideas or people together. Compartmentalisation is not a major feature of earliest longhouses, and becomes more prominent as the LBK continued to expand both outwards and within the area of its primary distribution, and as an earlier history became both more remote and more important.

Something of the same kind may have been important in the way longhouse lives were oriented. This may have varied. It has been argued that the general pattern of longhouse orientations can be related to the general direction from which LBK people came (Bradley 2001; 2002). Since the argument for orientation according to prevailing winter winds is unconvincing (Mattheusser 1991), this has much to recommend it, though it can be noted that in more northerly and westerly areas the idea of orientation in opposition to the coasts has also been mooted (Coudart 1998, 88–9). It is also to accept that the spread of the LBK was due to a colonisation which followed a regular path, which earlier discussion shows may be a simplification of a complex process. It remains plausible nonetheless to think in terms of a general orientation towards a sense of beginnings, even if this mental map should not be seen as a literal one. It is something that may have become more important with the passage of time, just as the movement of *Spondylus* down long paths from the east became a more marked feature as the LBK developed (Willms 1985; Sommer 2001, 262). The movement of axes is another feature which might have served to orientate people to far-away places. In all cases, however, there may have been other groundings. If the longhouse was not only a central metaphor but also a central physical fact in the LBK, then the layout of these structures, both as individual entities and as more or less nucleated or dispersed groupings depending on the case, must have encouraged a certain way of moving around the domestic focus, a combination, hard to put into words, of distancing between individual longhouses, progression around the long sides of buildings, movement past flanking ditches with their placed deposits of sherds and bones, and entry to and exit from the compartmentalised spaces within structures. There may in nearly all cases have been an important sense of local orientation, or grounding in the local landscape. This has hardly been explored in LBK studies at all. Bruchenbrücken provides an early example of orientation to the local river, and there are many others, such as Cuiry-lès-Chaudardes in the Aisne valley. In the same way, particular settlement clusters had local orientation in terms of their normal lithic sources (e.g. Zimmermann 1995; de Grooth 1997) as well as towards more exotic items coming from further afield. All these local aspects may have been as much at the heart of the experience of longhouse lives as the more metaphysical orientation to a sense of beginnings. It is tempting to speculate that the latter might have been a matter especially for older people, a kind of understanding reached with seniority.

We assume that while the LBK settlement was in existence, it contained long-houses. The longhouse stands as the central fact of residence. When one building came to an end, so another was constructed to replace it. The longhouse comes easily to stand for permanence and continuity, and this finds uncanny echoes in ethnographic accounts of the perpetuity of the house idea and of the 'metaphorical immortality of the social groups who identify with them' in many other settings (e.g. Waterson 2000, 177). Though the intention in this chapter is to focus on the archaeological evidence, it is worth quoting directly from Waterson's account of house dwellers in South Sulawesi, Indonesia, as a foil to what makes the LBK distinctive:

> The physical and spiritual components of house value – the heirlooms, bones, and spirits of the dead as well as the placentas of the newly born – anchor people to place and to their ancestral origins. People's identities are thus grounded in the landscape, the physical house functioning as a material sign for the social memories that localize groups to certain places (houses, fields, tombs). Houses create simultaneous spatial and temporal networks for conceptualizing how social groups are linked to one another, because of their references to specific historical memories of descent and affinal relationships that are construed as relationships between houses.
>
> (Waterson 2000, 177)

At least three features in combination mark out the distinctiveness of the LBK. We must envisage a steady pattern of recruitment to households, through local migra-tion and marriage. The potential value of the recent strontium isotope analyses (Price *et al.* 2001) in this regard is obvious. Simply because of the variation in their size and duration, apart from anything else, it is highly unlikely that individual longhouses all constituted closed social groupings. It is far more plausible that these were part of a network. One recent study of the distribution of distinctive motifs on pottery from sites on the Aldenhovener Platte, over a distance of only a few kilo-metres and across two or three local stream valleys, has shown how settlements, sometimes close neighbours but sometimes a little further apart, are linked by the use of such decorative techniques (Kolhoff 1999, figs 52–60). This is interpreted as part of an exogamous, virilocal residence pattern, in which daughters learn potting from their mothers and take their knowledge to local (and presumably other) settlements on marriage (Kolhoff 1999, 120–2). Neat though this scheme is, it might be as attractive to think in terms of a more generalised local network of material exchanges between kin groups, alliances or other social groupings. It presumably need not be the case that there was rigidly one daughter per household. Whoever did make pots, these patterns might also suggest a certain general fluidity in household membership.

If the house can be seen as a metaphor, so too can the human body be seen as standing for a lattice of relationships. Just as the individual longhouse came to an end, so too did the human body. There is a striking general contrast between the state and condition of bodies found within settlements on the one hand and in formal disposal areas or burial grounds on the other. In some areas, it may be that the cemetery was a feature that belonged to preeminent or senior settlements, or served a wider locality while placed closest to major settlements. The examples of both Niedermerz on the Aldenhovener Platte and Elsloo in Dutch Limburg could be thought of in this way. Whether this was a universal model is less clear. There is some basis for seeing burial grounds in tributary valleys of the Danube in southern Bavaria (Nieszery 1995) as belonging to a smaller orbit of settlements, if not to individual settlements. In both cases, however, the burial ground presented whole bodies, consciously positioned with material things carefully placed around them, redolent of identities appropriate to age and gender (Hofmann 2001). The history of an LBK burial ground often appears to begin a little later than that of the local settlements, the accretion of individual grave plots, in most cases presumably identifiable and in some way permanently marked, mirroring the succession of longhouses within settlement foci. But the body within the settlement was often treated very differently (Veit 1996; Orschiedt 1998). Here there is considerable variation in the placing of adult remains in relation to longhouses (mainly in various pits, at varying stages of *their* biographies), in the completeness of the skeleton (often partial) and its arrangement (often disordered in comparison to that seen in formal 'graves'), and in the association with material objects (often very few being present). Child burials often present a contrast, being both more complete and often apparently being placed close to particular longhouses. A series of contrasts could be suggested (cf. Pluciennik 2002). Just as the body selected for formal disposal in a separate burial ground could stand for the longhouse, or the idea of longhouses, so the partial and disordered remains found within settlements could stand for the possibility and reality of the finite existence and eventual dissolution of the longhouse. The force of the idea of longhouse continuity took its strength perhaps from the more mundane facts of frequent replacements, alterations and endings.

There are too many longhouses. For all their bulk, many if not most longhouses may have lasted for far shorter periods than their robust construction would have allowed. The sequence worked out for the Aldenhovener Platte (Lüning and Stehli 1994), probably currently the most detailed of its kind, and with fourteen or more phases, rests on the assumption of about twenty-five years per house generation. If the *älteste* LBK phase is to be seen as lasting longer, then this figure might even be seen as a maximum. But these structures could have lasted far longer than a generation (Bradley 1996, 247), being constructed of substantial oak timbers.[1] While seniority may have been one important principle guiding what was placed in graves with whom, and while the relative seniority of individual settlements may have been important at local or regional level, it does not seem – and in contrast to the ethnography of say the Malagasy Zafimaniry (Bloch 1992; 1998) – that ageing was an important consideration in the value placed on LBK longhouses. For all their bulk, these could be thought of as relatively ephemeral. What was important was their frequent replacement. If there is comparatively little evidence for the burning of LBK longhouses, then these were presumably simply abandoned, or possibly de-roofed and left, their timbers lasting for longer and eventually collapsing to form identifiable low mounds (Bradley 1996). There was then a play between endings and continuities. While the idea of the longhouse was maintained, any one example was definitely finite in its duration. The longhouse was therefore something constantly open to discussion, evaluation and negotiation.

We do not know the circumstances in which individual longhouses came to an end at this kind of generational pulse. They could as well be to do with shifting histories of the alliances or groupings which constituted them as with the deaths of prominent or leading members. To this house biography we should add the lives of others involved. What happened when a longhouse was abandoned, say on the death of a senior member? There would have been other older members, but also younger ones, recent incomers and children, who would all have been re-absorbed into another household. It often seems to be the case that the number of houses suggested per phase fluctuates through the history of a settlement, and in that situation relocation may have been to other existing households rather than in a direct house replacement. This potential discontinuity at the heart of longhouse lives has been little commented upon. Any LBK individuals surviving into mature adulthood might have belonged in the course of their existence to two or three different physical structures.

To this punctuated life course in turn can be added a variety of domains in the taskscape. These would have had diverse localities, temporalities and socialities. As I have noted in earlier chapters, the LBK taskscape extends outwards from the longhouse itself. Flint working, plant preparation and possibly animal butchery seem to have taken place in appointed places around the longhouse, and other activities were conducted in the spaces in between longhouses. Other activities would have taken people out into the landscape to varying distances and in varying groups. It is possible that by the established phases of the LBK cereal cultivation was practised in small fixed plots or gardens (summarised in Lüning 2000; see also Bogaard 2002), relatively close to longhouses. Such gardens would therefore often have been long-lasting, and part of the sense of place of a household or community.[2]

If the longhouse was merely part of a wider lattice of relationships, then people – perhaps particularly women if they were responsible for the maintenance of gardens – would probably have had access to or at least knowledge of a series of such places. This hypothetically female space, prominent especially in the spring and summer, would have been crossed by other, perhaps male activities. Let us suppose that animal herding and flint procurement were the responsibility principally of males. Cattle, sheep and pigs would have been tended at differing ranges from settlements. Taking animals to water must have been part of daily routine, and I have already noted the possible significance of wells as locales for social interaction. As we have seen, it has been argued from the Aisne valley evidence that there was some kind of specialisation in herding and hunting (Hachem 1995; 1997; 1999; 2000), which would give added significance to intersecting paths and routines involved in animal keeping, but I have suggested that this specialisation may also be to do with other factors such as household composition and history. Modest amounts of flint were procured at distances from settlements (Zimmermann 1995; de Grooth 1997), possibly on the basis of annual visits made perhaps chiefly by men.

The products and histories of these activities and socialities were in turn brought back to the communal spaces of the longhouses. It seems clear from various studies that life around the longhouse was carried on in a patterned kind of way, in so far as various sorts of deposition took place in a recurrent manner. This can be seen not only in the established phases of the LBK (e.g. Last 1998b; Hachem 2000) but in its earliest stage too (e.g. Stäuble 1997). There is also quite a lot of variability from setting to setting (Last 1998b, 35–6). It is also striking that the quantities of material remaining in LBK pits and the ditches flanking longhouses are comparatively modest (e.g. Last 1998b, 26). Two suggestions can be offered to make some sense of these observations. On the one hand, life around the longhouse may have been characterised not only by a more intense kind of sociality and gregariousness, but also by more formality or adherence to patterned ways of doing things. On the other hand, life was clearly not carried on only at longhouses. Unless we envisage original living surfaces thickly carpeted with the remains of occupation, the evidence could be taken to suggest, despite the sheer bulk of the longhouses themselves, modest numbers of people, not always present. Life away from the longhouse settlements might also have been, speculatively, carried on with a greater freedom. People came and went, some to a greater extent than others, depending on their age, gender and affiliations. Longhouses and associated places and socialities anchored people in particular locales, though not necessarily one only. It is as though there was a flow in the life course of these people, in which the longhouse, itself the product of a particular history at the beginning of it all, represented the possibility and means of periodic re-assembly of the social group. Something of that flow, it seems to me, is captured in the nature of the designs on LBK pottery, from the earliest but especially from the middle phase onwards: the bands as paths, straight or curving, going round the pot and round again without either starting point or ending, the infill motifs as footprints of people or animals,[3] or particular ones like the so-called music-note as punctuations or pauses in lives characterised by movement.

If no one model of LBK society has yet been agreed as acceptable (e.g. Sommer 2001, 258–60), this perhaps underlines the reality of multiple identities. Rather than seek to define a single structure, or uncover a dominant kind of agency, we could see the moral community of the LBK as a nexus constituted in varied dimensions. Memory of history brought an idea, perhaps an ideal, of fusion, together with a sense of orientation. The longhouse and longhouse groupings required a network of affiliations and allegiances, and the success of particular foci tended to concentrate people through time in places of prowess and renown. It is perhaps no accident that the striking new evidence for acts of interpersonal violence in the LBK is collective in nature: involving something like an extended household in the case of Talheim, and a larger grouping in the case of Asparn (summarised in Sommer 2001, 259).[4] There was some fluidity in residence and longhouse membership, and individuals can be thought of as constituted differently at different stages in their lives. A principle of seniority may have been important, marked in some cases in exotic items like amphibolite axes and with *Spondylus* shells being associated with older men (summarised in Sommer 2001, 259). In other cases, such as the Aiterhofen cemetery (Nieszery 1995), the oldest men had fewer *Spondylus* ornaments than their adult juniors and more local items such as fox mandibles and arrowheads, suggesting perhaps a passing on of exotic valuables and a turning to concern for the guarding and continuity of the community (Hofmann 2001, 56). The orbit of lives may have been largely local and regional, but there was interest too in things from farther afield. Whether there was any conscious sense of the totality of the LBK distribution is quite unclear. Involvement in exchange networks seems to have been a recurrent goal, and other values may have revolved around reputation, prowess and hospitality. The replacement and continuity of the longhouse itself was clearly a major concern. It is hard to see a single principle framing membership of the longhouse group, since memory, generalised ancestry and specific genealogies may all coincide in it. The descent principles of the longhouse grouping could as well have begun as open and bilateral as closed and unilineal. The tensions within LBK society suggested by the recent evidence for violence might in time have focused around issues of succession, rather than around the social costs of display (Bogucki 1996) or competition for scarce resources (Windl 1999).

Shorthouse settings

The wealth of evidence from the settlements of the Alpine foreland has been known since the mid-nineteenth century. Here there is no problem, as with the LBK, with non-existent house floors or occupation surfaces, though little survives absolutely intact or undamaged by various post-depositional processes. The wealth of timbers has allowed the development of detailed dendrochronologies, and sophisticated analyses of plant and animal remains have been noted in earlier chapters. Curiously, however, and almost in inverse proportion to the quantities of good data, the region does not figure large in broader discussions about the beginning of the Neolithic in its wider central and western European context, and certainly not so far in debates about identity and agency. In this section I want to explore some of the possibilities not only for a rich archaeology of daily routine but also for another set of beginnings, orientations and identities. While the term 'longhouse' is ubiquitous, its foil 'shorthouse' is rarely used. It is as though the evidence of this area, because of its preservation and abundance, has persuaded us of its typicality and normality. The shorthouse setting should emerge, however, not only as a contrast to that of the longhouse but as distinctive in its own right.

As with the LBK, but in different ways, beginnings and memory were important. Though at its geographical heart, this is the neglected Mesolithic–Neolithic transition of Europe. Much general attention has rightly been given to the striking delay between the arrival in the mid-sixth millennium BC of the LBK on the fringes of the north European plain and the eventual transitions in the Ertebølle culture which led to the rapid emergence of the south Scandinavian Neolithic at the very end of the fifth millennium BC. An almost comparable timelag in the Alpine foreland has not attracted similar comment. It seems legitimate to argue that the same sorts of process may have been at work: a strong sense of indigenous regional identity, and a satisfactory system of indigenous resource exploitation. This could have been coupled with awareness of developments on the outside and a willingness to experiment with some of them, as suggested by the apparently sixth millennium BC phase of cereal cultivation in the area of Lake Zürich and possible experimentation with sheep and goats in sites further west (Erny-Rodmann et al. 1997; Chaix 1997; Gronenborn 1999). It is possible that the orientation of people in the Alpine foreland at this time was as much to the west and south as to the north.

As in south Scandinavia, there is no convincing external factor which 'explains' the shift to new practices towards the end of the fifth millennium BC, though no doubt some would regard climatic variations around the Alpine foreland in the same way as suggested changes in the salinity of the Baltic at this time. If indigenous communities in the Alpine foreland had in some sense resisted full adoption of new practices earlier on, despite their ready and close availability, why did they choose to adopt them now? Was this simply the point at which convergence became more complete? Was there a broader awareness of things that were going on elsewhere, such that it is no accident that so much change is concentrated in the latter part of the fifth millennium BC in western Europe as a whole? If such a link were to be sought, it might have something to do with the end of longhouse existence. The chronologies suggest a beginning for the Alpine foreland Neolithic around 4300 BC; the last Rössen longhouses probably date a little before that. A changed character of existence in the area of primary Neolithic settlement – simply less *different* with the demise of the longhouse – might more easily have encouraged or enabled the adoption of new practices. The scale of change may not have been here as immediately profound as often imagined. There were additions rather than replacements. To patterns of residential and logistical mobility were added more durable structures, and to patterns of plant collection and large game hunting were added small-scale cultivations and varied herdings. As we have seen in earlier chapters, the subsistence patterns in the earlier centuries of the Alpine foreland Neolithic were far from fixed or stable. If there were difficulties with climatic deterioration around the thirty-seventh and thirty-sixth centuries BC, it was perhaps rather more a case of accentuating a still active tradition of use of wild resources, than a dramatic reversion to ways of doing things long abandoned. While this need not reflect the situation everywhere within the varied settings of the Alpine foreland, I find the evidence from the Wauwilermoos to be notable. Here there are both Mesolithic and Neolithic sites. Both sets tend to be arranged along short lengths of the lake- or marsh-edge. In particular, the layout of the Mesolithic site of Schötz 7 is strikingly similar to those of Egolzwil 3 and 5: both in terms of extent, and of the distribution, density and treatment of the animal remains and flint residues which are to be found in both (compare Wyss 1979, Faltplan 2 and 4 with Stampfli 1976, Faltplan 1). What really distinguishes the two situations is the presence of light timber buildings in Egolzwil 3 and 5, neither of which need have been long-lasting or indeed permanent occupations (Figure 6.2).

If there were notable links in the LBK to beginnings or to believed beginnings in the east, activated through longhouse orientations and the movement of axes and *Spondylus* shells, the *lack* of connection to the longhouse world is equally striking in the Alpine foreland. As noted earlier, it has been suggested that there is some echo of longhouse arrangements in the layout of functionally differentiated structures in east Jura lake sites (Pétrequin 1989, 504), and the terraced plan of sites like Niederwil might also evoke the compartmentalised linearity of the longhouse, but mostly the layouts of sites suggest a radically different sort of orientation. The emphasis from the beginning is on juxtaposition, clustering or close parallel alignment, on lake- or marsh-edges. The evidence of Schötz 7 and Egolzwil 3 and 5 again immediately suggests local continuities and orientations. Perhaps because of a strong sense of regional identity and the lack of a sense of beginnings from the outside, there is no common, strong or long-lasting pattern in the movement of things from the outside. The axe movements detailed in an earlier chapter (Pétrequin 1993; Pétrequin and Jeunesse 1995), for a while oriented to the north, for a while to the south, suggest other concerns: perhaps with shifting alliances conducted especially by men. Perhaps even, speculatively, there is some reflection here of differences in marriage residence rules. If the LBK system was sometimes or often patrilocal (Kolhoff 1999; Sommer 2001, 259), the converse might be true of the Alpine foreland.

This discussion, as of the LBK, has so far suggested a kind of unity across a broad area, but both the conditions of residence and the nature of the taskscape again highlight the probability of multiple identities. The overwhelming focus appears to be on quite small, close-knit social groupings. Houses are set cheek by jowl. Although normally built of stout timbers, it is doubtful whether any one structure would have afforded much privacy. There is no obvious evidence for separate or formalised sleeping arrangements; in winter at least one could envisage people sleeping close together near hearths. Patterns of deposition also suggest much more held in common than separate in terms of daily movements and consumption, as noted in earlier chapters. It is simply unclear whether individual houses held discrete households, and even if they did, these appear to have been very intimately linked, in a manner not evident in the LBK.

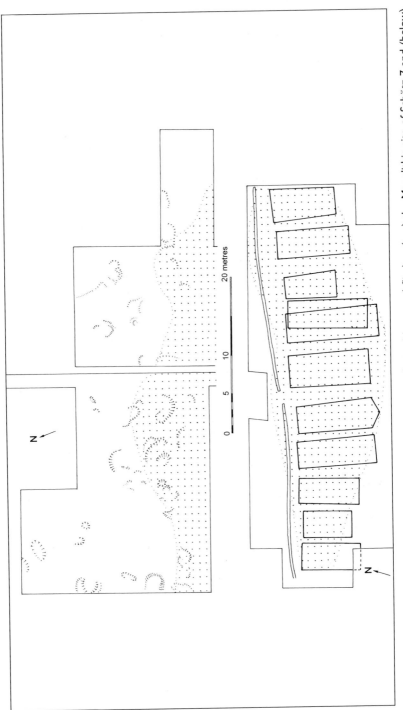

Figure 6.2 Outline plans of the main features and finds distributions (animal bone and flint) at (top) the Mesolithic site of Schötz 7 and (below) the Neolithic site of Egolzwil 5, Wauwilermoos, north-west Switzerland. After Wyss and Stampfli.

People were attached to place, but again the detailed study of this, as with the LBK, has hardly begun. They were also accustomed to the finite duration of particular settlements, and group identity was regularly re-affirmed through building. In strong contrast to elsewhere, the dead are little visible in the archaeological record. There are some remains scattered in some settlements, and the occasional separate burial ground has been identified, such as Lenzburg (Wyss 1967) or a little further afield Sion-Petit Chasseur (Gallay 1990), but taking the evidence at face value, it is as though the dead themselves normally mattered little for a sense of continuity and descent. This is therefore much more reminiscent of the situation with males in the Körös culture than with the LBK (though no connection of course is implied). If this was a population whose forebears had inhabited the same land, it must have been known that occupation of lake- and marsh-edges would entail periodic floodings through fluctuations in water levels, and even an incoming population would have recognised this basic fact of their environment in less than a generation. People nonetheless built in the expectation of future disruption of this kind. Repeated shorthouse rebuildings, at intervals of ten to twenty years, were a fundamental renewal of more than just shelter and place of residence, more a tangible link with what had gone before, a performance of community, a drawing on human cooperation on the one hand and the resources of surrounding woodland on the other, and a linking with the natural surroundings (Figure 6.3). Cycles of building mirrored cycles of land-use. Not all buildings came to an end through water level rises. As elsewhere, some were burnt, such as at Hornstaad and Chalain 3 (Dieckmann et al. 1997; Pétrequin 1997). It remains to be seen whether these were accidental fires or deliberate events initiated by the inhabitants themselves to close a period of house use. Nor can attacks by others be discounted.

A sense of closeness might have extended out into the taskscape and landscape. Some animals were stalled for some of the time, though others may have been excluded from settlements. The equal importance given in early centuries to deer and cattle may suggest that people did not make a rigid distinction between wild and domesticated; abundance, fertility, availability and movement may have been of greater importance. Rather than living a precarious existence of grinding hard work, easily threatened by climatic deterioration, I envisage people leading measured lives in patterns not greatly different from those of their forebears. The preservation of an abundance of artefacts suggests considerable skill in getting what was wanted from the surrounding landscape (cf. Ingold 2000, part III). There are, for example, organic containers, nets of diverse kinds, hafts and handles for large and small tools, points, and spoons. It is clear that the Ice Man, with his broad range of equipment, belonged to a long tradition of skill. One kind of artefact I find particularly intriguing: the wrapped weights at Clairvaux and sites in western Switzerland (Pétrequin 1989, 363–7). These consist of small stones wrapped in birch bark (Figure 6.4). It is suggested that these are weights for fixed nets. They are beautifully if simply made, and the fact that they recur in more than one context shows that they were part of an established way of doing something. To the importance of

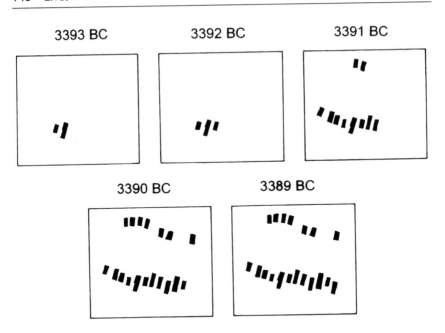

Figure 6.3 Biography of a settlement. Dendrochronology for the birth and growth of the settlement of Lattrigen Riedstation on the Bielersee, north-west Switzerland. After Hafner 2002.

place and shorthouse groupings for the sense of identity can therefore be added the dimension of work: skilful engagement in the taskscape.

From the evidence seen in earlier chapters, it is likely that people ranged to varying extents through their landscapes. Having so far emphasised differences between the Alpine foreland and the LBK, here there may be strong similarities. As well as the place of residence, with its familiar huddle of structures and small plots nearby, there were animals to herd further afield, hunting trips, and forays to procure axes. Speculatively, a male identity may have resided partly in these activities; in the 'dryland' burial cists at Lenzburg in the northern Swiss district of Aargau, males were associated with arrowheads and knives (Wyss 1967). It seems most unlikely from this perspective that the Ice Man represents anything new in terms of social figure or role in the later fourth millennium BC (contrast Hodder 1999; 2000). One of the many distinctive features of this archaeology is the lack not only of burials,[5] but also of other contexts of deposition or representation in which identities and roles could be symbolised or negotiated; despite their abundance elsewhere in the fourth millennium BC, there appear to be no enclosures in the Alpine foreland. So even if there were a separate male identity, created in part by activity out in the further reaches of the taskscape, to be remembered in stories and dreams when back in the settlement, it was subsumed in the moral community of the shorthouse,

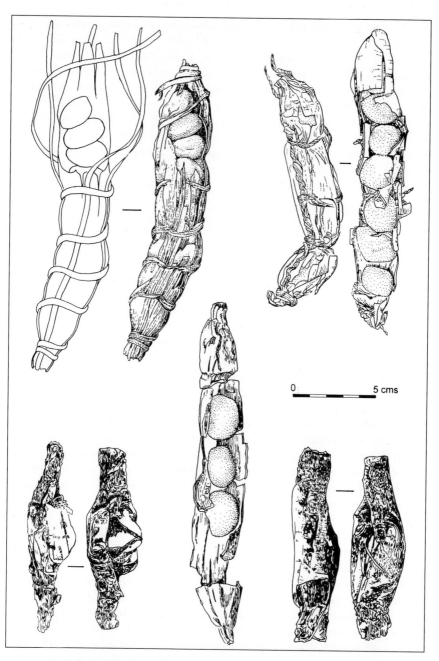

Figure 6.4 Stones wrapped in birch bark, perhaps net weights, from settlements in the Alpine foreland of Switzerland and the French Jura. Clockwise from top left: Twann; Auvernier Port; La Motte-aux-Magnins; Saint-Aubin, Port-Conty; La Motte-aux-Magnins. After Pétrequin 1989.

which literally embodied, in its placing, juxtapositions, layout, construction, biography and history, a long and perhaps closed tradition of ways of doing things. The evidence suggests to me that the adoption of cultivation here did not cause a fundamental shift in the patterns and style of this way of life. It accentuated perhaps the importance of the home base, but it did not create it. Even when the evidence does suggest a more established agriculture, longer clearances and gradually longer-lasting and larger settlements from the Horgen culture onwards, from the late fourth millennium BC on (e.g. Gross *et al.* 1990; Schibler, Hüster-Plogmann *et al.* 1997), the ideology of the shorthouse endured, lasting across the changes of the Late Neolithic until well into the middle Bronze Age.

Living by mounds and mountains

There is no one agreed hypothesis for the beginnings of the Neolithic in southern Britain. An older model of colonisation was replaced in the 1980s by models of indigenous acculturation, based in part on perceived continuities in lithic technology and mobility of lifestyle. These in turn have come under review more recently. On the one hand, the radiocarbon timescale has been reconsidered, and on the other, there is new isotopic evidence for a major diet shift in coastal areas from marine to terrestrial resources (Schulting 1998; 2000; Richards and Hedges 1999). This has brought the possibility of more rapid change once again to the fore. The view from Ireland has also rejected the comfortable model of indigenous continuity, slow change and a mobile existence (Cooney 2000). What was going on around 4000 BC remains stubbornly and frustratingly unclear, and certainly varied.

One solution might simply be to accept much more regional diversity: filtered colonisation through the western seaways into Ireland, with its distinctive insular conditions, and perhaps into other parts of western Britain as well; and rapid if partial acculturation elsewhere, including in inland southern Britain. Other scenarios can also be considered. Debate so far, in fact going right back to the initial discussions of the 1920s and 1930s, has tended to be in terms of the choice of one or the other major hypothesis. There has been very little attempt to consider the processes of filtered colonisation and indigenous acculturation at work together. There has been comparatively little effort to consider both daily routines and worldviews in the adoption of novel practices, since one or the other has tended to dominate explanations; Case (1969), for example, examined in detail the practical conditions of pioneer settlement, while Bradley (1998a) has stressed the importance of what people thought.[6] And there has been virtually no sense of regional inter-action; the perspective has been either thoroughly local or wholly generalising. Rather than a choice of 'east or west' (Piggott 1955), it may be fruitful now to consider the possible relationships *between* different areas. Unlike in the LBK and to a degree like the situation in the Alpine foreland, there were multiple orientations.

A general contrast between coastal and inland conditions may be a helpful start. There were Mesolithic populations in many parts of western Britain and in many though not necessarily all stretches of coastal Ireland. Taking the evidence of

Oronsay in the Inner Hebrides and elsewhere (Mithen 2000; Schulting 1998), these populations would have used a broad spectrum of resources, though favouring those of the coast and sea above all. Accepting the evidence of Ferriter's Cove for the introduction of a cow – dead or alive – into this milieu in the mid fifth millennium BC (Woodman *et al.* 1999), such people would also have been far from isolated. Indeed, it might be legitimate to argue that these two observations are connected, since attachment to the sea could have been strengthened as some kind of response to awareness of changes over the horizon. By contrast, though there need be no single pattern of inland settlement, it is far more likely that there were both empty spaces and little frequented regions among the populations of mobile foragers living inland; parts of the southern chalk downland are a case in point (Whittle 1990). As far as can be seen, a broad spectrum resource base is probable, without the kind of preferences or specialisation seen on the coast.

These sketches are simple, if not simplistic, but they begin to open the field for fresh speculation about beginnings. My first suggestions on this topic were to consider the conditions in which agricultural settlement began to expand in the earlier fifth millennium BC (Whittle 1977). Perhaps there was after all something in this idea, but the chronology was wrong, since at the time it was thought that the start of the British Neolithic could be put rather earlier. Now, with beginnings seemingly secured a little before 4000 BC, a different context can be evoked: filtered, small-scale and piecemeal colonisation, by fissioning communities or parts of communities, not just from the European coast itself but largely from the inland populations which constituted the major cultural groupings of Chasseen and Michelsberg. If such population movement is to be invoked to explain in part the rapidity with which novel material practices were adopted across many parts of Britain, it is likely that it was directed especially into inland areas. In a much earlier model, I suggested three possible fates for the indigenous population in this kind of situation: avoidance, disruption or absorption (Whittle 1977). Some kind of fusion is now an attractive possibility. Patterned movement through the seasonal cycles of the inland forager year would have been compatible with the patterned existence of pioneer agriculturalists. The routines of deer hunting and cattle herding, clearance to attract game and clearance for browse and cultivation, the occupation of base camps and the maintenance of small plots for cultivation, might all be thought of as leading to convergence. This could be seen as symbolised in material form in pottery: novel, transformative, in forms evoking a cultural relationship with European populations, but easy and quick to make, convenient in situations where food and drink was presented and shared, and spreading rapidly as a novelty through existing networks of exchange and interaction.

Better chronology has enabled not only greater precision about the likely start date for the British Neolithic, but also more awareness of subsequent development. And it turns out that some of the most striking monumental constructions probably belong not to the very beginning but to an established phase, beginning around 3700–3600 BC, perhaps as much as four centuries or more after it all began. It is likely in my view that most causewayed enclosures belong here, as well as the monumental mounds of many long barrows. At this date, the selective and creative rememberings discussed in the last chapter were of an older continental past, reinforcing an orientation to a real or perceived European homeland going back to the LBK. In nearly all cases, however, the monumentality of the long mound was preceded by something different: smaller in scale, not necessarily incompatible with the linearity of the long mound idea, but not so clearly owing form or content to the longhouse–long mound nexus. Instead, pavements, post settings, post façades, small post structures, pits, small parallel banks, and varied depositions of human bone, animal bone and artefacts, could all and variously owe as much to traditions of indigenous practice or again a fusion of ways of doing things in the first three or four centuries of the Neolithic in southern and eastern Britain.

By contrast, things may have been rather different in western Britain. It could be conjectured that colonisation of coastal areas already occupied by well-established indigenous communities is in fact unlikely, though that does not exclude colonisation of inland areas, as has been argued forcefully for Ireland (Cooney 2000), leading to their gradual infilling. It could be that the apparent turning away from use of the resources of the sea (Schulting 1998) belongs to this kind of context, and to a series of realignments in outlook and social practice. In other respects, there may have been continuity of belief systems. Much is still uncertain about the chronology of monument construction. It seems plausible, however, that some at least of the series of so-called portal dolmens on either side of the Irish Sea belong to the early stages of the Neolithic (see chapter 5), preceding perhaps court cairns or court tombs in Ireland and the Cotswold-Severn outliers of south-east Wales. In some parts of south-west Wales, the portal dolmens are found in areas which had had numerous Mesolithic occupations (Tilley 1994; Cummings 2001; Cummings and Whittle forthcoming). Many of these constructions are placed close to rocky outcrops or with a view of them and prominent hills. In striking instances, the architecture of the monument seems to mimic the form of the hills, Carn Ingli being referenced by Pentre Ifan and Llech y Dribedd among others. Unlike the situation in central southern Britain, where what eventually became monumentalised began with a series of smaller constructions and interventions, there is relatively little sign of gradual development (some sites do plausibly have sequences). These were probably constructions rapidly made: 'achievements of special virtue' in Frances Lynch's striking phrase (1972, 77). A possible exception is the instances where the portal dolmen stands directly above a shallow pit, as at Carreg Samson or Pentre Ifan, though this may equally be an integral part of a single phase of construction. Nor do successive rebuildings, as at Dyffryn Ardudwy (Powell 1973) or Trefignath (Smith and Lynch 1987), invalidate the general claim. There is no convincing instance of an enclosing cairn surviving around or over a portal dolmen. There is evidence, in some though not necessarily all cases, for a low surround or platform of small stones. Dyffryn Ardudwy and Trefignath are convenient examples. The same may be true of Pentre Ifan (Grimes 1949), and it is possible here, given the unusual addition of flanking façade stones, to see the horned platform or perhaps very low cairn as a later addition (Lynch 1972).

From this base arise the substantial uprights which hold an often massive 'cap-stone'. But here the conventional terminology of megalithic archaeology lets us down (cf. Tilley 1998). These top stones do indeed complete a box-like compart-ment, but there seems much more to them than this. They often overhang the uprights, and frequently are either pitched at a tilt or have an upper surface with a pronounced slope. These are surely stones which have been carefully selected for conspicuous presentation, after impressive amounts of labour to get them set up. They refer to or otherwise play on a connection with hills, mountains and rocky outcrops (Figure 6.5) (Tilley 1994; Cummings 2001). There is no surviving evidence, though admittedly the circumstances for such survival are not favourable, for any pronounced interest in the deposition of human remains inside the compart-ments.[7] Instead, these constructions could better be seen as to do with creation myths, involving perhaps figures who emerged from the earth through mountains or rose from the earth to the sky via mountains, at the beginning of it all. This kind of belief can be found widely in other situations (e.g. J. Middleton 1960, 2; Waterson 2000, 184–5; Martin 2001, 116). It seems more likely that, if this kind of interpret-ation is followed, this cosmology belonged to an indigenous population long familiar with the regional landscape. There are no directly comparable constructions in possible source areas for colonists, such as north-west France.

Why now? An answer must presumably lie in the changing situation over wide areas, even though contact between regions may have been fragmented and episodic. If there were a mixture of populations in western Britain and Ireland, the early monumental constructions could be seen as an assertion of indigenous identity, a statement that even if the sea was being slighted (Schulting 1998), the land endured. And interaction may have been played out at a wider scale too. If there were in fact more intrusive pioneer populations in southern and eastern Britain than in the Irish Sea zone, the early monumental constructions of the west could be seen as an assertion of regional indigenous identity. There is little in western areas which directly evokes the longhouse world, though a general connection might be sought in the cairns of the court monuments. Orientation was to a different past, previously taken for granted perhaps but now open to contestation and the possibility of replacement.

This kind of discussion tends to promote a view of agency as something operating at a rather large, collective and regional scale, and as also dominated by an orient-ation to the past. Thinking about conditions of residence and the taskscape offers a different kind of perspective, with different possible emphases: on short-term forward intentionality, ephemerality, cyclicity, and diversity. People may have been held within the flux of these rhythms and variations, such that no one fixed or absolute kind of identity can be easily defined. People undoubtedly planned ahead: in the creation of clearances, for example, or in the construction of such larger buildings as have been found. But it is not clear that they always thought far ahead. There was perhaps an expectation of a cycle of growth and decay or replacement, in the regeneration of woodland after clearance, in the lives of cattle, or in the setting up and falling or burning down of 'houses'. The Sweet Track (Coles and Coles 1986)

Figure 6.5 Stones that float to the sky: early monuments from the Irish Sea zone. Clockwise from top left: Carreg Coetan; Pentre Ifan; Maen y Bardd; Llech y Dribedd. Photos: Vicki Cummings.

still offers one of the most vivid illustrations of this kind of sense of time. It was preceded, at least over part of its course, by another construction some thirty years earlier. Some of the wood used in its own construction may have been stockpiled in advance. There was careful use of different wood species for different components, as well as of oak for major pieces from both primary and secondary woodland. Passing over patches of at least seasonally shallow water, the trackway would have offered a raised walkway, but it is far from clear that this was merely a device to keep feet dry. Its course was sanctified or otherwise marked from time to time not only by more ordinary pottery but also by the deposition of exotic axe blades of jadeite and flint. Judging by the state of preservation of the timbers, it is likely that the trackway was in use for something like a generation at most, and it was not replaced in the same massive form, even though this may well have been a construction easily within the labour compass of a small group of people, but by a series of other trackways built of wattle hurdles (themselves a product of cycles of hazel coppicing), set down at intervals subsequently. The taskscape here did not endure unaltered, but resided in a flow of changing activities.

Other striking examples of punctuated flow come from the recently published details of the causewayed enclosures of Etton and Windmill Hill (Pryor 1998; Whittle et al. 1999). The defining features of these places – ditch segments and on occasion accompanying low banks – were themselves probably created gradually over time. They were certainly subsequently much modified at Etton, though not it seems over the whole circuit at any one moment. Perhaps the possibility of recuts in the Windmill Hill ditches has been underplayed (Whittle et al. 1999). But it is the episodicity of the varied depositions in the ditches of both Etton and Windmill Hill which speaks for a cycle of activity, much of it at any one time rather small-scale. Overall emphases can be seen within the total distribution and spatially varying character of these depositions, and there were perhaps foundation deposits in significant primary locations such as ditch terminals. Nonetheless I remain most struck by the varied clusterings and scatters of material, interwoven in the accumulating ditch fills (Figure 6.6). In the Windmill Hill analysis we suggested a distinction between scatters and groups of material (Whittle et al. 1999, especially chapter 17), but this may be hard to sustain. The lasting impression is of varied, small-scale depositions. These may also themselves have had differing histories, some coming from events immediately prior to deposition, others at the end of a longer story of accumulation and temporary storage before final selection, in both cases accentuating the sense of a series of intersecting cycles. It could be that this pattern of deposition, seen both temporally and spatially, reflects the pattern of use of places of this kind. In that case, causewayed enclosures of this character would have been the scene of periodic gatherings, sometimes involving many people but at other times engaging few. And it could be that the pattern of deposition also in some way maps or echoes the nature of routine existence in a wider landscape beyond them, a way of life characterised by alternating movings and stayings, in a cycle of structured activities, rarely prolonged in any one place.

Figure 6.6 Depositions in the ditch segments at Etton. Clockwise from left: fox mandible, inverted pot, antler comb and pot, segment 7; cattle ribs, segment 1; wood, bone and pottery including nested sherds, segment 7; human cranium, antler baton and cattle bone, segment 6. Photos: Francis Pryor.

Until their final monumentalisation, there is something of the same character to the history of those other places where people both built and deposited: the long barrows of southern Britain. Recent analysis of the human remains from these has also shown much diversity in diet and activity. Isotopic studies (Richards and Hedges 1999) have indicated a variety of diets, from mixed ones to some rich in meat; what seems to be missing, on this evidence, is a major reliance on plant foods. The role of cereal cultivation is currently hotly debated (e.g. papers in Fairbairn 2000; cf. Monk 2000). Diversity may again be the key. In many situations, cereal cultivation may have been small-scale, even episodic, since relatively small amounts survive and because other plant remains can also be found. However, this supposition need not exclude the possibility of times when labour was invested on a greater scale. Study of human teeth, on admittedly small samples from long cairns in the Black Mountains group of south-east Wales, suggests diversity in this regard even within quite short distances. At Ty Isaf, the lack of caries, low ante-mortem tooth loss and low rate of enamel hypoplasia all suggested that carbohydrates including cereals played little part in a diet which was subject to few disruptions, while at Penywyrlod and Pipton, not far away, these trends are partially reversed (Wysocki and Whittle 2000). Even if those who were deposited in a particular cairn were not inhabitants of the immediately local area for their whole lives, the differences among the various mortuary groups are suggestive of differing kinds of livelihood.

The human bones themselves from these and related contexts bear other evidence suggesting the same conclusion. Musculoskeletal stress markers on the bones of adults suggest differences both between males and females, and between mortuary groups in separate areas (Wysocki and Whittle 2000). At West Kennet long barrow, not far from Windmill Hill, this evidence may suggest that the lifestyle of males involved more strenuous use of the right arm, shoulders and legs than was the case with females. On the other hand, females at West Kennet might have been more active than those from the chambered monument at Tinkinswood in the lowland Vale of Glamorgan in south-east Wales. Ideally, samples would be larger, but once again what matters is the apparent variation. Perhaps men were more involved in herding, hunting and longer-range movement, and women to varying degrees with labour-intensive routines or subsistence tasks, perhaps including cereal cultivation.

It has been customary to think of the introduction of 'Neolithic' diet and subsistence practices as more or less revolutionary. Much of the resistance to the notion of colonisation from the outside in the recent literature on the beginning of the Neolithic in Britain has been based in a belief that such changes were introduced gradually. This view has been severely challenged by the new isotopic evidence (Schulting 1998; Richards and Hedges 1999), at least from the standpoint of a few centuries after the start of new practices. This perspective in turn may obscure the nature of what had changed. In coastal areas of western Britain,[8] seals, fish, shellfish, deer, wild cattle, pigs and presumably wild plants were replaced by domesticated cattle, pigs and sheep and goats, supplemented by cereals; in inland areas, deer, wild cattle, pigs and presumably wild plants were replaced by domesticated cattle, pigs and sheep and goats, supplemented by cereals. The major inland substitutions could be seen as of deer and wild cattle by domesticated cattle, even if other elements of the diet were important to a degree; on the coasts the shifts would have been from seals to cattle. Now from this perspective, inland change can be seen as much of form as of substance, if the major focus of people's attention and values was still on large animals. It is often thought that one of the principal motives for adopting domestication would have been the greater degree of control to be exercised over the resource or resources in question. In this case, animals may still have caused people to follow in their wake around and about inland southern Britain. The enclosure sites indicate that it was through cattle and about cattle that people principally thought, and in the absence of evidence for prolonged settlement in one place and with so much evidence for woodland, it remains plausible that animals and people were normally on the move to some degree. On the coasts, the major replacement was again of one set of large creatures by another, and fish catches may have been substituted by cereal harvests. It is unclear what the advantages would have been in terms of control, abundance or predictability. The importance of the shift is likely to have been as much in values and location as in the resources in question alone.

In the area of the LBK and in the Alpine foreland, evidence for residential structures is the defining feature of early Neolithic archaeologies, whereas in southern Britain this is much more elusive. Long mounds seem to provide distant memories of those earlier buildings, while contemporary ones appear to be few and far between. The absences, however, are relative. The discovery under metres of col-luvium of a substantial structure at White Horse Stone, Kent (Current Archaeology 2000), and the survival of the large structure on the upper Thames floodplain at Yarnton, Oxfordshire (Hey 1997; and Gill Hey, pers. comm.), strongly suggest that other buildings of this kind are 'out there' waiting to be discovered in situations less subject to erosion or other destruction. These examples could be seen as part of a wider distribution which extends into Scotland and Ireland; there have been several recent discoveries in Ireland (Cooney 2000), and Claish Farm, near Stirling in central Scotland (G. Barclay et al. 2002), is the most recent northerly discovery. The Sweet Track itself is also a reminder that there was no lack of skill in working wood.

Though this may not always be the case in Ireland, in the British contexts such structures appear to occur on their own. Not only were they isolated, there also appears to have been little by way of other concentrations of features or material around them. There are only a few signs of post replacements or other repairs, and at face value these appear to have been relatively short-lived. The Claish Farm structure had been burned down (after one episode of repair or rebuilding). It might be legitimate to think of regional variations in the patterns or histories of settlement, but it may be more plausible to envisage again a flow or cycle of activity, within which from time to time larger structures were constructed, maintained for a relatively short time, possibly for special circumstances such as the fostering of alliances, feasting, or the celebration of ritual events, but then allowed to lapse if not deliberately destroyed to mark or to end their temporary significance. Whether any lasted longer than say the Sweet Track is not clear. Some were commemorated by the construction of mounds or cairns above them (or at least the places where they had stood were taken as significant by subsequent generations), such as Hazleton or Ascott-under-Wychwood (Saville 1990; A. Barclay 2000); below the outer bank of the Windmill Hill enclosure there are also the elements of what could have been a large timber structure (Darvill 1996; Whittle *et al*. 1999). In other instances, these buildings appear rapidly to have been forgotten. Few if any of the British examples appear to have been the residence of large numbers of people, though it is not excluded that some may have been the focus for unusual scales of production and consumption, including cereals (G. Jones 2000). If sedentism is defined as being in one place for more than a generation (Tringham 2000), it is far from clear, even when buildings can be found in southern Britain, that this was a sedentary population.

The implications of this issue are not confined to a purely practical sphere of shelter or subsistence. This body of evidence too, like that of the taskscape, strongly suggests a shifting, unstable, perhaps opportunistic social setting. If large buildings were briefly the focus for social groupings, those too may have lapsed, dispersed or otherwise re-formed on the abandonment of the structures in question. The other evidence for occupation (e.g. Pollard 1999b; C. Evans *et al*. 1999) also allows for a changing and changeable cast of co-residents through the cycles of agglomeration and dispersal. In this setting therefore identity and affiliation were presumably key issues, of perpetual significance and constantly to be negotiated. The most abundant evidence comes from the period a few centuries after the beginning of the Neolithic in southern Britain, as I have stressed already, when these questions may have become more pressing than they were initially. Though much is different, it may be revealing, as in the LBK and the Alpine foreland, to think in terms of several overlapping scales or dimensions of identity.

The evidence for the taskscape shows active people engaged in skilful performances. It is difficult to avoid thinking of people as self-reliant, and acting on their own: in herding cows through woodland, in longer-range movements to pro-cure axes, in walking in single file along the Sweet Track. The individual body was the start of many if not most mortuary rites, and the case for successive depositions in structures, mounds and cairns has strengthened rather than weakened in recent studies. Individual-ness was perhaps, however, at least in the mortuary sphere, a relative concept, as the re-assembled skeletons, composed of the bones of more than one individual, at Fussell's Lodge long barrow, strongly suggest; similar mixing to make up small, separate deposits can be seen in Penywyrlod and Pipton in the south Welsh Black Mountains (Wysocki and Whittle 2000). Categorisation in terms of age and sex or gender was also demonstrably a concern in many contexts where sorting of bones took place. This also involves the issue of individual-ness, since individuals had to be categorised before or as they were assigned to particular groupings. That transformation from fleshed, intact bodies to disarranged or re-arranged bones was a key organising principle in nearly all instances has been observed over and over again; less remarked has been the unstable history of treat-ment in some instances. There are certainly places where the same kind of practice seems essentially to have been repeated many times. Wayland's Smithy I is a case in point (Whittle 1991). In other instances, deposits may reflect a variety of practice, as in the mixture of stacked adult and juvenile remains, very scattered child remains and two reassembled individuals seen in the Fussell's Lodge long barrow (an alternative to what I suggested in chapter 3), or the mixture of articulated, semi-articulated and disarticulated remains in the West Kennet long barrow (Ashbee 1966; Piggott 1962).

The sense of unstable histories and fluid patterns extends to the organising principles behind the treatment of the human dead. Contrary to the claim that 'it is difficult to find any theoretical grounds for holding on to ancestors in the British Neolithic' (J. Whitley 2002, 121), the transformations of the dead, combined with their housing in a series of monuments in southern Britain whose form surely evokes in some way or other distant pasts, point interpretation firmly in this direction. But what has been too often left out of account is diversity of practice and especially the duration of the processes involved which allows further diversity to be considered. Inescapably, mortuary treatment begins with the individual dead person, and that was demonstrably the focus of rites in those cases where deposition directly into structures, rather than excarnation or exposure, was the first move. In many instances, we can suggest, as has long been mooted, a succession of individual depositions. And here it seems to me that we could consider genealogy as well as ancestry. On the way to the creation of more distant ancestors, there may have been much more vivid, personalised attention given to known, remembered individuals, back over say two to three or three to four generations. We have perhaps concentrated too much on the final form of deposits, and not enough on the process and associations of their formation. This perspective would allow us to think of concerns for position and descent, and for the immediacies of relationships among the living, *alongside* a wider principle of more generalised ancestry. The ancestors come into being through the lived concerns of their descendants.

This perspective may serve also to reduce the impression of communities or societies obsessed only with their dead and their past. The evidence of causewayed enclosures like those of Windmill Hill and Etton, noted above, points in other directions. The frame or the setting may again have echoes of distant pasts. The dead are certainly present, though in numbers and conditions that vary from site to site and even from ditch segment to ditch segment. For all the substantial numbers seen at Hambledon Hill, there are fewer at Windmill Hill, and an emphasis on children or younger people and their probably preferential placing in the outer circuit there (Whittle *et al.* 1999) indicates that the dead took their place in a wider scheme of things. At Etton, the emphasis in deposits on the east side of the enclosure, both in the ditches and the interior, may be on commemoration of individuals or small kin groups (Pryor 1998, 367–8). As Windmill Hill and Etton vividly show in their differing ways, the concerns writ large in the various deposits are for a very wide range of activities carried out by and important to the living. Practically every dimension of contemporary existence finds its representation here, which is why this kind of site has been such a powerful (if partially misleading) emblem of their period, from woodland existence to the working of flint tools, stone axes and querns. Animals find a central place here, their remains evoking a probably wide range of complex relationships, from ownership, the socialities of herding and daily tendings, and routine consumption (if there was such a thing), to the subtleties of systems of value, exchange, sacrifice, feasting, substitution and storage (Whittle *et al.* 1999, especially chapter 18). People might have thought far more consciously and more often about their living relations and their cows, and the immediate predecessors of these and their doings, than about generalised and more distant ancestors. But it is again not a choice between one or the other, if the moral community can be seen to be formed by long and fractured conversations about a variety of themes, from the contingencies of the present to the abstractions of pasts, otherworlds and 'nature'.

The enclosures seem to demand, from their size, and to some extent perhaps from their settings, a more than purely small or local audience. Their connections and connotations are wide. And yet the individual depositions that go to make up the eventual whole are characteristically both small and varied. Definition was the point at issue: of relationships, prowess, allegiances, histories. But what was being defined, or at least the way this was expressed, was never quite the same, and may have been witnessed by audiences of varying size and complexity. That instability speaks volumes for the nature of existence at this time.

Chapter 7

What happened in history?

Soon before and then in the middle of the Second World War, Gordon Childe published two books, *Man makes himself* and *What happened in history* (Childe 1936; 1942). These were in many ways remarkable, on the one hand for their scope and bold generalisations, and on the other for the employment of archaeological evidence to support an optimistic view of human development, which was not otherwise suggested by the conditions of the time. Of the two works, *Man makes himself* has perhaps the more sophisticated and detailed arguments, but it uses the same general thrust as *What happened in history*. The story in both is of progress and evolution, through a subtle combination of economic, technological, ideological and conceptual factors. Whereas the former work concentrates on the Neolithic revolution, the urban revolution and then the revolution in human knowledge, the main themes of the later work, perhaps because things in the contemporary world had become even worse, are couched in an older style, of development from savagery to barbarism and eventually to civilisation. This language now seems rather quaint, as few if any specialists today would think in terms of 'Neolithic barbarism' (Childe 1942, chapter 3) or the 'higher barbarism of the Copper Age' (Childe 1942, chapter 4). And, obviously, rather different evidence could be brought to bear compared to that available in the 1930s. This is not to deride Childe in any way, as it is part of his enduring appeal that his general arguments have seemed to last so well. Perhaps, for all the accumulation of new data since his day, this is not in fact so surprising, since his main successors were 'processualists', and in turn their successors or protagonists, 'post-processualists', have often been little interested in the same sort of long-term perspectives.

Because 'the whole long process', as Childe called it in *What happened in history*, can be broken down into chronological stages, and because it is obvious that profound changes did occur in the long term, it was easy for Childe and has been easy too for successors to assume that change took place steadily. The nineteenth-century idea of evolution has had a long hold on archaeology. There has also been a kind of *horror vacui*, an unwillingness to conceive of periods of human history in which not much went on, as Colin Renfrew (2001) has hinted for the Upper Palaeolithic. For Renfrew (2001), the key shift was to sedentary existence, whose material and especially cognitive consequences were to realise the potential of the loitering brain of *Homo sapiens*. His argument is truncated, but the implication seems clear that a more active time followed the kickstart of sedentism, with monuments, commodities and property among the foci which kept people busy, and changing.

In this book, I have concentrated mainly on the early parts of sequences in just a few regions of Europe. I have tried to explore different layers of human activity, relationships, values and identity in those times, in order to suggest a complexity to human existence which resists being reduced to a single dimension. In this brief coda, I want to begin to consider some further implications of this point of view. I am not arguing for a lack of change through time, which would be more or less absurd, and have given plenty of examples, from the Hungarian plain to the loesslands to the Alpine foreland, of things shifting over the generations. But what if the till now dominant model of steady and ultimately directed change is incomplete? Childe's title is now more challenging with a question mark added: what *did* happen in Neolithic history?

Subjects for discussion

I have set out these arguments in more detail elsewhere (Whittle 2001) but it is useful briefly to touch on some of the key themes again.

In the first chapter of *What happened in history* Childe wrote that a 'single directional trend is most obvious in the economic sphere in the methods whereby the most progressive societies secure a livelihood. In this domain it will be possible to recognize radical and indeed revolutionary innovations, each followed by such increases in population that, were reliable statistics available, each would be reflected by a conspicuous kink in the population graph.' To Childe's general argument of the emergence of a food-producing economy, Andrew Sherratt (1981; 1987) added the idea of a 'secondary products revolution'. I have already discussed and criticised this model in chapter 4, and Sherratt himself (1995a, 6) has subsequently characterised it as an example of 'block thinking'. It is not as though no changes took place in the domestic and other economies of the Neolithic. The Alpine foreland, for example, offers some of the most striking evidence of a combination of gradual changes in the scale and duration of clearances, and the conditions of preservation allow very specific markers of ecological difference, such as birds, small mammals and plants, to be identified (Schibler and Jacomet 1999). But in this context, the longer-term trend in animal husbandry seems to be a consolidation of the importance of cattle (e.g. Gross *et al.* 1990; Schibler, Hüster-Plogmann *et al.* 1997) rather than the emergence of the large sheep herds necessary for the predicted rise in importance of textiles. The same thing may be reflected elsewhere, to the north and east, in the importance given to cattle in fourth to third millennium BC burial practices (e.g. Pollex 1999 and references). In other regions, such as the Paris basin, trends may have been different again (e.g. Tresset 2000, fig. 4). The kind of dramatic and universal trends long proposed prove very hard to find, and the search for them has obscured the extent of regional diversity and local development.

Another favourite search has been for a clear pattern in the development of social formation and social difference. Despite prolonged attempts to find chiefdoms or other kinds of social formation with ranking and structured difference, one of the best observations remains that of Andrew Sherratt (1982a, 14), who commented on Europe after the introduction of farming in the seventh millennium BC that 'the long intervening period cannot adequately be described by a simple evolutionary succession of increasingly ranked societies'. In one of the most sophisticated examples of 'social evolutionary' modelling, developed for peninsular Italy, a Big Man society was still seen as characterising the early second millennium BC, to be followed by a semi-stratified tribal confederacy (Figure 7.1) (Robb 1994, table 1). Many other authors agree that it is not until as late as the mid-second millennium BC that small-scale chiefdoms appear in central Europe (e.g. S.J. Shennan 1993), coinciding in part with the appearance of a male warrior elite or aristocracy (Treherne 1995; Kristiansen 1998). Even thereafter, there is no convincing case to be made for state formation, nor even necessarily of elaborate or large-scale chiefdoms, in temperate Europe before the arrival of the Romans.

A more recent concern has been with gender relations. I have already discussed views of the significance of the Ice Man in relation to his wider context, and criticised the view that he can be seen as standing for a newer world of the male-dominated and more aggressive *agrios*. In a similar vein, it has been argued by several other authors that the nature of gender relations altered from the third to the second millennium BC. The outcome, in this view, was the appearance of a warrior ideology in the mid second millennium BC (Treherne 1995), and beginnings have been sought in gender distinctions claimed in Corded Ware mortuary practices from the earlier third millennium BC onwards, leading to a process whereby male activities and associations were increasingly emphasised, with a concomitant downplaying

Period	Gender emphases/oppositions	Social regulation
6000 BC Early–Middle Neolithic	Male/female balanced	Formal ritualisation Great Man?
3500 BC Late Neolithic	Proto male hierarchy Exclusion of women	Formal ritualism/incipient male prestige competition
3000 BC Eneolithic/EBA	Male hierarchy Exclusion of women	Male prestige competition Big Man
1400 BC LBA inland/upland	Male hierarchy Exclusion of women	Male prestige competition Big Man
1400 BC LBA lowland/coastal	Male hierarchy/proto female hierarchy Exclusion of women/ peripheral males	Elite male prestige competition Semi-stratified tribal confederacy

Figure 7.1 Suggested aspects of gender relations and social formations in the Italian sequence from Early Neolithic to Late Bronze Age. After Robb 1994.

of the value of women (S.J. Shennan 1993, 149), to the point where some women buried with valuable items in the Early Bronze Age of the earlier second millennium BC have been regarded as possessing such valuables by virtue of their husbands' wealth or as bridewealth in a pattern of exogamy (S.E. Shennan 1975). A related model has been argued in detail for Italy (Robb 1994). A central problem with this view in central Europe is the instability of representations of gender relations in mortuary ritual from place to place and through time (S.J. Shennan 1994, 124–5). In one account, the development of the use of 'secondary products' should have led to an *increase* in female power (Chapman 1997a, 137). There was much variation within the vast Corded Ware area, and cemeteries in central Europe in the second millennium BC (e.g. S.E. Shennan 1975; 1982; O'Shea 1996; Harding 2000) have much in common – apart from their size – with earlier examples of the Early and Middle Copper Age of the later fifth and earlier fourth millennia BC (e.g. Chapman 1997a; Derevenski 1997; 2000). The treatment of women in death can be distinguished from that of men, but age and life process are at least as important as biological sex (Derevenski 1997; 2000), and the scale of difference is hardly ever extreme. As has been argued throughout this book, it is not clear anyway that we should be seeking a simple or single pattern. In one example from elsewhere, the Hua of eastern highland New Guinea, Meigs (1990) has emphasised a threefold male ideology, of accentuated chauvinism on the one hand, but of envy of women and of complementary interdependence on the other.

Curiously, what does seem to have been neglected in explanations since Childe's time, apart from a brief flurry of interest in the early years of processualism, is the possibility and role of population increase. As we have seen above, Childe seems to have regarded population increase as the effect of economic-technological innovation. In the Neolithic context, he is presumably in general right, in that the conditions were created in which subtle changes in fertility and mortality resulted in more people across the European landscape. The settlements of the Alpine foreland might again be one of the best indices at our disposal, since they last from the late fifth to the second millennium BC. Not only do clearances in this area get bigger and last longer, but so too do settlements themselves (e.g. Schibler, Hüster-Plogmann *et al.* 1997). Another useful index might be the sheer size of single-grave cemeteries by the time of the Early Bronze Age in central Europe (e.g. Harding 2000, chapter 3). But this process may have been much more gradual than Childe's reference to 'conspicuous kinks' presupposes. And while population increase might have followed other change to begin with, there is the interesting but neglected possibility that in time it could have come to be one of the most influential factors with the potential to alter what John Barrett (2000) has called 'structural conditions'.

Different kinds of history

The kind of view of existence and identity which I have explored in the book for early Neolithic situations may therefore have considerable implications for what came after. It looks as though it is in fact, despite evolutionary assumptions to the contrary, very difficult to claim profound or sustained structural change before the second millennium BC. (And it is a moot point, far beyond the scope of this book, whether change from the second millennium BC onwards was as complete as often characterised in the past.) In local contexts, in regional settings and in wider networks, things did not stay the same. The early longhouse did not last more than about a millennium, and even within that span it altered in form and setting. There were fluctuations in the distribution and concentration of people across the landscape, and variations in preferred animals and crops. At different times, this and that material was of greater importance. By the second millennium BC the production and circulation of bronze is often taken as distinctive in scale and complexity, but it is debatable whether the winning, use and deposition of copper and bronze really exceeded in complexity those of stone. And there may have been cycles of change. The Hungarian evidence explored in earlier chapters is one informative case of gradual change towards a concentration of people in potentially dominant places in the landscape, but followed by dispersal and different kinds of relationship and community played out partly in the mortuary domain.

These are different kinds of history to the single story of directed change, with its consistent and persistent trend towards greater social differentiation and economic specialisation and intensification, which has dominated generalising accounts since Childe's day and even earlier. If there are different kinds of history, they are no less interesting or valuable simply because they do not resemble the nature of change from the second millennium BC onwards. And this perspective puts two questions into sharp focus. If what I am suggesting is valid, why should it be so, and what happened finally in or by the second millennium BC for things to change?

My suggested answer to the first question rests in the complexity and layered nature of existence which has been the substance of this book. People cannot be reduced to single dimensions, because they existed inescapably in a complex web of routines, socialities and networks, relationships with animals, memories and attitudes to the past, and sanctioning values created by the shared moral community. I have argued for fluid identities in many situations, and this lack of fixity may have made people hard to pin down. I have not wanted to imply a cosy, wholly peaceful world. Discussing the use and duration of enclosures in Denmark, Nick Thorpe (2001) has referred to the possibilities for competition, a kind of jostling for position, that taking part in special arenas would afford, and suggested that their apparently episodic and generally short-lived use can be seen as the result of the inability to maintain aggregations or combined activity before conflict or worse broke out. People normally had the option to go elsewhere. But in seeing people as hard to pin down, I am not thinking only of the physical conditions of their residence and daily routines. It seems to me that profound and lasting structural change would require alterations in many if not all the dimensions of what constituted identity, and I cannot think of any generalising explanations of long-term change so far which have addressed this problem.

An answer to the second question would require another book. It is informative, however, to contemplate what an answer might encompass, in the terms of reference considered here. We would need to explain how people came to adopt or fit into changed routines, how they thought differently about animals, perhaps more as commodities or objects than partners or subjects of value, how they began to draw on different memories and pasts, perhaps more immediate ones with a different sort of creativity at work, and how they were now channelled into more fixed identities. Such processes were, I suggest, incomplete even in the second millennium BC. They may be partly the result – perhaps an old-fashioned view – of the very gradual increase in human numbers, of more people on the ground. The effect of social distancing (see again the discussion in chapter 3) has normally been neglected, except in discussions of hunter-gatherer existence. Intimate networks might have changed very little through time, but the 'worlds of otherness', in Neustupný's phrase, may gradually have widened. Some of what is often summoned in support of the emergence of social differentiation, such as the building of very large monuments in the third millennium BC, or the creation of more extensive field systems in the second millennium BC, might have been an attempt in part to counter this tendency, and to re-emphasise commonality. But a very gradual widening of worlds of otherness may have made its mark in the long term. It might have become very gradually easier for groups, small networks or individuals to have avoided or escaped the demands of the wider network and the sanctions of the wider moral community. And finally, people were not on their own for ever. The focus in this book has tended to be on the local, on small-scale settings and immediate socialities, in relation to a wider frame of value. When other worlds began to impinge to a much greater extent, first in the third millennium (the Corded Ware complex) and then in the second millennium BC (as interactions with the changing Mediterranean intensified), an older Europe began to alter for ever.

Notes

Preface

1 Part of a series called *Chroniques de la nuit des temps*, with 'direction scientifique' by the experienced and respected prehistorian Alain Gallay. *Le couteau de pierre* deals with a situation a little earlier, at the end of the fourth millennium BC.

I Being there

1 Although I am using this skeleton to illustrate aspects of the Körös culture, it is possible that it belongs a little later, to the AVK, which stands for the Hungarian label 'Alföldi vonaldíszes kerámiai' (see chapter 3). Radiocarbon dating of samples from Ecsegfalva is not yet completed.
2 Which I maintain despite the new evidence, so far reported in the press, of an arrowhead in the left shoulder, shot through the back.
3 I am referring to the striking title *We, the Tikopia* by Raymond Firth (1936). For a critical view of this in the context of its time, see Kuper 1996, 70–1.

2 The daily round

1 Though clearly much more work needs to be done on both the variations in the geological setting and increasing the numbers of samples.
2 I am very grateful to Dr Peter Walter of the Phahlbaumuseum, Unteruhldingen, for information and references.
3 Manambu warfare required enemies temporarily to lose their human form and transform themselves into dangerous spirit-beings.
4 Referring to the North Pacific rim, Maschner and Reedy-Maschner (1998) argue that warfare, both short- and long-range, was more often over revenge, status and women than critical subsistence resources.
5 The Amazonian Nukak also subsist by fishing and some small-scale horticulture.
6 Again, wider study and further analysis are required.

3 Difficult individuals

1 Consider the universalising tendencies of structuralism, post-structuralism and neo-Marxism/structural Marxism, compared with hermeneutics, phenomenology and critical theory.
2 These are the most comprehensive summaries in English. I have discussed this topic in Whittle 1998a.

3 AVK stands for the Hungarian label 'Alföldi vonaldíszes kerámiai'.
4 Note that Neustupný (1998) uses 'settlement area' to denote the transformation of a living community area into part of the archaeological record.
5 In regional terminology, 'Rubané Récent du Bassin Parisien', dating to around 5000 BC.
6 The average number of bones per house was 1,386; the minimum number was about 1,000, or 10 kg. This is a tiny amount for up to a generation of use.

4 What animals were like

1 It is worth quoting the paragraph in full (Lévi-Strauss 1964, 89):
   Radcliffe-Brown's demonstration ends decisively the dilemma in which the adversaries as well as the proponents of totemism have been trapped because they could assign only two roles to living species, viz., that of a natural stimulus, or that of an arbitrary pretext. The animals in totemism cease to be solely or principally creatures which are feared, admired, or envied: their perceptible reality permits the embodiment of ideas and relations conceived by speculative thought on the basis of empirical observations. We can understand, too, that natural species are chosen not because they are 'good to eat' but because they are 'good to think'.
2 Terms used include 'Existenzminimum', defined as 'knappe Versorgung, Mangel an Arbeitskraft, und lange Arbeitstage', and 'Mangelwirtschaft' (Gross et al. 19909, 96).
3 Perhaps not entirely novel. Whittle (1978), for example, suggested excess population and subsequent problems as a reason for reduction in new clearances and the closing in of existing ones, as suggested by pollen diagrams for the later fourth millennium BC in Britain and Ireland. Apart from anything else, there now appears little good evidence for such high population levels.
4 The author of the 'secondary products revolution' model has more recently seen it as an example of 'block thinking' (Sherratt 1995a, 6).
5 For emerging complications in using the chronology of Srejović (1972), see among others Radovanović 1996; Garašanin and Radovanović 2001; Borić 1999; Cook et al. 2002. This example, 7a at the rear of house 21, was assigned to LV1d by Srejović (1972); in Radovanović 1996, it is assigned to her LV1 phase 2.

5 Looking back

1 I am grateful to Tim Ingold for pointing me in this direction.
2 I acknowledge here all the colleagues who have worked on this project and who will be contributing to our final report: see Whittle 2000a.
3 Obtained jointly with Alex Bayliss and Mick Wysocki, with the support of English Heritage and the Leverhulme Trust. They are to be published in a forthcoming monograph.
4 See note 3.
5 Note that the difficulties of translating indigenous conceptions into English are fully recognised (J. Middleton 1960, 32–4). Kopytoff (1971) does not discuss this case study.
6 This has yet to be confirmed in detail, plausible though the general case is. Cooney 2000 sets out the dating evidence from Ireland.

6 Lives

1 The oak posts which hold up the front gate of my own house have been in the ground, which has a high water table, for over twenty years. They show some signs of decay at ground level but remain strong. They are about 17 cm square. It was the roof of the

longhouse, susceptible to the weather, which was perhaps its weakest element, and in this general regard the older arguments about concern for the effects of winter winds are still relevant.

2 I am grateful to Amy Bogaard for discussion of this issue.

3 This idea began with Rick Schulting, who suggested during our time together on fieldwork in Hungary that the pinched-up motif on Körös pottery resembled animal footprints. I do not implicate him in this outcome. The history of reading meaning into LBK pot decoration has been sadly limited: from Soudský and Pavlů (1966) to Hodder (1984).

4 It remains to be seen, however, whether the deposits at enclosures like Asparn and Herxheim are the result of single episodes of deposition as at Talheim.

5 Could the Ice Man, whatever the circumstances leading up to his death, be seen as a deliberate deposition, a burial by exposure, up in some of the high places he had known, carefully placed with representative equipment, even if some of it, like the bow, was not operational?

6 The account of Edmonds (1999) perhaps comes closest, but this is still a very generalised picture of established Neolithic settlement.

7 The portal tomb at Poulnabrone, Co. Clare, does have human remains, though the chronological relationship between bones and stones is unclear (Cooney 2000, 94–7).

8 Note again the different postglacial fauna of Ireland, probably lacking both wild cattle and red deer (Cooney 2000; Woodman et al. 1999).

Bibliography

Aaris-Sørensen, K. 1999. The Holocene history of the Scandinavian aurochs (*Bos primigenius* Bojanus, 1827). In G.-C. Weniger (ed.), *Archäologie und Biologie des Auerochsen*, 49-57. Mettmann: Neanderthal Museum.

Akeret, Ö. and Jacomet, S. 1997. Analysis of plant macrofossils in goat/sheep faeces from the Neolithic lake shore settlement of Horgen Scheller – an indication of prehistoric trans-humance? *Vegetation History and Archaeobotany* 6, 235-9.

Allen, M. 1998. Male cults revisited: the politics of blood versus semen. *Oceania* 68, 189-99.

Allen, M.J. 2000. Soils, pollen and lots of snails. In M. Green, *A landscape revealed: 10,000 years on a chalkland farm*, 36-49. Stroud: Tempus.

Ammerman, A.J., Shaffer, G.D. and Hartmann, N. 1988. A Neolithic household at Piana di Curinga, Italy. *Journal of Field Archaeology* 15, 121-40.

Andersen, N.H. 1997. *The Sarup enclosures: the Funnel Beaker culture of the Sarup site including two causewayed camps compared to the contemporary settlements in the area and other European enclosures*. Moesgaard: Jysk Arkæologisk Selskab.

Anderson, A. and Smith, I. 1996. The transient village in southern New Zealand. *World Archaeology* 27, 359-71.

Arbogast, R.M., Pétrequin, A.-M. and Pétrequin, P. 1995. Fonctionnement de la cellule domestique d'après l'étude des restes osseux d'animaux: le cas d'un village Néolithique du Lac de Chalain (Jura, France). *Anthropozoologica* 21, 131-46.

Arima, E. 1983. *The West Coast (Nootka) people*. Victoria: British Columbia Provincial Museum.

Armour-Chelu, M. 1998. The animal bone. In F. Pryor, *Etton: excavations at a Neolithic cause-wayed enclosure, near Maxey, Cambridgeshire, 1982-7*, 273-88. London: English Heritage.

Ashbee, P. 1966. Fussell's Lodge long barrow excavations, 1957. *Archaeologia* 100, 1-80.

Ashbee, P., Smith, I.F. and Evans, J.G. 1979. Excavation of three long barrows near Avebury, Wiltshire. *Proceedings of the Prehistoric Society* 45, 207-300.

Baddeley, A.D. 1999. *Essentials of human memory*. Hove: Psychology Press.

Baert, P. 1998. *Social theory in the twentieth century*. Cambridge: Polity Press.

Bailey, D.W. 2000. *Balkan prehistory: exclusion, incorporation and identity*. London: Routledge.

Bailloud, G., Boujot, C., Cassen, S. and Le Roux, C.-T. 1995. *Carnac: les premières architectures en pierre*. Paris: CNRS.

Bakker, J.A., Kruk, J., Lanting, A.E. and Milisauskas, S. 1999. The earliest evidence of wheeled vehicles in Europe and the Near East. *Antiquity* 73, 778-90.

Balasse, M., Tresset, A., Bocherens, H., Mariotti, A. and Vigne, J.-D. 2000. Un abattage 'post-lactation' sur des bovins domestiques néolithiques. Étude isotopique des restes osseux du site de Bercy (Paris, France). *Anthropozoologica* 31, 39-48.

Bánffy, E. 2000. Starčevo und/oder LBK? Die ersten Ergebnisse der westungarischen Ausgrabungen aus der Entstehungsphase der Bandkeramik. *Varia neolithica* 1, 47-60.

Barclay, A. 2000. Spatial histories of the Neolithic: a study of the monuments and material culture of southern central England. Unpublished PhD thesis, Reading University.

Barclay, G., Brophy, K. and MacGregor, G. 2002. A Neolithic building at Claish Farm, near Callander, Stirling Council, Scotland, UK. *Antiquity* 76, 23-4.

Barrett, J.C. 1994. *Fragments from antiquity: an archaeology of social life in Britain, 2900-1200 BC*. Oxford: Blackwell.

Barrett, J.C. 2000. A thesis on agency. In M.-A. Dobres and J. Robb (eds), *Agency in archaeology*, 61-68. London: Routledge.

Bartlett, F.C. 1932. *Remembering: a study in experimental and social psychology*. Cambridge: Cambridge University Press.

Bartosiewicz, L. 1999. Aurochs (*Bos primigenius* Bojanus, 1827) in the Holocene of Hungary. In G.-C. Weniger (ed.), *Archäologie und Biologie des Auerochsen*, 103-17. Mettmann: Neanderthal Museum.

Basso, K.H. 1984. 'Stalking with stories': names, places, and moral narratives among the Western Apache. In E.M. Bruner (ed.), *Text, play and the story: the reconstruction of self and society*, 19-55. Washington, DC: American Ethnological Society.

Battaglia, D. 1990. *On the bones of the serpent: person, memory and mortality in Sabarl Island society*. Chicago and London: Chicago University Press.

Bell, C. 1992. *Ritual theory, ritual practice*. Oxford: Oxford University Press.

Benedict, R. 1934. *Patterns of culture*. Boston: Houghton Mifflin.

Bennike, P. 1999. The Early Neolithic Danish bog finds: a strange group of people! In B. Coles, J. Coles and M.S. Jørgensen (eds), *Bog bodies, sacred sites and wetland archaeology*, 27-32. Exeter: Wetland Archaeology Research Project.

Bergson, H. 1911. *Matter and memory* (translated by N.M. Paul and W.S. Palmer, first published 1908). London: Allen and Unwin.

Bird-David, N. 1990. The giving environment: another perspective on the economic system of gatherer-hunters. *Current Anthropology* 31, 189-96.

Bird-David, N. 1999. The Nyaka of the Wynaad, south India. In L.B. Lee and R. Daly (eds), *The Cambridge encyclopedia of hunters and gatherers*, 257-60. Cambridge: Cambridge University Press.

Bloch, M. 1971. *Placing the dead: tombs, ancestral villages, and kinship organization in Madagascar*. London: Seminar Press.

Bloch, M. 1977. The past and the present in the past. *Man* 12, 278-92.

Bloch, M. 1985. Almost eating the ancestors. *Man* 20, 631-46.

Bloch, M. 1992. What goes without saying: the conceptualization of Zafimaniry society. In A. Kuper (ed.), *Conceptualizing society*, 127-46. London: Routledge.

Bloch, M. 1993. Domain specificity, living kinds and symbolism. In P. Boyer (ed.), *Cognitive aspects of religious symbolism*, 111-19. Cambridge: Cambridge University Press.

Bloch, M. 1994. Ancestors. In A. Barnard and J. Spencer (eds), *Encyclopedia of social and cultural anthropology*, 43. London: Routledge.

Bloch, M. 1995a. Questions not to ask of Malagasy carvings. In I. Hodder, M. Shanks, A. Alexandri, V. Buchli, J. Carmen, J. Last and G. Lucas (eds), *Interpreting archaeology: finding meaning in the past*, 212-15. London: Routledge.

Bloch, M. 1995b. The resurrection of the house amongst the Zafimaniry of Madagascar. In J. Carsten and S. Hugh-Jones (eds), *About the house: Lévi-Strauss and beyond*, 69-83. Cambridge: Cambridge University Press.

Bloch, M. 1998. *How we think they think: anthropological approaches to cognition, memory and literacy*. Boulder: Westview.

Bloch, M. and Parry, J. 1982, Introduction: death and the regeneration of life. In M. Bloch and J. Parry (eds), *Death and the regeneration of life*, 1-44. Cambridge: Cambridge University Press.

Bogaard, A. 2002. Questioning the relevance of shifting cultivation to Neolithic farming in the loess belt of Europe: evidence from the Hambach Forest experiment. *Vegetation History and Archaeobotany* 11, 155-68.

Bognár-Kutzián, I. 1963. *The Copper Age cemetery of Tiszapolgár-Basatanya*. Budapest: Akadémiai Kiadó.

Bognár-Kutzián, I. 1972. *The Early Copper Age Tiszapolgár culture in the Carpathian basin*. Budapest: Akadémiai Kiadó.

Bogucki, P. 1988. *Forest farmers and stockherders: early agriculture and its consequences in north-central Europe*. Cambridge: Cambridge University Press.

Bogucki, P. 1993. Animal traction and household economies in Neolithic Europe. *Antiquity* 67, 492-503.

Bogucki, P. 1996. Sustainable and unsustainable adaptations by early farming communities of northern Poland. *Journal of Anthropological Archaeology* 15, 289-311.

Bohannan, L. 1952. A genealogical charter. *Africa* 22, 301-15.

Boissevain, J. 1974. *Friends of friends: networks, manipulators and coalitions*. Oxford: Blackwells.

Bökönyi, S. 1974. *History of domestic mammals in central and eastern Europe*. Budapest: Akadémiai Kiadó.

Bökönyi, S. 1992. The Early Neolithic vertebrate fauna of Endrőd 119. In S. Bökönyi (ed.), *Cultural and landscape changes in south-east Hungary*, 195-299. Budapest: Archaeolingua.

Bonsall, C., Cook, G., Lennon, R., Harkness, D., Scott, M., Bartosiewicz, L. and McSweeney, K. 2000. Stable isotopes, radiocarbon and the Mesolithic-Neolithic transition in the Iron Gates. *Documenta Praehistorica* 27, 119-32.

Bonsall, C., Lennon, R., McSweeney, K., Stewart, C., Harkness, D., Boroneanţ, V., Bartosiewicz, L., Payton, R. and Chapman, J. 1997. Mesolithic and Early Neolithic in the Iron Gates: a palaeodietary perspective. *Journal of European Archaeology* 5, 51-92.

Borić, D. 1999. Places that created time in the Danube Gorges and beyond, c. 9000-5500 BC. *Documenta Prehistorica* 26, 41-70.

Botenschlager, S. and Öggl, K. (eds) 2000. *The Iceman and his natural environment: The Man in the Ice 4*. Vienna and New York: Springer.

Bouchet, F., Pétrequin, P., Paichelier, J.C. and Dommelier, S. 1995. Première approche paléoparasitologique du site néolithique de Chalain (Jura, France). *Bulletin de la Société de Pathologie Exotique* 88, 265-8.

Bouchet, F., Bentrad, S., Dommelier, S., Paichelier, J.C. and Pétrequin, P. 1997. Capillarioses intestinales: nematodoses du Néolithique? *Bulletin de la Société Française de Parasitologie* 15, 49-54.

Boujot, C., Cassen, S. and Vaquero Lastres, J. 1998. Some abstraction for a practical subject: the Neolithization of western France seen through funerary architecture. *Cambridge Archaeological Journal* 8, 193-206.

Bourdieu, P. 1977. *Outline of a theory of practice* (translated by R. Nice, first published 1972). Cambridge: Cambridge University Press.

Bradley, R. 1993. *Altering the earth*. Edinburgh: Society of Antiquaries of Scotland.

Bradley, R. 1996. Long houses, long mounds and Neolithic enclosures. *Journal of Material Culture* 1, 239-56.

Bradley, R. 1998a. *The significance of monuments: on the shaping of human experience in Neolithic and Bronze Age Europe*. London: Routledge.

Bradley, R. 1998b. Ruined buildings, ruined stones: enclosures, tombs and natural places in the Neolithic of south-west England. *World Archaeology* 30, 13-22.

Bradley, R. 2000. *An archaeology of natural places*. London: Routledge.

Bradley, R. 2001. Orientations and origins: a symbolic dimension to the long house in Neolithic Europe. *Antiquity* 75, 50-6.

Bradley, R. 2002. *The past in prehistoric societies*. London: Routledge.

Brück, J. 2001. Monuments, power and personhood in the British Neolithic. *Journal of the Royal Anthropological Institute* 7, 649-67.

Bulmer, R. 1967. Why is the cassowary not a bird? A problem of zoological taxonomy among the Karam of the New Guinea highlands. *Man* 2, 5-25.

Burl, A. 1987. *The Stonehenge people*. London: Dent.

Busby, C. 1997. Permeable and partible persons: a comparative analysis of gender and body in south India and Melanesia. *Journal of the Royal Anthropological Institute* 3, 261-78.

Butler, J. 1993. *Bodies that matter: on the discursive limits of 'sex'*. London: Routledge.

Campen, I. and Stäuble, H. 1999. Holzfunde im Braunkohlentagebau Zwenkau: Ausnahme oder Regel? *Plattform (Zeitschrift des Vereins für Pfahlbau und Heimatkunde)* 7/8 (1998/99), 46-57.

Capasso, L. 1995. Ungueal morphology and pathology of the "Ice Man". In K. Spindler, E. Rastbichler-Zissernig, H. Wilfing, D. zur Nedden and H. Nothdurfter (eds), *Der Mann im Eis: neue Funde und Ergebnisse*, 231-9. Springer: Vienna.

Carman, J. and Harding, A. (eds) 1999. *Ancient warfare: archaeological perspectives*. Stroud: Sutton.

Case, H. 1969. Neolithic explanations. *Antiquity* 43, 176-86.

Chagnon, N.A. 1968. *Yanomamo: the fierce people*. New York: Holt, Rinehart and Winston.

Chaix, L. 1997. La transition Méso-Néolithique: quelques données de l'archéozoologie dans les Alpes du Nord et le Jura. In C. Jeunesse (ed.), *Le Néolithique danubien et ses marges entre Rhin et Seine*, 191-6. Strasbourg: Cahiers de l'Association pour la Promotion de la Recherche Archéologique en Alsace.

Chapdelaine, C. 1993. The sedentarization of the prehistoric Iroquians: a slow or rapid transformation? *Journal of Anthropological Archaeology* 12, 173-209.

Chapman, J. 1982. 'The Secondary Products Revolution' and the limitations of the Neolithic. *Bulletin of the Institute of Archaeology* 19, 107-22.

Chapman, J. 1993. Social power in the Iron Gates Mesolithic. In J.C. Chapman and P. Dolukhanov (eds), *Cultural transformations and interactions in eastern Europe*, 61-106. Aldershot: Avebury.

Chapman J. 1994. The living, the dead and the ancestors, time, life cycles and the mortuary domain in later European prehistory. In J. Davies (ed.), *Ritual and remembrance: responses to death in human societies*, 40-85. Sheffield: Sheffield Academic Press.

Chapman, J. 1997a. Changing gender relations in Hungarian prehistory. In J. Moore and E. Scott (eds), *Invisible people and processes: writing gender and childhood into European archaeology*, 131-49. London: Leicester University Press.

Chapman, J. 1997b. The origin of tells in eastern Hungary. In P. Topping (ed.), *Neolithic landscapes*, 139-64. Oxford: Oxbow.

Chapman, J. 1997c. Places as timemarks: the social construction of prehistoric landscapes in eastern Hungary. In J. Chapman and P. Dolukhanov (eds), *Landscapes in flux: central and eastern Europe in antiquity*, 209-30. Oxford: Oxbow.

Chapman, J. 2000a. *Fragmentation in archaeology: people, places and broken objects in the prehistory of south-eastern Europe*. London: Routledge.

Chapman, J. 2000b. *Tensions at funerals: micro-tradition analysis in later Hungarian prehistory.* Budapest: Archaeolingua.

Childe, V.G. 1936. *Man makes himself.* London: Watts and Co.

Childe, V.G. 1942. *What happened in history.* Harmondsworth: Penguin.

Clason, A.T. 1968. The animal bones of the Bandceramic and Middle Age settlements near Bylany in Bohemia. *Palaeohistoria* 14, 1-17.

Cleal, R. 1992. Significant form: ceramic styles in the Earlier Neolithic of southern England. In N. Sharples and A. Sheridan (eds), *Vessels for the ancestors*, 286-304. Edinburgh: Edinburgh University Press.

Coles, J.M. and Coles, B.J. 1986. *Sweet Track to Glastonbury: the Somerset Levels in prehistory.* London: Thames and Hudson.

Connerton, P. 1989. *How societies remember.* Cambridge: Cambridge University Press.

Connor, L.H. 1995. The action of the body on society: washing a corpse in Bali. *Journal of the Royal Anthropological Institute* 1, 537-59.

Cook, G.T., Bonsall, C., Hedges, R.E.M., McSweeney, K., Boroneanţ, V., Bartosiewicz, L. and Pettitt, P.B. 2002. Problems of dating human bones from the Iron Gates. *Antiquity* 76, 77-85.

Cooney, G. 2000. *Landscapes of Neolithic Ireland.* London: Routledge.

Coser, L.A. (ed.) 1992. *Maurice Halbwachs: on collective memory.* Chicago and London: University of Chicago Press.

Coudart, A. 1998. *Architecture et société néolithique: l'unité et la variance de la maison danubienne.* Paris: Éditions de la Maison des Sciences de L'Homme.

Crandall, D.P. 1998. The role of time in Himba valuations of cattle. *Journal of the Royal Anthropological Institute* 4, 101-14.

Crossley, N. 1995. Merleau-Ponty: the illusive body and carnal sociology. *Body and Society* 1, 43-64.

Cullen, B.S. 2000. *Contagious ideas: on evolution, culture, archaeology and cultural virus.* Oxford: Oxbow.

Cummings, V. 2001. Landscapes in transition?: exploring the origins of monumentality in south-west Wales and south-west Scotland. Unpublished PhD thesis, Cardiff University.

Cummings, V. and Whittle, A. forthcoming. *Places of special virtue: megaliths in the Neolithic landscapes of Wales.* Oxford: Oxbow.

Current Archaeology 2000. White Horse Stone: a Neolithic longhouse. *Current Archaeology* 168, 450-3.

Dahl, G. 1979. Ecology and equality: the Boran case. In *Production and society*, 261-81. Cambridge: Cambridge University Press.

Dahl, G. and Hjort, A. 1976. *Having herds: pastoral herd growth and household economy.* Stockholm: Department of Social Anthropology, University of Stockholm.

Darvill, T. 1996. Neolithic buildings in England, Wales and the Isle of Man. In T. Darvill and J. Thomas (eds), *Neolithic houses in northwest Europe and beyond*, 77-111. Oxford: Oxbow.

Darvill, T. and Thomas, J. (eds) 1996. *Neolithic houses in northwest Europe and beyond.* Oxford: Oxbow.

de Beaune, S.A. 2000. *Pour une archéologie du geste: broyer, moudre, piler, des premiers chasseurs aux premiers agriculteurs.* Paris: CNRS Éditions.

de Grooth, M.E.Th. 1997. Social and economic interpretations of the chert procurement strategies of the Bandkeramik settlement at Hienheim, Bavaria. *Analecta Praehistorica Leidensia* 29, 91-8.

de Grooth, M. 1999. Review of A. Zimmermann 1995. *Germania* 77, 731-4.

De Laguna, F. 1990. Tlingit. In W. Suttles (ed.), *Handbook of North American Indians. Volume 7. Northwest Coast*, 203-28. Washington: Smithsonian Institution.

Derevenski, J.S. 1997. Age and gender at the site of Tiszapolgár-Basatanya, Hungary. *Antiquity* 71, 875-89.

Derevenski, J.S. 2000. Rings of life: the role of early metalwork in mediating the gendered life course. *World Archaeology* 31, 389-406.

De Roever-Bonnet, H., Rijpstra, A.C., van Renesse, M.A. and Peen, C.H. 1979. Helminth eggs and gregarines from coprolites from the excavations at Swifterbant (Swifterbant Contribution 10). *Helinium* 19, 7-12.

Descola, P. 1992. Societies of nature and the nature of society. In A. Kuper (ed.), *Conceptualizing society*, 107-26. London: Routledge.

Descola, P. 1994. *In the society of nature: a native ecology in Amazonia* (translated by N. Scott). Cambridge: Cambridge University Press.

Dickens, P. 1990. *Urban sociology: society, locality and human nature*. Hemel Hempstead: Harvester Wheatsheaf.

Dieckmann, B., Maier, U. and Vogt, R. 1997. Hornstaad-Hörnle, eine der ältesten jungstein-zeitlichen Ufersiedlungen am Bodensee. In H. Schlichtherle (ed.), *Pfahlbauten rund um die Alpen*, 15-21. Stuttgart: Theiss.

Dobres, M.-A. 2000. *Technology and social agency: outlining a practice framework for archaeology*. Oxford: Blackwell.

Dobres, M.-A. and Robb, J. (eds) 2000a. *Agency in archaeology*. London: Routledge.

Dobres, M.-A. and Robb, J. 2000b. Agency in archaeology: paradigm or platitude? In M.-A. Dobres and J. Robb (eds), *Agency in archaeology*, 3-17. London: Routledge.

Döhle, H.-J. 1993. Haustierhaltung und Jagd in der Linienbandkeramik – ein Überblick. *Zeitschrift für Archäologie* 27, 105-24.

Domboróczki, L. 1997. Füzesabony-Gubakút. In P. Raczky, T. Kovács and A. Anders (eds), *Utak a múltba: az M3-as autópálya régészeti leletmentései*, 19-27. Budapest: Magyar Nemzeti Múzeum and Eötvös Loránd Tudományegyetem Régészettudományi Intézet.

Douglas, M. 1957. Animals in Lele religious symbolism. *Africa* 27, 46-58.

Douglas, M. 1966. *Purity and danger: an analysis of concepts of pollution and taboo*. London: Routledge and Kegan Paul.

Douglas, M. 1996. *Natural symbols: explorations in cosmology, with a new introduction* (first published 1970). London: Routledge.

Douglas, M. and Isherwood, B. 1996. *The world of goods: towards an anthropology of consumption*. London: Routledge.

Ebersbach, R., Favre, P. and Akeret, Ö. 1999. Horgen-Scheller – ein Bauerndorf? *Archäologie der Schweiz* 22, 18-21.

Edmonds, M. 1999. *Ancestral geographies of the Neolithic: landscape, monuments and memory*. London: Routledge.

Eliade, M. 1968. *Myths, dreams and mysteries*. London: Collins Fontana Library.

Erny-Rodmann, C., Gross-Klee, E., Haas, J.N., Jacomet, S. and Zoller, H. 1997. Früher 'human impact' und Ackerbau im Übergangsbereich Spätmesolithikum-Frühneolithikum im schweizerischen Mittelland. *Jahrbuch der Schweizerischen Gesellschaft für Ur- und Frühgeschichte* 80, 27-56.

Evans, C., Pollard, J. and Knight, M. 1999. Life in woods: tree-throws, 'settlement' and forest cognition. *Oxford Journal of Archaeology* 18, 241-54.

Evans, J.G. and Smith, I.F. 1983. Excavations at Cherhill, north Wiltshire, 1967. *Proceedings of the Prehistoric Society* 49, 43-117.

Evans-Pritchard, E.E. 1940. *The Nuer*. London: Oxford University Press.

Evans-Pritchard, E.E. 1956. *Nuer religion*. New York and Oxford: Oxford University Press.

Fairbairn, A. (ed.) 2000. *Plants in Neolithic Britain and beyond*. Oxford: Oxbow.

Fairweather, A.D. and Ralston, I.B.M. 1993. The Neolithic timber hall at Balbridie, Grampian Region, Scotland: the building, the date and the plant macrofossils. *Antiquity* 67, 313-23.

Falk, P. 1994. *The consuming body*. London: Sage Publications.

Fardon, R. 1999. *Mary Douglas: an intellectual biography*. London: Routledge.

Featherstone, M., Hepworth, M. and Turner, B.S. 1991. *The body: social process and cultural theory*. London: Sage Publications.

Feist, E. and Feist, W. 1999. Die Häuser der Nivchi, Ostsiberien. *Plattform (Zeitschrift des Vereins für Pfahlbau und Heimatkunde)* 7/8 (1998/99), 2-21.

Fentress, J. and Wickham, C. 1992. *Social memory*. Oxford: Blackwell.

Firth, R. 1936. *We, the Tikopia*. London: George Allen and Unwin.

Forty, A. and Küchler, S. (eds) 1999. *The art of forgetting*. Oxford and New York: Berg.

Foster, J.K. (ed.) 1999. *Neuroimaging and memory*. Hove: Psychology Press.

Foucault, M. 1978. *The history of sexuality*. London: Allen Lane.

Fowler, C. 2000. The individual, the subject, and archaeological interpretation. Reading Luce Irigaray and Judith Butler. In C. Holtorf and H. Karlsson (eds), *Philosophy and archaeological practice: perspectives for the 21st century*, 107-33. Göteborg: Bricoleur Press.

Fowler, C. 2001. Personhood and social relations in the British Neolithic with a case study from the Isle of Man. *Journal of Material Culture* 6, 137-63.

Fraser, S. 1998. The public forum and the space between: the materiality of social strategy in the Irish Neolithic. *Proceedings of the Prehistoric Society* 64, 203-24.

Gallay, A. 1990. Historique des recherches enterprises sur le nécropole mégalithique du Petit-Chasseur à Sion (Valais: Suisse). In J. Guilaine and X. Gutherz (eds), *Autour de Jean Arnal*, 335-57. Montpellier: École des Études en Sciences Sociales.

Gamble, C. 1999. *The Palaeolithic societies of Europe*. Cambridge: Cambridge University Press.

Garašanin, M. and Radovanović, I. 2001. A pot in house 54 at Lepenski Vir. *Antiquity* 75, 118-25.

Gardner, A. 1999. The impact of Neolithic agriculture on the environments of south-east Europe. Unpublished PhD thesis, Cambridge University.

Gardner, P.M. 2000. Respect and nonviolence among recently sedentary Paliyan foragers. *Journal of the Royal Anthropological Institute* 6, 215-36.

Garfinkel, H. 1967. *Studies in ethnomethodology*. Englewood Cliffs, NJ: Prentice-Hall.

Gatens, M. 1992. Power, bodies and difference. In M. Barrett and A. Phillips (eds), *Destabilising theory: contemporary feminist debates*, 120-37. Cambridge: Polity Press.

Gell, A. 1998. *Art and agency: an anthropological theory*. Oxford: Clarendon Press.

Gell, A. 1999. Strathernograms, or the semiotics of mixed metaphors. In A. Gell (edited by E. Hirsch), *The art of anthropology: essays and diagrams*, 29-75. London: Routledge.

Gero, J.M. 2000. Troubled travels in agency and feminism. In M.-A. Dobres and J. Robb (eds), *Agency in archaeology*, 34-9. London: Routledge.

Giddens, A. 1979. *Central problems in social theory: action, structure and contradiction in social analysis*. Cambridge: Polity Press.

Giddens, A. 1984. *The constitution of society: outline of the theory of structuration*. Cambridge: Polity Press.

Goffman, E. 1963. *Behaviour in public places: notes on the social organization of gatherings*. New York: Free Press.

Goffman, E. 1969. *The presentation of self in everyday life*. London: Allen Lane.

Goldman, G. 1978. Gesichtsgefässe und andere Menschendarstellungen aus Battonya. *A Békés Megyei Múzeum Közleményei* 5, 13-60.

Gopnik, A., Meltzoff, A. and Kuhl, P. 1999. *How babies think: the science of childhood*. London: Weidenfeld and Nicholson.

Gosden, C. 1994. *Social being and time*. Oxford: Blackwell.

Gosden, C. 1999. *Archaeology and anthropology: a changing relationship*. London: Routledge.

Gosden, C. 2001. Making sense: archaeology and aesthetics. *World Archaeology* 33, 163-7.

Gosden, C. and Hather, J. (eds) 1999. *The prehistory of food: appetites for change*. London: Routledge.

Gow, P. 1991. *Of mixed blood: kinship and history in Peruvian Amazonia*. Oxford: Clarendon Press.

Graham, M. 1994. *Mobile farmers: an ethnographic approach to settlement organization among the the Raramuri of northwestern Mexico*. Ann Arbor: International Monographs in Prehistory.

Grigson, C. 1999. The mammalian remains. In A. Whittle, J. Pollard and C. Grigson, *The harmony of symbols: the Windmill Hill causewayed enclosure, Wiltshire*, 164-252. Oxford: Oxbow.

Grimes, W.F. 1949. Pentre-ifan burial chamber, Pembrokeshire. *Archaeologia Cambrensis* 100, 3-23.

Grinker, R.R. 1994. *Houses in the rainforest: ethnicity and inequality among farmers and foragers in central Africa*. Berkeley: University of California Press.

Gronenborn, D. 1997. *Silexartefakte der ältestbandkeramischen Kultur*. Bonn: Habelt.

Gronenborn, D. 1999. Variations on a basic theme: the transition to farming in southern central Europe. *Journal of World Prehistory* 13, 123-210.

Gross, E., Jacomet, S. and Schibler, J. 1990. Stand und Ziele der wirtschaftsarchäologischen Forschung an neolithischen Ufer- und Inselsiedlungen im unteren Zürichseeraum (Kt. Zürich, Schweiz). In J. Schibler, J. Sedlmeier and H. Spycher (eds), *Festschrift für Hans R. Stampfli: Beiträge zur Archäozoologie, Archäologie, Anthropologie, Geologie und Paläontologie*, 77-100. Basel: Helbing and Lichtenhahn.

Guenther, M. 1999. From totemism to shamanism: hunter-gatherer contributions to world mythology and spirituality. In L.B. Lee and R. Daly (eds), *The Cambridge encyclopedia of hunters and gatherers*, 426-33. Cambridge: Cambridge University Press.

Hachem, L. 1995. La réprésentation de la chasse dans les espaces villageois rubanés de la vallée de l'Aisne (France). *Anthropozoologica* 21, 197-205.

Hachem, L. 1997. Structuration spatiale d'un village du Rubané Récent, Cuiry-lès-Chaudardes (Aisne). Analyse d'une catégorie de rejets domestiques: la faune. In A. Bocquet (ed.), *Espaces physiques, espaces sociaux dans l'analyse interne des sites du Néolithique à l'Âge du Fer*, 245-61. Paris: Éditions du Comité des Travaux Historiques et Scientifiques.

Hachem, L. 1999. Apport de l'archéozoologie à la connaissance de l'organisation villageoise rubanée. In F. Braemer, S. Cleuziou and A. Coudart (eds), *Habitat et société*, 325-38. Antibes: Éditions APDCA.

Hachem, L. 2000. New observations on the Bandkeramik house and social organization. *Antiquity* 74, 308-12.

Hachem, L. and Auxiette, G. 1995. La faune. In M. Ilett and M. Plateaux (eds), *Le site néolithique de Berry-au-Bac, "Le Chemin de la Pêcherie" (Aisne)*, 128-99. Paris: CNRS Éditions.

Hachem, L., Guichard, Y., Farruggia, J.-P., Dubouloz, J. and Ilett, M. 1998. Enclosure and burial in the earliest Neolithic of the Aisne valley. In M. Edmonds and C. Richards (eds), *Understanding the Neolithic of north-west Europe*, 127-40. Glasgow: Cruithne Press.

Hafner, A. 2002. Unter Wasser: retten und bewahren. *Archäologie in Deutschland* 2, 54–9.

Hagen, J.M. 1999. The good behind the gift: morality and exchange among the Maneo of eastern Indonesia. *Journal of the Royal Anthropological Institute* 5, 361-76.

Halbwachs, M. 1925. *Les cadres sociaux de la mémoire*. Paris: Presse Universitaire de France.

Halbwachs, M. 1950. *La mémoire collective*. Paris: Presse Universitaire de France.

Halpern, J.M. 1999. The ecological transformation of a resettled area, pig herders to settled farmers in Central Serbia (Šumadija, Yugoslavia) during the 19th and 20th centuries. In L. Bartosiewicz and H.M. Greenfield (eds), *Transhumant pastoralism in southern Europe: recent perspectives from archaeology, history and ethnology*, 79-95. Budapest: Archaeolingua.

Halstead, P. 1989. Like rising damp? An ecological approach to the spread of farming in south-east and central Europe. In A. Milles, D. Williams and N. Gardner (eds), *The beginnings of agriculture*, 23-53. Oxford: British Archaeological Reports.

Halstead, P. 1996. Pastoralism or household herding? Problems of scale and specialisation in early Greek animal husbandry. *World Archaeology* 28, 20-42.

Halstead, P. 1998. Mortality models and milking: problems of uniformitarianism, optimality and equifinality reconsidered. *Anthropozoologica* 27, 3-20.

Halstead, P. 1999. Neighbours from hell? The household in Neolithic Greece. In P. Halstead (ed.), *Neolithic society in Greece*, 77-95. Sheffield: Sheffield Academic Press.

Hampel, A. 1995. *Frankfurt am Main Niedereschbach: ein ältestbandkevamischer Siedlungsplatz. Teil 1: Die Befunde*. Nussloch: Rolf Angerer.

Harding, A.F. 2000. *European societies in the Bronze Age*. Cambridge: Cambridge University Press.

Harris, M. 1998. The rhythm of life on the Amazon floodplain: seasonality and sociality in a riverine village. *Journal of the Royal Anthropological Institute* 4, 65-82.

Harris, M. 2000. *Life on the Amazon: the anthropology of a Brazilian peasant village*. Oxford: Oxford University Press.

Harrison, S. 1995. Transformations of identity in Sepik warfare. In M. Strathern (ed.), *Shifting contexts: transformations in anthropological knowledge*, 81-97. London: Routledge.

Häusser, A. (ed.) 1998. *Krieg oder Frieden? Herxheim vor 7000 Jahren*. Herxheim: Landesamt für Denkmalplfege.

Hayden, B. 1995. Pathways to power: principles for creating socioeconomic inequalities. In T.D. Price and G. Feinman (eds), *The foundations of social inequality*, 15-86. New York: Plenum Press.

Hegedűs, K. and Makkay, J. 1987. Vésztő-Mágor: a settlement of the Tisza culture. In P. Raczky (ed.), *The Late Neolithic of the Tisza region*, 93-111. Budapest and Szolnok: Szolnok Museum.

Hertz, M. 1960. *Death and the right hand*. Aberdeen: Cohen and West.

Hey, G. 1997. Neolithic settlement at Yarnton, Oxfordshire. In P. Topping (ed.), *Neolithic landscapes*, 99-111. Oxford: Oxbow.

Higgs, E. and Jarman, M. 1969. The origins of agriculture: a reconsideration. *Antiquity* 43, 31-41.

Hillman, G.C. 1981. Reconstructing crop husbandry practices from charred remains of crops. In R. Mercer (ed.), *Farming practice in British prehistory*, 123-62. Edinburgh: Edinburgh University Press.

Hillson, S. 1996. *Dental anthropology*. Cambridge: Cambridge University Press.

Hodder, I. 1982. *Symbols in action: ethnoarchaeological studies of material culture*. Cambridge: Cambridge University Press.

Hodder, I. 1984. Burials, houses, women and men in the European Neolithic. In D. Miller and C. Tilley (eds), *Ideology, power and prehistory*, 51-68. Cambridge: Cambridge University Press.

Hodder, I. 1986. *Reading the past*. Cambridge: Cambridge University Press.

Hodder, I. 1990. *The domestication of Europe*. Oxford: Blackwell.

Hodder, I. 1999. *The archaeological process: an introduction*. Oxford: Blackwell.

Hodder, I. 2000. Agency and individuals in long-term process. In M.-A. Dobres and J. Robb (eds), *Agency in archaeology*, 21-33. London: Routledge.

Hofmann, D. 2001. The representation of personal identity in the mortuary record of early Neolithic Bavaria. Unpublished MA dissertation, Cardiff University.

Horváth, F. 1987. Hódmezővásárhely-Gorzsa: a settlement of the Tisza culture. In P. Raczky (ed.), *The Late Neolithic of the Tisza region*, 33-49. Budapest and Szolnok: Szolnok Museum.

Houot, A. 1992. *Le soleil des morts*. Brussels and Paris: Éditions du Lombard.

Hugh-Jones, C. 1996. Houses in the Neolithic imagination: an Amazonian example. In T. Darvill and J. Thomas (eds), *Neolithic houses in northwest Europe and beyond*, 185-93. Oxford: Oxbow.

Hugh-Jones, S. 1995. Inside-out and back-to-front: the androgynous house in northwest Amazonia. In J. Carsten and S. Hugh-Jones (eds), *About the house: Lévi-Strauss and beyond*, 226-52. Cambridge: Cambridge University Press.

Hüster-Plogmann, H., Schibler, J. and Jacomet, S. 1999. The significance of aurochs as a hunted animal in the Swiss Neolithic. In G.-C. Weniger (ed.), *Archäologie und Biologie des Auerochsen*, 151-60. Mettmann: Neanderthal Museum.

Hymes, D. 1990. Mythology. In W. Suttles (ed.), *Handbook of North American Indians. Volume 7. Northwest Coast*, 593-601. Washington: Smithsonian Institution.

Ilett, M., Constantin, C., Demoule, J.-P. and Coudart, A. 1982. The late Bandkeramik of the Aisne valley: environment and spatial organisation. *Analecta Praehistorica Leidensia* 15, 45-61.

Ilett, M., Plateaux, M. and Coudart, A. 1986. Analyse spatiale des habitats du Rubané Récent: problèmes actuels. In J.-P. Demoule and J. Guilaine (eds), *Le Néolithique de la France*, 131-40. Paris: Picard.

Ingold, T. 1980. *Hunters, pastoralists and ranchers: reindeer economies and their transformations*. Cambridge: Cambridge University Press.

Ingold, T. (ed.) 1988. *What is an animal?* London: Unwin Hyman.

Ingold, T. 1993. The temporality of the landscape. *World Archaeology* 25, 152-73.

Ingold, T. 1995. Building, living, dwelling: how animals and people make themselves at home in the world. In M. Strathern (ed.), *Shifting contexts: transformations in anthropological knowledge*, 57-80. London: Routledge.

Ingold, T. 1996. Hunting and gathering as ways of perceiving the environment. In R. Ellen and K. Fukui (eds), *Redefining nature*, 117-55. Oxford: Berg.

Ingold, T. 2000. *The perception of the environment: essays in livelihood, dwelling and skill*. London: Routledge.

Jacomet, S., Brombacher, C. and Dick, M. 1989. *Archäobotanik am Zürichsee: Ackerbau, Sammelwirtschaft und Umwelt von neolithischen und bronzezeitlichen Seeufersiedlungen im Raum Zürich*. Zürich: Verlag Orell Füssli.

Jacomet, S. and Kreuz, A. 1999. *Archäobotanik: Aufgaben, Methoden und Ergebnisse vegetations- und agrargeschichtlicher Forschung*. Stuttgart: Verlag Eugen Ulmer.

Jankovich, B.D., Makkay J. and Szőke B.M. 1989. *Magyarország Régészeti Topográfiája: a Szarvasi járás IV/2*. Budapest: Akadémiai Kiadó.

Jarman, M.1972. European deer economies and the advent of the Neolithic. In E.S. Higgs (ed.), *Papers in economic prehistory*, 125-48. Cambridge: Cambridge University Press.

Jeunesse, C. 1997. *Pratiques funéraires au Néolithique ancien: sépultures et nécropoles des sociétés danubiennes (5500-4900 av. J.-C.)*. Paris: Éditions Errance.

Jeunesse, C. and Arbogast, R.-M. 1997. À propos du statut de la chasse au Néolithique moyen. La faune sauvage dans les déchets domestiques et dans les mobiliers funéraires. In C. Jeunesse (ed.), *Le Néolithique danubien et ses marges entre Rhin et Seine*, 81-102. Strasbourg: Cahiers de l'Association pour la Promotion de la Recherche Archéologique en Alsace, Supplément 3.

Johnson, D.H. 1994: *Nuer prophets: a history of prophecy from the Upper Nile in the nineteenth and twentieth centuries*. Oxford: Clarendon Press.

Jones, A. 1998. Where eagles dare: landscape, animals and the Neolithic of Orkney. *Journal of Material Culture* 3, 301-24.

Jones, A. 1999. The world on a plate: ceramics, food technology and cosmology in Neolithic Orkney. *World Archaeology* 31, 55-77.

Jones, A. 2000. Life after death: monuments, material culture and social change in Neolithic Orkney. In A. Ritchie (ed.), *Neolithic Orkney in its European context*, 127-38. Cambridge: McDonald Institute for Archaeological Research.

Jones, G. 2000. Evaluating the importance of cultivation and collecting in Neolithic Britain. In A. Fairbairn (ed.), *Plants in Neolithic Britain and beyond*, 79-84. Oxford: Oxbow.

Kalicz, N. and Koós, J. 1997. Mezőkövesd-Mocsolyás. In P. Raczky, T. Kovács and A. Anders (eds), *Utak a múltba: az M3-as autópálya régészeti leletmentései*, 28-33. Budapest: Magyar Nemzeti Múzeum and Eötvös Loránd Tudományegyetem Régészettudományi Intézet.

Kalicz, N. and Makkay, J. 1977: *Die Linienbandkeramik in der grossen ungarischen Tiefebene*. Budapest: Akadémiai Kiadó.

Kalicz, N. and Raczky, P. 1984. Preliminary report on the 1977-82 excavations at the Neolithic and Bronze Age tell settlement at Berettyóújfalu-Herpály. *Acta Archaeologica Academiae Scientiarum Hungaricae* 36, 85-136.

Kalicz, N. and Raczky, P. 1987. Berettyóújfalu-Herpály: a settlement of the Herpály culture. In P. Raczky (ed.), *The Late Neolithic of the Tisza region*, 113-34. Budapest and Szolnok: Szolnok Museum.

Kalicz, N., Virág, Z.M. and Biró, K.T. 1998. The northern periphery of the Early Neolithic Starčevo culture in south-western Hungary: a case study of an excavation at Lake Balaton. *Documenta Praehistorica* 25, 151-88.

Keeley, L.H. and Cahen, D. 1989. Early Neolithic forts and villages in NE Belgium: a preliminary report. *Journal of Field Archaeology* 16, 157-76.

Kelly, R.C. 1993. *Constructing inequality: the fabrication of a hierarchy of virtue among the Etoro*. Ann Arbor: University of Michigan Press.

Kennedy, D.I.D. and Bouchard, R.T. 1990. Bella Coola. In W. Suttles (ed.), *Handbook of North American Indians. Volume 7. Northwest Coast*, 323-39. Washington: Smithsonian Institution.

Kertész, R. 1996. The Mesolithic in the Great Hungarian Plain. In L. Tálas (ed.), *At the fringes of three worlds: hunter-gatherers and farmers in the middle Tisza valley*, 5-34. Szolnok: Damjanich Museum.

Kinnes, I. and Hibbs, J. 1989. Le Gardien du Tombeau: further reflections on the Initial Neolithic. *Oxford Journal of Archaeology* 8, 159-66.

Kokkinidou, D. and Nikolaidou, M. 1997. Body imagery in the Aegean Neolithic: ideological implications of anthropomorphic figurines. In J. Moore and E. Scott (eds), *Invisible people and processes: writing gender and childhood into European prehistory*, 88-112. London: Leicester University Press.

Kolhoff, C. 1999. Die Keramik des bandkeramischen Fundplatzes Weisweiler 110. Unpublished Magisterarbeit im Fach Ur- und Frühgeschichte der Philosophischen Fakultät der Universität zu Köln.

Kopytoff, I. 1971. Ancestors as elders in Africa. *Africa* 41, 129-42.

Korek, J. 1989. *Die Theiss-Kultur in der mittleren und nördlichen Theissgegend*. Budapest: Magyar Nemzeti Múzeum.

Kosse, K. 1979. *Settlement ecology of the Early and Middle Neolithic Körös and Linear Pottery cultures in Hungary*. Oxford: British Archaeological Reports.

Krause, R. 1997. Un village rubané avec fossé d'enceinte et nécropole près de Vaihingen/Enz, dept. Ludwigsburg. In C. Jeunesse (ed.), *Le Néolithique danubien et ses marges entre Rhin et Seine*, 45-56. Strasbourg: Cahiers de l'Association pour la Promotion de la Recherche Archéologique en Alsace, Supplément 3.

Kreuz, A. 1990. *Die ersten Bauern Mitteleuropas - eine archäobotanische Untersuchung zu Umwelt und Landwirtschaft des ältesten Bandkeramik*. Analecta Praehistorica Leidensia 13.

Kristiansen, K. 1998. *Europe before history*. Cambridge: Cambridge University Press.

Küchler, S. 1987. Malangan - art and memory in a Melanesian society. *Man* 22, 238-55.

Kuper, A. 1988. *The invention of primitive society: transformations of an illusion*. London: Routledge.

Kuper, A. 1996. *Anthropology and anthropologists: the modern British school* (third revised and enlarged edition). London: Routledge.

Kuper, A. 1999. *Culture: the anthropologists' account*. Cambridge, MA: Harvard University Press.

Kwint, M., Breward, C. and Aynsley, J. (eds) 1999. *Material memories: design and evocation*. Oxford and New York: Berg.

Larsen, C.S. 1997. *Bioarchaeology: interpreting human behaviour from the human skeleton*. Cambridge: Cambridge University Press.

Last, J. 1998a. Books of life: biography and memory in a Bronze Age barrow. *Oxford Journal of Archaeology* 17, 43-53.

Last 1998b. The residue of yesterday's existence: settlement space and discard at Miskovice and Bylany. In I. Pavlů (ed.), *Bylany: Varia I*, 17-45. Prague: Archeologický ústav AV ČR.

Latour, B. 1993. *We have never been modern*. New York: Harvester Wheatsheaf.

Lawrence, P. 1984. *The Garia: an ethnography of a traditional cosmic system in Papua New Guinea*. Melbourne: Melbourne University Press.

Layard, J. 1942. *Stone men of Malekula*. London: Chatto and Windus.

Layton, R. 2000. *Anthropology and history in Franche-Comté: a critique of social theory*. Oxford: Oxford University Press.

Leach, E. 1954. *The political systems of Highland Burma*. London: G. Bell and Sons.

Leach, E. 1961. *Pul Eliya, a village in Ceylon: a study in land tenure and kinship*. Cambridge: Cambridge University Press.

Leach, E. 1964. Anthropological aspects of language: animal categories and verbal abuse. In E. Lenneberg (ed.), *New directions in the study of language*, 23-63. Cambridge, MA: MIT Press.

Leach, E. 1973. Concluding address. In C. Renfrew (ed.), *The explanation of culture change: models in prehistory*, 761-771. London: Duckworth.

Leach, M. 1992. Women's crops in women's spaces: gender relations in Mende rice farming. In E. Croll and D. Parkin (eds), *Bush base: forest farm. Culture, environment and development*, 76-96. London: Routledge.

Lech, J. 1990. The organization of siliceous rock supplies to the Danubian early farming communities (LBK): central European examples. In D. Cahen and M. Otte (eds), *Rubané et Cardial*, 51-9. Liège: Études et Recherches Archéologiques de l'Université de Liège.

Lech, J. 1997. Remarks on prehistoric flint mining and flint supply in European archaeology.

In A. Ramos-Millán and M.A. Bastille (eds), *Siliceous rocks and culture*, 611-37. Granada: Universidad de Granada.

Lenneis, E. 1997. Houseforms of the central European Linear Pottery culture and of the Balkan Early Neolithic - a comparison. *Poročilo o raziskovanju paleolitika, neolitika in eneolitika v Sloveniji* 24, 143-9.

Lenneis, E. and Lüning, J. 2001. *Die altbandkeramischen Siedlungen von Neckenmarkt und Strögen*. Bonn: Habelt.

Lepowsky, M. 1990. Gender in an egalitarian society: a case study from the Coral Sea. In P.G. Sanday and R.G. Goodenough (eds), *Beyond the second sex: new directions in the anthropology of gender*, 171-223. Philadelphia: University of Pennsylvania Press.

Leslie, E. 1999. Souvenirs and forgetting: Walter Benjamin's memory-work. In M. Kwint, C. Breward and J. Aynsley (eds), *Material memories: design and evocation*, 107-22. Oxford and New York: Berg.

Lévi-Strauss, C. 1964. *Totemism* (translated by R. Needham, first published 1962). London: Merlin Press.

Lienhardt, G. 1961. *Divinity and experience: the religion of the Dinka*. Oxford: Oxford University Press.

Lourandos, H. 1980. Change or stability? Hydraulics, hunter-gatherers and population in temperate Australia. *World Archaeology* 11, 245-64.

Louwe Kooijmans, L.P. 1993. An Early/Middle Bronze Age multiple burial at Wassenaar, the Netherlands. *Analecta Praehistorica Leidensia* 26, 1-20.

Lowenstein, T. 1993. *Ancient land: sacred whale. The Inuit hunt and its rituals*. New York: North Point Press.

Lucas, G.M. 1996. Of death and debt. A history of the body in Neolithic and Early Bronze Age Yorkshire. *Journal of European Archaeology* 4, 99-118.

Lüning, J. (ed.) 1997a. *Studien zur neolithischen Besiedlung der Aldenhovener Platte und ihrer Umgebung*. Bonn: Habelt.

Lüning, J. (ed.) 1997b. *Ein Siedlungsplatz der ältesten Bandkeramik in Bruchenbrücken, Stadt Friedberg/Hessen*. Bonn: Habelt.

Lüning, J. 2000. *Steinzeitliche Bauern in Deutschland: die Landwirtschaft im Neolithikum*. Bonn: Habelt.

Lüning, J. and Stehli, P. (eds) 1994. *Die Bandkeramik im Merzbachtal auf der Aldenhovener Platte*. Bonn: Habelt.

Lynch, F. 1972. Portal dolmens in the Nevern valley, Pembrokeshire. In F. Lynch and C. Burgess (eds), *Prehistoric man in Wales and the west*, 67-83. Bath: Adams and Dart.

MacDonald, D.H. and Hewlett, B.S. 1999. Reproductive interests and forager mobility. *Current Anthropology* 40, 501-23.

MacDonald, G.F. 1981. Cosmic equations in Northwest Coast Indian art. In D.N. Abbott (ed.), *The world is as sharp as a knife*, 225-37. Victoria: British Columbia Provincial Museum.

Mack, J. 1986. *Madagascar: island of the ancestors*. London: British Museum Publications.

Makkay, J. 1992. Excavations at the Körös culture settlement of Endrőd-Öregszőlők 119 in 1986-1989. In S. Bökönyi (ed.), *Cultural and landscape changes in south-east Hungary*, 121-93. Budapest: Archaeolingua.

Makkay, J. 2000. *Egy ösi háború: Az esztergályhorváti kédö neolithikus tömegsír [An early war: the late Neolithic mass grave from Esztergályhorváti]*. Budapest: Janos Makkay.

Maltby, M. 1990. Animal bones. In J. Richards, *The Stonehenge environs project*, 57-61. London: English Heritage.

Manning, A. and Serpell, J. (eds) 1994. *Animals and human society: changing perspectives*. London: Routledge.

Martin, J.W. 2001. *The land looks after us: a history of native American religion*. Oxford: Oxford University Press.

Maschio, T. 1998. The narrative and counter-narrative of the gift: emotional dimensions of ceremonial exchange in southwestern New Britain. *Journal of the Royal Anthropological Institute* 4, 83-100.

Maschner, H.D.G. and Reedy-Maschner, K.L. 1998. Raid, retreat, defend (repeat): the archaeology and ethnohistory of warfare on the North Pacific rim. *Journal of Anthropological Archaeology* 17, 19-51.

Mateiciucová, I. 2001. Silexindustrie in der ältesten Linearbandkeramik-Kultur in Mähren und Niederösterreich auf der Basis der Silexindustrie des Lokalmesolithikums. In R. Kertész and J. Makkay (eds), *From the Mesolithic to the Neolithic*, 283-99. Budapest: Archaeolingua.

Mattheusser, E. 1991. Die geographische Ausrichtung bandkeramischer Häuser. In *Studien zur Siedlungsarchäologie 1*, 1-49. Bonn: Habelt.

Mauss, M. 1985. A category of the human mind: the notion of person, the notion of self. In M. Carrithers, S. Collins and S. Lukes (eds), *The category of the person: anthropology, philosophy, history*, 1-25. Cambridge: Cambridge University Press.

Mayes, A.R. and Montaldi, D. 1999. The neuroimaging of long-term memory encoding processes. In J.K. Foster (ed.), *Neuroimaging and memory* (a special issue of *Memory*), 613-59. Hove: Psychology Press.

Mead, M. 1943. *Coming of age in Samoa: a study of adolescence and sex in primitive societies* (first published 1928). Harmondsworth: Penguin.

Meigs, A. 1984. *Food, sex and pollution: a New Guinea religion*. New Brunswick: Rutgers University Press.

Meigs, A. 1990. Multiple gender ideologies and statuses. In P.G. Sanday and R.G. Goodenough (eds), *Beyond the second sex: new directions in the anthropology of gender*, 99-112. Philadelphia: University of Pennsylvania Press.

Meillassoux, C. 1972. From reproduction to production. *Economy and society* 1, 93-105.

Meisenheimer, M. 1989. *Das Totenritual, geprägt durch Jenseitsvorstellungen und Gesellschafts-realität: Theorie des Totenrituals eines kupferzeitlichen Friedhofs zu Tiszapolgár-Basatanya (Ungarn)*. Oxford: British Archaeological Reports.

Méniel, P. 1984. *Contribution à l'histoire de l'élevage en Picardie du Néolithique à l'Âge du Fer. Revue Archéologique de Picardie*, numéro spécial.

Méniel, P. 1987. Les dépôts d'animaux du fossé chasséen de Boury-en-Vexin (Oise). *Revue Archéologique de Picardie* 1, 3-21.

Mercer, R.J. 1999. The origins of warfare in the British Isles. In J. Carman and A. Harding (eds), *Ancient warfare: archaeological perspectives*, 143-56. Stroud: Sutton.

Merleau-Ponty, M. 1962. *Phenomenology of perception* (translated by C. Smith). London: Routledge and Kegan Paul.

Meskell, L. 1996. The somatisation of archaeology: institutions, discourses and corporeality. *Norwegian Archaeological Review* 29, 1-16.

Meskell, L. 1998. Intimate archaeologies: the case of Kha and Merit. *World Archaeology* 29, 363-79.

Middleton, D. and Edwards, D. 1990. Introduction. In D. Middleton and D. Edwards (eds), *Collective remembering*, 1-22. London: Sage.

Middleton, J. 1960. *Lugbara religion: ritual and authority among an East African people*. London: Oxford University Press.

Middleton, J. 1970. *The study of the Lugbara: expectation and paradox in anthropological research*. New York: Holt, Rinehart and Winston.

Middleton, J. 1982. Lugbara death. In M. Bloch and J. Parry (eds), *Death and the regeneration of life*, 134-54. Cambridge: Cambridge University Press.

Mithen, S. (ed.) 2000. *Hunter-gatherer landscape archaeology: the Southern Hebrides Mesolithic project 1988-98*. Cambridge: McDonald Institute for Archaeological Research.

Modderman. P.J.R. 1988. *The Linear Pottery culture: diversity in uniformity*. Berichten van de Rijksdienst voor het Oudheidkundig Bodemonderzoete, Jaargang 38.

Molleson, T. 1994. The eloquent bones of Abu Hureyra. *Scientific American* 271, 59-65.

Momaday, N.S. 1976. Native American attitudes to the environment. In W.H. Capps (ed.), *Seeing with a native eye: essays on Native American religion*, 79-85. New York: Harper and Row.

Monk, M. 2000. Seeds and soils of discontent: an environmental archaeological contribution to the nature of the Early Neolithic. In A. Desmond, G. Johnson, M. McCarthy, J. Sheehan and E. Shee Twohig (eds), *New agendas in Irish prehistory: papers in commemoration of Liz Anderson*, 67-87. Bray: Wordwell.

Montgomery, J., Budd, P. and Evans, J. 2000. Reconstructing the lifetime movements of ancient people: a Neolithic case study from southern England. *European Journal of Archaeology* 3, 370-85.

Moore, H.L. 1988. *Feminism and anthropology*. Cambridge: Polity Press.

Moore, H.L. 1994. *A passion for difference: essays in anthropology and gender*. Cambridge: Polity Press.

Moore, H.L. 2000. Ethics and ontology: why agents and agency matter. In M.-A. Dobres and J. Robb (eds), *Agency in archaeology*, 259-63. London: Routledge.

Mordant, D. 1997. Le complexe des Réaudins à Balloy: enceinte et nécropole monumentale. In C. Constantin, D. Mordant and D. Simonin, *La culture du Cerny: nouvelle économie, nouvelle société au Néolithique*, 449-77. Nemours: Mémoires du Musée de Préhistoire d'Ile de France.

Morris, B. 1995. Woodland and village: reflections on the 'animal estate' in rural Malawi. *Journal of the Royal Anthropological Institute* 1, 301-15.

Morris, B. 1998. *The power of animals: an ethnography*. Oxford: Berg.

Morris, B. 2000. *Animals and ancestors: an ethnography*. Oxford: Berg.

Morris, I. 1991. The archaeology of ancestors: the Saxe/Goldstein hypothesis revisited. *Cambridge Archaeological Journal* 1, 147-69.

Müller, H.-H. 1964. *Die Haustiere der mitteldeutschen Bandkeramiker*. Berlin: Akademie-Verlag.

Neth, A. 1999. *Eine Siedlung der frühen Bandkeramik in Gerlingen, Kreis Ludwigsburg*. Stuttgart: Theiss.

Neustupný, E. 1998. Structures and events: the theoretical basis of spatial archaeology. In E. Neustupný (ed.), *Space in prehistoric Bohemia*, 9-44. Praha: Institute of Archaeology, Academy of Sciences of the Czech Republic.

Newell, W.H. (ed.). 1976. *Ancestors*. Paris and The Hague: Mouton.

Nieszery, N. 1995. *Linearbandkeramische Gräberfelder in Bayern*. Espelkamp: Marie Leidorf.

Orschiedt, J. 1998. *Bandkeramische Siedlungsbestattungen in Südwestdeutschland: archäologische und anthropologische Befunde*. Rahden: Marie Leidorf.

O'Shea, J. 1996. *Villagers of the Maros: a portrait of an Early Bronze Age society*. New York: Plenum Press.

Oswald, A., Dyer, C. and. Barber, M. 2001. *The creation of monuments: Neolithic causewayed enclosures in the British Isles*. London: English Heritage.

Palmer, R. 1976. Interrupted ditch enclosures in Britain: the use of aerial photography for comparative studies. *Proceedings of the Prehistoric Society* 42, 161-86.

Parker Pearson, M. 1992. Tombs and monumentality in southern Madagascar: preliminary results of the central Androy survey. *Antiquity* 66, 941-8.

Parker Pearson, M. 2000. Eating money: a study in the ethnoarchaeology of food. *Archaeological Dialogues* 7, 217-32.

Parker Pearson, M. and Richards, C. 1994. Architecture and order: spatial representation and archaeology. In M. Parker Pearson and C. Richards (eds), *Architecture and order: approaches to social space*, 38-72. London: Routledge.

Pavlů, I. 1966. Early 'myths' relating to the Neolithic society. *Archeologické Rozhledy* 18, 700-17.

Pétrequin, P. 1984. *Gens de l'eau, gens de la terre: ethno-archéologie des communautés lacustres.* Paris: Hachette.

Pétrequin, P. (ed.) 1989. *Les sites littoraux néolithiques de Clairvaux-les-Lacs (Jura). II. Le Néolithique moyen.* Paris: Éditions de la Maison des Sciences de L'Homme.

Pétrequin, P. 1993. North wind, south wind: Neolithic technical choices in the Jura mountains, 3700-2400 BC. In P. Lemonnier (ed.), *Technical choices: transformations in material culture since the Neolithic*, 36-76. London: Routledge.

Pétrequin, P. 1996. Management of architectural woods and variations in population density in the fourth and third millennia B.C. (Lakes Chalain and Clairvaux, Jura, France). *Journal of Anthropological Archaeology* 15, 1-19.

Pétrequin, P. (ed.) 1997. *Les sites littoraux néolithiques de Clairvaux-les-Lacs et de Chalain (Jura) III. Chalain station 3. 3200-2900 av. J.-C. Volume 2.* Paris: Éditions de la Maison des Sciences de L'Homme.

Pétrequin, P. and Jeunesse, C. (eds) 1995. *La hache de pierre: carrières vosgiennes et échanges de lames polies pendant le Néolithique (5400-2100 av. J.-C.).* Paris: Éditions Errance.

Piggott, S. 1955. Windmill Hill – east or west? *Proceedings of the Prehistoric Society* 21, 96-101.

Piggott, S. 1962. *The West Kennet long barrow: excavations 1955-56.* London: HMSO.

Pluciennik, M. 2002. Art, artefact, metaphor. In Y. Hamilakis, M. Pluciennik and S. Tarlow (eds), *Thinking through the body: archaeologies of corporeality*, 217-32. New York: Kluwer Academic/Plenum Publishers.

Politis, G.G. 1996. Moving to produce: Nukak mobility and settlement patterns in Amazonia. *World Archaeology* 27, 492-511.

Pollard, J. 1999a. The Keiller excavations. In A. Whittle, J. Pollard and C. Grigson, *The harmony of symbols: the Windmill Hill causewayed enclosure, Wiltshire*, 24-72. Oxford: Oxbow.

Pollard, J. 1999b. 'These places have their moments': thoughts on settlement practices in the British Neolithic. In J. Brück and M. Goodman (eds), *people, place and tradition: new dimensions in settlement archaeology*, 76-93. London: UCL Press.

Pollard, J. 2001. The aesthetics of depositional practice. *World Archaeology* 33, 315-33.

Pollex, A. 1999. Comments on the interpretation of the so-called cattle burials of Neolithic central Europe. *Antiquity* 73, 542-50.

Powell, T.G.E. 1973. Excavation of the megalithic chambered cairn at Dyffryn Ardudwy, Merioneth, Wales. *Archaeologia* 104, 1-49.

Power, C. and Watts, I. 1997. The woman with the zebra's penis: gender, mutability and performance. *Journal of the Royal Anthropological Institute* 3, 537-60.

Price, T.D., Bentley, R.A., Lüning, J., Gronenborn, D. and Wahl, J. 2001. Prehistoric human migration in the *Linearbandkeramik* of central Europe. *Antiquity* 75, 593-603.

Prummel, W., Niekus, M.J.L.Th., van Gijn, A.L. and Cappers, R.T.J. 2002. A Late Mesolithic kill site of aurochs at Jardinga, Netherlands. *Antiquity* 76, 413-24.

Pryor, F. 1998. *Etton: excavations at a Neolithic causewayed enclosure near Maxey, Cambridgeshire, 1982-7.* London: English Heritage.

Pucher, E. 1987. Viehwirtschaft und Jagd zur Zeit der ältesten Linearbandkeramik von Neckenmarkt (Burgenland) und Strögen (Niederösterreich). *Mitteilungen der Anthropologischen Gesellschaft in Wien* 117, 141-55.

Pucher, E. 1998. Die Tierknochen des linearbandkeramischen Siedlungsplatz Brunn am Gebirge (Niederösterreich). In P. Anreiter, L. Bartosiewicz, E. Jerem and W. Meid (eds), *Man and the animal world*, 465-79. Budapest: Archaeolingua.

Raczky, P. 1983. Origins of the custom of burying the dead inside houses in south-east Europe. *Szolnok Megyei Múzeumi Évkönyve* 1982-3, 5-10.

Raczky, P. (ed.) 1987a. *The Late Neolithic of the Tisza region*. Budapest and Szolnok: Szolnok Museum.

Raczky, P. 1987b. Öcsöd-Kováshalom: a settlement of the Tisza culture. In P. Raczky (ed.), *The Late Neolithic of the Tisza region*, 61-83. Budapest and Szolnok: Szolnok Museum.

Raczky, P., Anders, A., Nagy, E., Kurucz, K., Hajdú, Z. and Meier-Arendt, W. 1997a. Polgár-Csőszhalom-dűlő. In P. Raczky, T. Kovács and A. Anders (eds), *Utak a múltba: az M3-as autópálya régészeti leletmentései*, 34-43. Budapest: Magyar Nemzeti Múzeum and Eötvös Loránd Tudományegyetem Régészettudományi Intézet.

Raczky, P., Anders, A., Nagy, E., Kriveczky, B., Hajdú, Z. and Szalai, T. 1997b. Polgár-Nagy Kasziba. In P. Raczky, T. Kovács and A. Anders (eds), *Utak a múltba: az M3-as autópálya régészeti leletmentései*, 47-50. Budapest: Magyar Nemzeti Múzeum and Eötvös Loránd Tudományegyetem Régészettudományi Intézet.

Raczky, P., Meier-Arendt, W., Kurucz, K., Hajdú, Z. and Szikora, A. 1994. A Late Neolithic settlement in the Upper Tisza region and its cultural connections (preliminary report). *A Nyíregyházi Jósa András Múzeum Évkönyve* 36, 231-6.

Radovanović, I. 1996. *The Iron Gates Mesolithic*. Ann Arbor: International Monographs in Prehistory.

Radovanović, I. 1997. The Lepenski Vir culture: a contribution to interpretation of its ideological aspects. In I. Radovanović (ed.), *ΑΝΤΙΔΩΡΟΝ Dragoslavo Srejović*, 85-93. Belgrade: Centre for Archaeological Research, Faculty of Philosophy, University of Belgrade.

Rappaport, R.A. 1968. *Pigs for the ancestors: ritual in the ecology of a New Guinea people*. New Haven and London: Yale University Press.

Rapport, N. 1996. Individualism. In A. Barnard and J. Spencer (eds), *Encyclopaedia of social and cultural anthropology*, 298-302. London: Routledge.

Rapport, N. 1997. *Transcendent individual: towards a literary and liberal anthropology*. London: Routledge.

Reddy, W.M. 1997. Against constructionism: the historical ethnography of emotions. *Current Anthropology* 38, 327-51.

Renfrew, C. 1976. Megaliths, territories and populations. In S.J. de Laet (ed.), *Acculturation and continuity in Atlantic Europe*, 198-220. Bruges: de Tempel.

Renfrew, C. 2000. At the edge of knowability: towards a prehistory of languages. *Cambridge Archaeological Journal* 10, 7-34.

Renfrew, C. 2001. Commodification and institution in group-oriented and individualizing societies. In W.G. Runciman (ed.), *The origin of human social institutions*, 93-117. Oxford: Oxford University Press.

Richards, M. 2000. Human consumption of plant foods in the British Neolithic: direct evidence from bone stable isotopes. In A.S. Fairbairn (ed.), *Plants in Neolithic Britain and beyond*, 123-35. Oxford: Oxbow.

Richards, M. and Hedges, R.E.M. 1999. A Neolithic revolution? New evidence of diet in the British Neolithic. *Antiquity* 73, 891-7.

Robb, J. 1994. Gender contradictions, moral coalitions, and inequality in prehistoric Italy. *Journal of European Archaeology* 2, 20-49.

Robb, J. 1999. Secret agents: culture, economy, and social reproduction. In J.E. Robb (ed.), *Material symbols: culture and economy in prehistory*, 3-15. Carbondale: Center for Archaeological Investigations, Southern Illinois University.

Rosaldo, R. 1993. *Culture and truth: the remaking of social analysis*. London: Routledge.

Russell, M. 2000. *Neolithic flint mines in Britain*. Stroud: Tempus.

Sahlins, M. 1999. Two or three things that I know about culture. *Journal of the Royal Anthropological Institute* 5, 399-421.

Santos-Granero, F. 1991. *The power of love: the moral use of knowledge among the Amuesha of central Peru*. London and Atlantic Highlands, NJ: Athlone Press.

Sassaman, K.E. 2000. Agents of change in hunter-gatherer technology. In M.-A. Dobres and J. Robb (eds), *Agency in archaeology*, 148-67. London: Routledge.

Saville, A. 1990. *Hazleton North: the excavation of a Neolithic long cairn of the Cotswold-Severn group*. London: English Heritage.

Scarre, C. and Raux, P. 2000. A new decorated menhir. *Antiquity* 74, 757-8.

Scheffler, H.W. 1966. Ancestor worship in anthropology: or, observations on descent and descent groups. *Current Anthropology* 7, 541-51.

Scheffler, H.W. 1985. Filiation and affiliation. *Man* 20, 1-21.

Schibler, J. and Jacomet, S. 1999. Archaeozoological and archaeobotanical evidence of human impact on Neolithic environments in Switzerland. In N. Benecke (ed.), *The Holocene history of the European vertebrate fauna: modern aspects of research*, 339-54. Berlin: Archäologie in Eurasien 6.

Schibler, J., Hüster-Plogmann, H., Jacomet, S., Brombacher, C., Gross-Klee, E. and Rast-Eicher, A. 1997. *Ökonomie und Ökologie neolithischer und bronzezeitlicher Ufersiedlungen am Zürichsee*. Zürich: Monographien der Kantonsarchäologie Zürich.

Schibler, J., Jacomet, S., Hüster-Plogmann, H. and Brombacher, C. 1997. Economic crash in the 37th and 36th centuries cal. BC in Neolithic lake shore sites in Switzerland. *Anthropozoologica* 25/26, 553-70.

Schulting, R. 1998. Slighting the sea: stable isotope evidence for the transition to farming in northwestern Europe. *Documenta Praehistorica* 25, 203-18.

Schulting, R. 2000. New AMS dates from the Lambourn long barrow and the question of the earliest Neolithic in southern England: repacking the Neolithic package? *Oxford Journal of Archaeology* 19, 25-35.

Schulting, R. and Richards, M. 2001. Dating women and becoming farmers: new AMS and stable isotope evidence from the Breton Mesolithic cemeteries of Téviec and Hoëdic. *Journal of Anthropological Archaeology* 20, 314-44.

Schwartz, A.C. 1998. Eastern Hungary: animal bones from Polgár-Csőszhalom. In P. Anreiter, L. Bartosiewicz, E. Jerem and W. Meid (eds), *Man and the animal world*, 511-14. Budapest: Archaeolingua.

Seip, L.P. 1999. Transformations of meaning: the life history of a Nuxalk mask. *World Archaeology* 31, 272-87.

Sené, G. 1996. Les coprolithes du Néolithique final de Clairvaux-les-Lacs et de Chalain. In P. Pétrequin (ed.), *Les sites littoraux néolithiques de Clairvaux-les-Lacs et de Chalain (Jura). III. Chalain station 3, 3200-2900 av. J.-C., volume 2*, 747-56. Paris: Éditions de la Maison des Sciences de L'Homme.

Seremetakis, C.N. 1991. *The last word: women, death, and divination in inner Mani*. Chicago: University of Chicago Press.

Shaffer, G.D. 1999. An examination of architectural stability and change: contributions from southern Italy. In R.H. Tykot, J. Morter and J.E. Robb (eds), *Social dynamics of the prehistoric Mediterranean*, 97-110. London: Accordia Research Institute.

Shanks, M. and Tilley, C. 1982. Ideology, symbolic power and ritual communication: a reinterpretation of Neolithic mortuary practices. In I. Hodder (ed.), *Symbolic and structural archaeology*, 129-54. Cambridge: Cambridge University Press.

Shanks, M. and Tilley, C. 1987. *Social theory and archaeology*. Cambridge: Polity Press.

Sharples, N. 1991. *Maiden Castle: excavations and field survey 1985-6*. London: Historic Buildings and Monument Commission for England.

Sharples, N. 2000. Antlers and Orcadian rituals: an ambiguous role for red deer in the Neolithic. In A. Ritchie (ed.), *Neolithic Orkney in its European context*, 107-16. Cambridge: McDonald Institute for Archaeological Research.

Shee Twohig, E. 1981. *The megalithic art of western Europe*. Oxford: Clarendon Press.

Shennan, S.E. 1975. The social organisation at Brank. *Antiquity* 49, 279-88.

Shennan, S.E. 1982. From minimal to moderate ranking. In C. Renfrew and S. Shennan (eds), *Ranking, resource and exchange*, 27-32. Cambridge: Cambridge University Press.

Shennan, S.J. 1986. Central Europe in the third millennium BC: an evolutionary trajectory for the beginning of the Bronze Age. *Journal of Anthropological Archaeology* 5, 115-46.

Shennan, S.J. 1993. Settlement and social change in central Europe, 3500-1500 BC. *Journal of World Prehistory* 7, 121-61.

Shennan, S.J. 1994. Grounding arguments about burials. *Archaeological Dialogues* 1, 124-5.

Sherratt, A. 1981. Plough and pastoralism: aspects of the secondary products revolution. In I. Hodder, G. Isaac and N. Hammond (eds), *Pattern of the past: studies in honour of David Clarke*, 261-305. Cambridge: Cambridge University Press.

Sherratt, A. 1982a. Mobile resources: settlement and exchange in early agricultural Europe. In C. Renfrew and S. Shennan (eds), *Ranking, resource and exchange*, 13-26. Cambridge: Cambridge University Press.

Sherratt, A. 1982b. The development of Neolithic and Copper Age settlement in the Great Hungarian Plain. Part 1: the regional setting. *Oxford Journal of Archaeology* 1, 287-316.

Sherratt, A. 1983. The development of Neolithic and Copper Age settlement in the Great Hungarian Plain. Part II: site survey and settlement dynamics. *Oxford Journal of Archaeology* 2, 13-41.

Sherratt, A. 1987. Cups that cheered. In W.H. Waldren and R.C. Kennard (eds), *Bell Beakers of the western Mediterranean*, 81-114. Oxford: British Archaeological Reports.

Sherratt, A. 1995a. Reviving the grand narrative: archaeology and long-term change. *Journal of European Archaeology* 3, 1-32.

Sherratt, A. 1995b. Instruments of conversion? The role of megaliths in the Meso-lithic/Neolithic transition in north-west Europe. *Oxford Journal of Archaeology* 14, 245-60.

Siemoneit, B. 1997. *Das Kind in der Linienbandkeramik: Befunde aus Gräberfeldern und Siedlungen in Mitteleuropa*. Rahlen: Marie Leidorf.

Smith, C.A. and Lynch, F.M. 1987. *Trefignath and Din Dryfol: the excavation of two megalithic tombs in Anglesey*. Bangor: Cambrian Archaeological Association.

Snyder, K.S. 1997. Elders' authority and women's protest: the *masay* ritual and social change among the Iraqw of Tanzania. *Journal of the Royal Anthropological Institute* 3, 561-76.

Sommer, U. 2001. 'Hear the instruction of thy father, and forsake not the law of thy mother': change and persistence in the European early Neolithic. *Journal of Social Archaeology* 1, 244-70.

Soudský, B. and Pavlů, I. 1966. Interprétation historique de l'ornament linéaire. *Památky Archeologické* 57, 91-125.

Spatz, H. 1997. La nécropole du Néolithique moyen (Hinkelstein, Grossgartach) de Trebur (Gross-Gerau, Hesse). In C. Jeunesse (ed.), *Le Néolithique danubien et ses marges entre Rhin et Seine*, 157-70. Strasbourg: Cahiers de l'Association pour la Promotion de la Recherche Archéologique en Alsace, Supplément 3.

Spector, J.D. 1991. What this awl means: towards a feminist archaeology. In J.M. Gero and M.W. Conkey (eds), *Engendering archaeology: women and prehistory*, 388-476. Oxford: Blackwell.

Spindler, K. 1996. Iceman's last weeks. In K. Spindler, H. Wilfing, E. Rastbichler-Zissernig, D. zur Nedden and H. Nothdurfter (eds), *Human mummies: a global survey of their status and the techniques of conservation*, 249-63. Vienna: Springer.

Spindler, K., Rastbichler-Zissernig, E., Wilfing, H., zur Nedden, D. and Nothdurfter, H. (eds) 1995. *Der Mann im Eis: neue Funde und Ergebnisse*. Springer: Vienna.

Srejović, D. 1972. *Europe's first monumental sculpture: new discoveries at Lepenski Vir*. London: Thames and Hudson.

Stampfli, H.R. 1976. Die Tierknochen von Egolzwil 5: osteoarchäologische Untersuchungen. In R. Wyss (ed.), *Das jungsteinzeitliche Jäger-Bauerndorf von Egolzwil 5 im Wauwilermoos*, 125-40. Zürich: Schweizerisches Landesmuseum Zürich.

Starnini, E. 2000. Stone industries of the Early Neolithic cultures in Hungary and their relationships with the Mesolithic background. *Società Preistoria Protostoria Friuli-Venezia Giulia, Trieste* 8, 207-19.

Stäuble, H. 1990. Die ältestbandkeramische Grabenanlage in Eitzum, Ldkr. Wolfenbüttel. Überlegungen zur Verfüllung und Interpretation von Befunden. *Jahresschrift für mitteldeutsche Vorgeschichte* 73, 331-44.

Stäuble, H. 1995. Radiocarbon dates of the earliest Neolithic in central Europe. *Radiocarbon* 37, 227-37.

Stäuble, H. 1997. Häuser, Gruben und Fundverteilung. In J. Lüning (ed.), *Ein Siedlungsplatz der ältesten Bandkeramik in Bruchenbrücken, Stadt Friedberg/Hessen*, 17-150. Bonn: Habelt

Stäuble, H. and Campen, I. 1998. 7000 Jahre Brunnenbau im Südraum von Leipzig. In H. Koschik (ed.), *Brunnen der Jungsteinzeit*, 51-71. Köln: Rheinland-Verlag.

Steadman, L.B., Palmer, C.T. and Tilley, C.F. 1996. The universality of ancestor worship. *Ethnology* 35, 63-76.

Stehli, P. 1994. Chronologie der Bandkeramik im Merzbachtal. In J. Lüning and P. Stehli (eds), *Die Bandkeramik im Merzbachtal auf der Aldenhovener Platte*, 79-191. Bonn: Habelt.

Steppan, K. 1999. Aurochs in the food economy of the Jungneolithikum (Upper Neolithic) in south-west Germany. In G.-C. Weniger (ed.), *Archäologie und Biologie des Auerochsen*, 161-71. Mettmann: Neanderthal Museum.

Sterner, J. 1989. Who is signalling whom? Ceramic style, ethnicity and taphonomy among the Sirak Bulahay. *Antiquity* 63, 451-9.

Stevanovic, M. 1997. Production of architecture in the age of clay. *Journal of Anthropological Archaeology* 16, 334-95.

Stewart, S. 1999. Prologue: from the museum of touch. In M. Kwint, C. Breward and J. Aynsley (eds), *Material memories: design and evocation*, 17-36. Oxford and New York: Berg.

Strathern, A. and Stewart, P. 1999. Dangerous woods and perilous pearl shells: the fabricated politics of a longhouse in Pangia, Papua New Guinea. *Journal of Material Culture* 5, 69-89.

Strathern, M. 1980. No nature, no culture: the Hagen case. In C. MacCormack and M. Strathern (eds), *Nature, culture and gender*, 174-222. Cambridge: Cambridge University Press.

Strathern, M. 1987. Introduction. In M. Strathern (ed.), *Dealing with inequality: analysing gender relations in Melanesia and beyond*, 1-32. Cambridge: Cambridge University Press.

Strathern, M. 1988. *The gender of the gift: problems with women and problems with society in Melanesia*. Berkeley: University of California Press.

Strathern, M. 1992a. Parts and wholes: refiguring relationships in a post-plural world. In A. Kuper (ed.), *Conceptualizing society*, 75-104. London: Routledge.

Strathern, M. 1992b. *After nature: English kinship in the late twentieth century*. Cambridge: Cambridge University Press.

Strathern, M. 1996. Cutting the network. *Journal of the Royal Anthropological Institute* 2, 517-35.

Suttles, W. (ed.) 1990. *Handbook of North American Indians, Volume 7: Northwest Coast*. Washington: Smithsonian Institution.

Sykes, B. 1999. The molecular genetics of European ancestry. *Proceedings of the Royal Society of London* B 354, 131-39.

Szynkiewicz, S. 1994. Sheep bone as a sign of descent: tibial symbolism among the Mongols. In R. Willis (ed.), *Signifying animals: human meaning in the natural world*, 74-84. London: Routledge.

Takács, I. 1992. Fish remains from the Early Neolithic site of Endrőd 119. In S. Bökönyi (ed.), *Cultural and landscape changes in south-east Hungary*, 301-11. Budapest: Archaeolingua.

Tambiah, S.J. 1969. Animals are good to think and good to prohibit. *Ethnology* 8, 423-59.

Tambiah, S.J. 1998. Edmund Ronald Leach, 1910-1989. *Proceedings of the British Academy* 97, 293-344.

Taylor, A.C. 1993. Remembering to forget: identity, mourning and memory among the Jivaro. *Man* 28, 653-78.

Taylor, A.C. 1996. The soul's body and its states: an Amazonian perspective on the nature of being human. *Journal of the Royal Anthropological Institute* 2, 201-15.

Teschler-Nicola, M. 1996. Anthropologische Spurensicherung – Die traumatischen und postmortalen Veränderungen an den linearbandkeramischen Skelettresten von Asparn/Schletz. In *Rätsel um Gewalt und Tod vor 7,000 Jahren: eine Spurensicherung*, 47-64. Asparn a.d.Zaya: Museum für Urgeschichte.

Thomas, J. 1988. The social significance of Cotswold-Severn burial rites. *Man* 23, 540-59.

Thomas, J. 1996. *Time, culture and identity: an interpretive archaeology*. London: Routledge.

Thomas, J. 1999. *Understanding the Neolithic*. London: Routlege.

Thorpe, N. 2001. Danish causewayed enclosures – temporary monuments? In T. Darvill and J. Thomas (eds), *Neolithic enclosures in Atlantic northwest Europe*, 190-203. Oxford: Oxbow Books.

Tilley, C. 1994. *A phenomenology of landscape: places, paths and monuments*. Oxford: Berg.

Tilley, C. 1996. *An ethnography of the Neolithic: early prehistoric societies in southern Scandinavia*. Cambridge: Cambridge University Press

Tilley, C. 1998. Megaliths in texts. In M. Edmonds and C. Richards (eds), *Understanding the Neolithic of north-western Europe*, 141-60. Glasgow: Cruithne Press.

Tilley, C. 1999. *Metaphor and material culture*. Oxford: Blackwell.

Tilley, C. and Bennett, W. 2001. An archaeology of supernatural places: the case of West Penwith. *Journal of the Royal Anthropological Institute* 7, 335-62.

Tomka, S.A. 1993. Site abandonment among transhumant agro-pastoralists: the effects of delayed curation on assemblage composition. In C.M. Cameron and S.A. Tomka (eds), *Abandonment of settlements and regions: ethnoarchaeological and archaeological approaches*, 11-24. Cambridge: Cambridge University Press.

Treherne, P. 1995. The warrior's beauty: the masculine body and self-identity in Bronze Age Europe. *Journal of European Archaeology* 3, 105-44.

Tresset, A. 2000. Early husbandry in Atlantic areas. Animal introductions, diffusions of techniques and native acculturation at the north-western fringe of Europe. In J.C. Henderson (ed.), *The prehistory and early history of Atlantic Europe*, 17-32. Oxford: British Archaeological Reports.

Tresset, A. and Vigne, J.-D. forthcoming. Le dépôt d'animaux de la structure et d'Er Grah: une illustration de la symbolique des bovins à la charnière du Mésolithique et du Néolithique bretons? *Gallia Préhistoire*.

Tringham, R. 1991. Households with faces: the challenge of gender in prehistoric architectural remains. In J.M. Gero and M.W. Conkey (eds), *Engendering archaeology: women and prehistory*, 93-131. Oxford: Blackwell.

Tringham, R. 2000. The continuous house: a view from the deep past. In S. Gillespie and R. Joyce (eds), *Beyond kinship: social and material reproduction in house societies*, 115-34. Philadelphia: University of Pennsylvania Press.

Trogmayer, O. 1969. Die Bestattungen der Körös-Gruppe. *A Móra Ferenc Múzeum Évkönyve* 2, 5-15.

Turner, B.S. 1996. *The body and society: explorations in social theory* (second edition). London: Sage Publications.

Turner, V. 1969. *The ritual process: structure and anti-structure*. Chicago: Aldine.

Uerpmann, H.-P. 1977. Betrachtungen zur Wirtschaftsform neolithischer Gruppen in Südwestdeutschland. *Fundberichte aus Baden-Württemberg* 3, 144-61.

Uerpmann, M. and Uerpmann, H.-P. 1997. Remarks on the faunal remains of some early farming communities in central Europe. *Anthropozoologica* 25/26, 571-8.

Veit, U. 1996. *Studien zum Problem der Siedlungsbestattung im europäischen Neolithikum*. Münster: Waxmann.

Vogt, E. 1951. Das steinzeitliche Uferdorf Egolzwil 3 (Kt Luzern). *Zeitschrift für Schweizerische Archäologie und Kunstgeschichte* 12, 193-211.

Wagner, R. 1967. *The curse of Souw: principles of Daribi clan definition and alliance in New Guinea*. Chicago: Chicago University Press.

Wagner, R. 1978. *Lethal speech: Daribi myth as symbolic obviation*. Ithaca, NY: Cornell University Press.

Wahl, J. and König, G. 1987. Anthropologisch-traumatische Untersuchung der menschlichen Skelettreste aus dem bandkeramischen Massengrab bei Talheim, Kreis Heilbronn. *Fundberichte Baden-Württemberg* 12, 65-186.

Waterson, R. 2000. House, place and memory in Tana Toraja (Indonesia). In R.A. Joyce and S.D. Gillespie (eds), *Beyond kinship: social and material reproduction in house societies*, 177-88. Philadelphia: University of Pennsylvania Press.

Weiner, J. 1994. Myth and mythology. In A. Barnard and J. Spencer (eds), *Encyclopedia of social and cultural anthropology*, 386-9. London: Routledge.

Weiner, J. 1998. Drei Brunnenkasten, aber nur zwei Brunnen: eine neue Hypothese zur Baugeschichte des Brunnens von Erkelenz-Kückhoven. In H. Koschik (ed.), *Brunnen der Jungsteinzeit*, 95-112. Köln: Rheinland-Verlag.

Weiner, J.F. 1988. *The heart of the pearl shell: the mythological dimension of Foi sociality*. Berkeley: University of California Press.

Weiner, J.F. 1991. *The empty place: poetry, space, and being among the Foi of Papua New Guinea*. Bloomington and Indianapolis: Indiana University Press.

Weiner, J.F. 1995. *The lost drum: the myth of sexuality in Papua New Guinea and beyond*. Madison: University of Wisconsin Press.

Whitley, D.S. 1998. Finding rain in the desert: landscape, gender and far western North American rock-art. In C. Chippindale and P. Taçon (eds), *The archaeology of rock-art*, 11-29. Cambridge: Cambridge University Press.

Whitley, J. 2002. Too many ancestors. *Antiquity* 76, 119-26.

Whittle, A. 1977. *The Earlier Neolithic of southern England and its continental background*. Oxford: British Archaeological Reports.

Whittle, A. 1978. Resources and population in the British Neolithic. *Antiquity* 52, 34-42.

Whittle, A. 1985. *Neolithic Europe: a survey*. Cambridge: Cambridge University Press.

Whittle, A. 1990. A model for the Mesolithic-Neolithic transition in the upper Kennet valley, north Wiltshire. *Proceedings of the Prehistoric Society* 56, 101-10.

Whittle, A. 1991. Wayland's Smithy, Oxfordshire: excavations at the Neolithic tomb in 1962-3 by R.J.C. Atkinson and S. Piggott. *Proceedings of the Prehistoric Society* 57(2), 61-101.

Whittle, A. 1994. Excavations at Millbarrow chambered tomb, Winterbourne Monkton, north Wiltshire. *Wiltshire Archaeological and Natural History Magazine* 87, 1-53.

Whittle, A. 1996. *Europe in the Neolithic: the creation of new worlds*. Cambridge: Cambridge University Press.

Whittle, A. 1997. Moving on and moving around: Neolithic settlement mobility. In P. Topping (ed.), *Neolithic landscapes*, 15-22. Oxford: Oxbow.

Whittle, A. 1998a. Beziehungen zwischen Individuum und Gruppe: Fragen zur Identität im Neolithikum der ungarischen Tiefebene. *Ethnographisch-Archäologische Zeitschrift* 39, 465-87.

Whittle, A. 1998b. Fish, faces and fingers: presences and symbolic identities in the Mesolithic-Neolithic transition in the Carpathian basin. *Documenta Praehistorica* 25, 133-50.

Whittle, A. 2000a. New research on the Hungarian Early Neolithic. *Antiquity* 74, 13-14.

Whittle, A. 2000b. Bringing plants into the taskscape. In A. Fairbairn (ed.), *Plants in Neolithic Britain and beyond*, 1-7. Oxford: Oxbow.

Whittle, A. 2000c. 'Very like a whale': menhirs, motifs and myths in the Mesolithic-Neolithic transition of northwest Europe. *Cambridge Archaeological Journal* 10, 243-59.

Whittle, A. 2001. Different kinds of history: on the nature of lives and change in central Europe, c. 6000 to the second millennium BC. In W.G. Runciman (ed.), *The origin of human social institutions*, 39-68. Oxford: Oxford University Press.

Whittle, A., Bartosiewicz, L., Borić, D., Pettitt, P. and Richards, M. 2002. In the beginning: new radiocarbon dates for the Early Neolithic in northern Serbia and south-east Hungary. *Antaeus* 25, 63–117.

Whittle, A., Davies, J.J., Dennis, I., Fairbairn, A.S. and Hamilton, M.A. 2000. Neolithic activity and occupation outside Windmill Hill causewayed enclosure, Wiltshire: survey and excavation 1992-93. *Wiltshire Archaeological and Natural History Magazine* 93, 131-80.

Whittle, A., Pollard, J. and Grigson, C. 1999. *The harmony of symbols: the Windmill Hill causewayed enclosure, Wiltshire*. Oxford: Oxbow.

Whittle, A., Rouse, A.J. and Evans, J.G. 1993. A Neolithic downland monument in its environment: excavations at the Easton Down long barrow, Bishops Cannings, north Wiltshire. *Proceedings of the Prehistoric Society* 59, 197-239.

Widlok, J. 1997. Orientation in the wild: the shared cognition of Hai‖om Bushpeople. *Journal of the Royal Anthropological Institute* 3, 317-32.

Willis, R. 1994. Introduction. In R. Willis (ed.), *Signifying animals: human meaning in the animal world*, 1-24. London: Routledge (first published 1990).

Willms, C. 1985. Neolithischer Spondylusschmuck. Hundert Jahre Forschung. *Germania* 63, 331-43.

Windl, H.J. 1999. Makabres Ende einer Kultur? *Archäologie in Deutschland* 1999(1), 54-7.

Woodman, P.C., Anderson, E. and Finlay, N. 1999. *Excavation at Ferriter's Cove, 1983-95: last foragers, first farmers in the Dingle peninsula*. Bray: Wordwell.

Wysocki, M. and Whittle, A. 2000. Diversity, lifestyles and rites: new biological and archaeological evidence from British Earlier Neolithic mortuary assemblages. *Antiquity* 74, 591-601.

Wyss, R. 1967. Ein jungsteinzeitliches Hockergräberfeld mit Kollektivbestattungen bei Lenzburg, Kt. Aargau. *Germania* 45, 20-34.

Wyss, R. 1976. *Das jungsteinzeitliche Jäger-Bauerndorf von Egolzwil 5 im Wauwilermoos*. Zürich: Schweizerisches Landesmuseum Zürich.

Wyss, R. 1979. *Das mittelsteinzeitliche Hirschjägerlager von Schötz 7 im Wauwilermoos*. Zürich: Schweizerisches Landesmuseum Zürich.

Zimmermann, A. 1995. *Austauschsysteme von Silexartefakten in der Bandkeramik Mitteleuropas*. Bonn: Habelt.

Index